Dynamics of a creole system

Dynamics of a creole system

DEREK BICKERTON
Associate Professor of Linguistics
University of Hawaii

CAMBRIDGE UNIVERSITY PRESS

Published by the Syndics of the Cambridge University Press
Bentley House, 200 Euston Road, London NW1 2DB
American Branch: 32 East 57th Street, New York, N.Y. 10022

© Cambridge University Press 1975

Library of Congress Catalogue Card Number: 74-12971

ISBN: 0 521 20514 X

First published 1975

Printed in the United States of America
by Vail-Ballou Press, Inc., Binghamton, New York

Contents

Acknowledgements

The present volume represents the fruits of a four-year period (1967–71) spent in teaching and research at the University of Guyana. The research on which it is actually based was initiated with the help of the University of Guyana Research and Publications Committee, but the major part of the fieldwork was completed with the aid of a generous grant from the Ford Foundation, which is here gratefully acknowledged. I am also indebted to the University of Lancaster for allowing me three months' study leave in the spring of 1972, during which the first draft of the earlier chapters was completed, and to the University of Hawaii for a half-time research post in 1972–3, which gave me time to complete the final draft.

To my colleagues Joyce Trotman and George Cave at the University of Guyana I owe a deep debt of gratitude for introducing me to some of the many complexities of Guyanese language and culture. Many other linguists have helped me in more ways than I can well list; however, some names stand out. Mervyn Alleyne and David DeCamp both provided me with mental and moral stimuli at times when I almost despaired of ever unravelling the complexities of the data with which I found myself confronted. Many other Caribbean scholars, in particular Beryl Bailey, Richard Allsopp, Lawrence Carrington, Dennis Craig and Dennis Solomon, greatly helped me with their friendly but critical discussions of papers presented by me at various conferences and seminars held in the area. However, there are two linguists in particular whose contribution to this work was so great that no mere acknowledgement can hope to repay it. William Labov gave unsparingly of his advice and encouragement, and his generous assistance is the more noteworthy in that we first met through an article of mine which had sharply attacked one of his papers. Charles-James Bailey was largely instrumental in assisting me, through long correspondence and personal discussion, to formulate and develop the theoretical framework within which this book is written. Needless to say, neither of these two, nor any other colleague, is responsible for the opinions herein expressed, nor for the errors and omissions which the book still doubtless contains.

For their assistance in obtaining recordings of Guyanese speech, I am grateful to a number of my former students, in particular Walter Edwards,

Ahad Ishoop, Arnold Persaud and Waveney Seaforth; also to Wendella Gittens, Geoffrey Jardim and Arnold Persaud for their many hours of tedious work in transcribing the tapes, and to Wendella Gittens for typing and other secretarial tasks.

But perhaps the greatest contribution to this study was made by the many Guyanese citizens who gave willingly of their time and energies to provide the raw material on which it is based. That material, earthy, shot through with wit and irreverence, filled with lively turns of speech and vivid anecdote, has inevitably been made almost unrecognisable through the abstraction of its formal linguistic patterns. However, something of its warmth and vigour may still show through here and there, as well as some suggestion of the satisfaction I myself derived from being admitted, however partially and briefly, to the pleasures of Guyanese working-class society and the richness and diversity of its cultural heritage. All speakers have been kept completely anonymous, as they would have wished, but the unique personality of each will remain in my memory as long as memory lasts.

Finally, to my wife, Yvonne, whose loving kindness sustained me through the few hardships and many tediums that such a work entails, my dearest thanks are due.

Derek Bickerton

April 1974

1 Problems in the description of creole systems

No less than two centuries have elapsed since the publication of the first grammar of a creole language (Magens 1770), and the subsequent scope and amplitude of pidgin and creole studies are well attested by the wealth of entries in Reinecke et al. 1974. However, and irrespective of their theoretical bias, practically all published descriptions of pidgin and creole languages have had at least one thing in common: they have assumed that the objects of description were unitary, homogeneous languages that could be adequately described in terms of a single monolithic grammar. It is true that in some areas (especially Jamaica; cf. DeCamp 1961, 1964; B. L. Bailey 1966, etc.) the heterogeneity of the primary speech data was explicitly recognised. But until the appearance of such papers as DeCamp 1971a and Tsuzaki 1971, such recognition had little practical influence on published descriptions.

However, the changed approach which these two papers exemplify was in part at least a reflection of changing priorities in general linguistics. While a concern with linguistic variation (traditionally the terrain of dialectology) had always been maintained by a minority of scholars in both historical (e.g. Politzer 1949) and synchronic (e.g. Pulgram 1961) linguistics, it was not until the appearance of Labov's early work (Labov 1963, 1966) that variation began to be seen as central rather than peripheral to major linguistic issues. Since then, a number of publications (of which perhaps the most influential have been Weinreich et al. 1968, Labov 1970 and C.-J. N. Bailey 1971) have posed cogent alternatives to the monosystemic assumptions about language which had for so long appeared to dominate the discipline. It was only natural that such a development should affect creole studies (since variation in some creoles is more widespread and involves 'deeper' categories than is normally the case in non-creole languages), and that, in turn, new approaches to creoles should contribute in both theory and methodology to the study of language in general.

Yet, despite the pioneering work of the last decade, it would be wrong to suggest that linguistic variation is thoroughly understood, or that an adequate formalism for its description has been devised. The linguist confronted by highly variable data has still the task of determining exactly what he is going to describe, and exactly how he is going to describe it. A sizeable part of the present study will concern itself with precisely these issues, and will try to resolve them in ways which, hopefully, will have a general application. For, although it is limited in coverage to the creole English of Guyana, and, within that, to a single, if crucial, area of the grammar (the system of tense and aspect), the decisions it has to make and the procedures it has to follow should be relevant, not merely in other creole-speaking areas, but wherever 'normal' languages (e.g. Fijian; cf. Schütz 1972) show a high degree of internal variation.

These are, of course, not the only issues involved in the study of creole variation. A study such as the present one must inevitably make some contribution to a number of other open questions in current linguistics. One of these is how to determine the bounds of a linguistic system (Labov 1971a, 1971b): at what stage, if any, can we say that English stops and Guyanese Creole begins? Another is whether it is possible to study syntactic change synchronically; so far, writings on syntactic change (e.g. Closs 1965) have assumed that it is not, and have indeed complained about the constraints that a limited corpus and the absence of informants place upon the investigator. If, however, that end of what DeCamp (1971a) has called a 'post-creole continuum' which is furthest from English in fact represents an 'older' form, and varieties between it and English, progressively younger ones, then it should, in theory, be possible to 'do diachronic syntax synchronically' (Bickerton MS.).

However, questions of this type, interesting though they are, are methodologically posterior to an adequate description of the primary data, and the problem most immediately before us is, therefore, how such a description may best be provided. The type as well as the magnitude of this problem may perhaps best be illustrated by looking at three samples of the type of material we shall have to deal with:

> A1. And in none of the many chapters they have in there have this fellow condemn white man for all that he did. All he said is that for you to achieve your aim you will have to do it, ahm, constitutionally. By the other side with the two names I have mentioned, Stokeley Carmichael and Rap Brown, they are talking about change also but from a different angle – just talking about gun bullet. How the hell they going use gun bullet pon the white people and they are the very people who are controlling the armoury and the arms? Is silly, man, silly.

> B1. As he see blood he does get eye turn, you know, and I tell he when you weeding mustn't hold grass and fire chop. He hold grass and fire chop till he

chop he finger. See little blood, he begin run. And by the time he meet the trench he fall down . . . And how he drink. You know the estate give five dollar advance to buy cutlass and file for the commencement to this crop. Well he never buy cutlass neither file. Well he take the money and yesterday he start drink at Lenora. He come. He run out the wife out of the house. Last night whole night he been do this do that. He come back. What little he had he mussy buy one little thing and he bounce up.

C1. But in awe village been get one black lady he name Aunty Punch. He son them come for carry am away because she a the only black woman what dey in this village and them frighten sey them go kill out am so them come night time for start carry away the lady. And when them people see that in Bushlot, them start beat them drum again and them – and all them people start come out again in flock flock. One of them chap been get gun and when them run they run go see. When they see sey nobody not come, soldier run in pon am. A chap drop a gun, you see he lay down flat in a potopoto and them blackman a other side run for go way a other place . . . Man a that the only thing what me can say.

Even when, as here, these passages have been 'normalised' by being reduced, in so far as that is possible, to standard English orthography, the differences between them are still very considerable. Moreover, a common hypothesis about variable situations – that they arise simply through un-equal mixtures of two 'pure' ingredients – is very difficult to maintain in the face of such evidence. It could, it is true, be argued that A1 is simply an En-glish marked by a few surviving creole features – copula omission in *they going*, absence of both determiner and pluraliser in the (itself non-standard) 'generic' noun phrase *gun bullet*, dummy-pronoun deletion in *is silly* [1] and so on. Equally, it could be argued that C1 represents a creole with a pre-dominantly English lexicon. But what is B1? The fact that it combines ele-ments as opaque to the naive standard-English-speaker as anything in C1 (*eye turn*, giddiness, *fire chop*, to strike a blow with a sharp instrument) with elements that suggest an attempt to master some 'frozen' variety of English (*for the commencement to this crop*) might suggest, to a supporter of the 'mix-ture' hypothesis, that the passage resulted from the struggles of a socially in-secure speaker of a creole vernacular to adjust his speech 'upwards' in the presence of some representative of the superordinate culture. In fact, noth-ing could be farther from the truth. The passage was surreptitiously recorded by a relative of the speaker, and probably represents, as nearly as one can

---

[1] It should be noted that this *is* is phonetically [ɪz] and thus non-identical with the sandhi form (phonetically [ɪs]) in U.S. Black English arises through deletion of the apical stop in *it's*. Most Guyanese speakers lack dummy *it*.

ever determine such things, the undiluted vernacular of that speaker – a vernacular, incidentally, by no means untypical for one of his particular background.[2] Moreover, while such a speaker can certainly vary his output in an upward and perhaps even a downward direction, it is unlikely that he could for long maintain consistently the varieties illustrated by A1 and C1 – the 'pure' varieties which his output is supposed to 'mix'. In other words, the 'mixture' is certainly not in the perception of the speaker – rather in that of the standard-speaking observer, who automatically dichotomises the data into 'what is like English' and 'what is not'.

It would, however, be equally false to suggest that we are merely in the presence of three discrete language-varieties rather than two. As DeCamp 1971a showed for Jamaica, there are many (if not, perhaps, infinitely many) varieties intermediate between A1 and B1, and between B1 and C1. Moreover, while (as stated above) a speaker whose uninhibited speech falls near the middle of the continuum might have difficulty in attaining or at least in maintaining speech at or near its limits, this must not be taken to mean that he cannot approach those limits when occasion arises. Of the following three samples from the same speaker, the second, B2 (taken from free conversation with a peer-group member, with the author present), probably represents something close to if a little above his vernacular, while A2 represents his formal narrative style to the author, and C2, his simulated dialogue of non-standard-speaking characters within the context of that same narrative:

> A2. He got up – he went and he put on his chocolate on the fire to boil. He wasn't sleeping because his noise arouse me. And I was watching him through my hammock bar. I see the boy went and he took up the double barrel gun and he have it at side of him. I wonder what is this boy doing with this gun? Catch his fire, put on his saucepan. As a matter of fact in every crew they has a man they calls him the general. You know as, ahm, we may have a set of men working, you have a leading hand, the general is the leading hand. He got up and this man went and he pick up what-do-you-call, yari-yari, a wood they call yari-yari, young ones he had as a ramrod to punch out cartridges from the gun. When he pick up he give the boy two lashes and the boy took the hot boiling cup of chocolate, a saucepan of chocolate off the fire and dash it on him and burn him.

[2] This speaker is identical with speaker 99/125 in Bickerton 1973a, 1973b; some personal data on him are given in the latter paper, as well as in Appendix II in the present volume. His speech is fairly typical of that of rural Africans in manual jobs within a twenty-mile radius of Georgetown.

B2. [Interlocutor's comments omitted]
I give it name Brownie, you can't pass that there.

. . . . .

You pick up a stick at it, it worse. The eyes become green green green. You can't pass.

. . . . .

And a great hunter. Hunt anything. Would hunt until –

. . . . .

He hunt until he hunt heself in the tiger mouth.

. . . . .

Yes it hunt until he hunt himself, he hunt heself in the tiger mouth. One night I see somebody passing. When I open this window there was nobody but this dog barking, jumping in the bush and coming up, jumping in the bush until he –

. . . . .

– jump in the tiger mouth: wow!

. . . . .

Next morning we see little bit of blood and the tiger gone.

C2. 'And you ain't know what for do?' he say. 'Them not got gun?' He say, 'Yes.' 'You take the gun, load the gun, hide am. You doesn't get up pon a morning for make tea?' He say, 'Yes, them a wake me. If me a sleep some time them a beat me and wake me for go make tea.' He say, 'All right. When them beat you and wake you,' he say, 'cry. But me go tell you what for do.' He say, 'When you put that chocolate for boil,' he say, 'but make sure that you hide the gun, and when that chocolate start for boil, quarrel, cry, say you want money for go home.' . . . . 'Me want me money. This a eighteen month me dey here and me can't get for go home and me grandmama a hungry. And ayou no want for give me money, ayou a send home money.'

It is true that, if the varieties represented by A1 and C1 are their respective targets, A2 and C2 fall somewhat short of them. As well as a number of hyper-corrections absent from A1 ('I see the boy went', 'they has', 'they calls'), there are in A2 more non-standard [3] features, e.g. auxiliary inversion in embedded Ss ('I wonder what is this boy doing'), and failure to apply gapping in co-ordinate conjoined Ss ('the boy went and he took up . . . and he have it . . .'). Likewise C2 contains several items that do not occur in the 'deepest' form of Guyanese Creole: negation with *ain't*, *does*, internal verb-

---

[3] The term 'non-standard' is used here in preference to 'creole' because the features which distinguish this passage from standard English are by no means all characteristic of the creole extreme. For instance, while failure to apply gapping is a creole feature, Aux-movement is definitely not; the creole equivalent of the sentence in question, *mi aks misef se wa di bai-dis a du*, could under no circumstances be realised as **mi aks misef se wa a di bai-dis du*. This issue is further discussed in Bickerton MS.

phrase negation, complementiser-deletion after *say* [4] and so on. However, A2, C2 are respectively closer to A1, C1 than they are to one another, and the distance between them is far greater than that which normally separates speech styles of the same speaker; both these points seem to me to constitute powerful arguments for a unitary treatment of Guyanese speech data.

However, at least one further aspect of such a treatment should be made clear immediately. During recent years, attempts have been made to draw the study of creoles ever further under the umbrella of sociolinguistics. It is assumed (e.g. Hymes 1971) that the observer confronted by variable data such as we have just examined will be mainly if not exclusively concerned with determining the social and cultural correlates of the different varieties, and indeed much recent work on Anglo-Caribbean speech (e.g. Reisman 1965; Edwards 1968, 1970, 1972; Abrahams and Bauman 1971) has followed this approach. However, interesting though some of its results may be, it is no substitute for linguistic analysis. Indeed, one could well argue that accurate linguistic analysis is methodologically prior to it, in that one can hardly determine the sociocultural function of a given speech-variety unless that variety itself has been very precisely defined; one might further suggest that failure to appreciate this point is what underlies the above-mentioned studies' failure to find a middle way between the purely anecdotal ('Well, this is how it happened on one particular occasion') on the one hand, and generalities too broad to be of interest on the other. On this issue, Labov has surely had the last word:

> If [sociolinguistics] refers to the use of data from the speech community to solve problems of linguistic theory, then I would agree that it applies to the research described here. But sociolinguistics is more frequently used to suggest a new interdisciplinary field – the comprehensive description of the relations of language and society. This seems to me an unfortunate notion, foreshadowing a long series of purely descriptive studies with little bearing on the central theoretical problems of linguistics or sociology (1966:v).

Similarly, while the present writer is far from uninterested in the culture and social organisation of the community under study, his concerns here will be exclusively linguistic – linguistic, moreover, in the sense of Chomsky's statement that the 'goals of linguistic theory' are 'to characterize

---

[4] The creole version of the sentence in question would actually be *taak se yu waan moni* . . . The verb *say* is unknown at this level, where the phonologically similar complementiser *se* (equivalent to English *that*) is obligatory before sentential complements. This construction, and the dubious etymology for it offered by Cruikshank (1916), is mentioned again in Chapter 2.

in the most neutral possible terms the knowledge of the language that provides the basis for actual use of language by a speaker–hearer' [5] and thereby
shed light on 'the general character of one's capacity to acquire knowledge'
(1965:9, 59). The only important difference between my position and
Chomsky's lies in my belief that an heuristic model of a uniform and
homogeneous speech-community does not necessarily constitute the best
means of attaining these goals. On the contrary, it would seem that a line
of approach which made different languages look as unalike as possible (an
inevitable consequence of Chomskyan idealisation) would be rather less
likely to 'develop an account of linguistic universals that . . . will not be fal-
sified by the actual diversity of languages' (Chomsky 1965:28) than one
which recognised the existence of dialect chains, creole continuums and
similar phenomena which link many languages traditionally treated as discrete. Some attempt to justify this position will be made in the final chapter;
our primary task is, first, to demonstrate that a true continuum exists, and
second, to show how it works.

Having established the general nature of the problem before us, we must
now examine not only works that deal specifically with Guyanese Creole
and related Caribbean dialects, but treatments of linguistic variation of other
types and in other areas, to see to what extent these can offer us assistance.

Most of the little written on Guyanese Creole prior to 1970 followed
traditional lines. Apart from notes in travellers' tales, collections of songs
and/or proverbs, and a few non-technical articles, [6] the only useful sources are
Quow (1877), van Sertima (1905), Cruikshank (1916) and Allsopp (1958a,
1958b, 1962). The first-named of these, though not a linguistic work in any

---

[5] Note the transition in this passage from '*the* language' to 'language' *tout court*. Chomsky
is far from being alone in this particular sleight-of-hand, in which two totally different
things are equated or confused. As a result, it is seldom clear whether it is the speaker's
'language capacity' or 'capacity to speak a (given) language' that is at issue, and therefore
impossible to determine what might be the relationship between the two. Chomsky's
theory of knowledge attributes tacit knowledge of universals to the child, and defines his
'problem' as 'being to determine which of the (humanly) possible languages is that of the
community in which he is placed' (1965:27). This seems perfectly reasonable; but what
is supposed to happen to the child's knowledge of universals, once he has 'chosen the
right language'? Arguments by Halle (1964) and Lenneberg (1967), attacked on quite
other grounds in Chapter 5 below, would imply that he somehow 'forgets' them – an
implausible conclusion, if one adopts the only plausible explanation of universal knowledge, that it is based on physiological features of brain structure. I would prefer to argue
that it is precisely because of such knowledge that we can learn other languages and
other varieties of our own.

[6] A reasonably complete list of these is given in Reinecke, DeCamp, Hancock, Tsuzaki
and Wood 1974.

accepted sense of the term, deserves some mention, since it represents an attempt by a writer with ample first-hand experience [7] to re-create the vernacular of working-class Afro-Guyanese in the third quarter of the nineteenth century. Either it is an unusually accurate record of this vernacular, or the author, by some remarkable feat of prognostication, was able to specify nearly all of the features characteristic of Indo-Guyanese rural working-class vernacular in the third quarter of the twentieth century. Since the former hypothesis is intrinsically more probable, we may legitimately conclude that the massive influx of Indian indentured labourers into nineteenth-century Guyana did not bring about any significant repidginisation or recreolisation of pre-1837 Creole, [8] but that the latter was learnt as a foreign language by the immigrants and preserved with a fair degree of accuracy. It is worth mentioning in passing that much of Quow's work is of a high literary standard and deserves a wider audience than it has yet received.

Van Sertima 1905 and Cruikshank 1916 are both brief works by talented amateurs. The former, while it attempts a higher degree of rigour – there is a chapter on 'accidence', and tables of verb-paradigms (*I go, you go, he go* etc.) – is the less helpful of the two, since, without ever explicitly avowing this restriction, it limits itself exclusively to a variety of partially decreolised creole found nowadays mainly in urban areas. Again, there are two possibilities: that the author, either through unfamiliarity with rural speech or because of the difficulties of multidialectal description, deliberately limited himself to the urban vernacular of his time, or that the extremer forms of creole recorded in Quow's work had somehow died out only to be resurrected later in the present century. Again, the first seems the more probable. If it is correct, we have the further interesting suggestion that the continuum of Guyanese speech, far from being a recent innovation, is at least the better part of a century old.

---

[7] Michael McTurk, the pseudonymous author, was a Resident Magistrate in rural districts of Guyana for many years during the mid-nineteenth century. The nature of his work must have brought him into daily contact with creole speakers.

[8] This issue raises a number of questions, such as: is a language such as Krio, native to some but used as a (second) contact language by many more, a pidgin, a creole, or both at the same time? Is a speaker who acquires a creole as a second language a pidgin-speaker, or merely a foreign-language speaker of a creole? – and so on. There is not space to deal with such matters here. That Indian immigration could have brought about repidginisation is a hypothesis worth considering, though inherently unlikely – pidgins, as Whinnom (1971) points out, seem to need more than two parents, and the bulk of immigrants were monolingual in Hindi. In fact, however, the linguistic evidence for such a process, some of which will be examined later in this volume, seems very slight indeed.

In contrast, Cruikshank 1916 has all the virtues as well as some of the vices of good amateur work. It is lively, observant and readable – ready, too, long before Herskovits and Herskovits 1934 [9] to give the contributions of African languages their due. However, it falls victim to what Dillard (1970) has aptly termed the 'Cafeteria Principle' of deriving creole phonology from a variety of disparate British dialects, and it perpetuates a number of folk-etymologies such as that of *talk say*. [10] For our present purposes, its virtual limitation to the contents of the lexicon sharply reduces its relevance.

The work of Allsopp, however, is on a different level altogether, representing as it does the first attempt to handle the Guyanese situation with the tools of (relatively) modern linguistic analysis; moreover, the area of grammar covered by Allsopp 1962 is virtually identical with that covered in the present study. Allsopp 1958a contains the first clear example which showed how the variety of forms found in the Guyanese continuum could be arranged hierarchically on a scale from nearest-to-English to farthest-from-English, and that this scale corresponded to that of social stratification. [11] The example was that of possible realisations of the sentence 'I told him':

1. *ai tɔuld hɪm.*	6. *ai tɛl i.*
2. *ai to:ld hɪm.*	7. *a tɛl i.*
3. *ai to:l ɪm.*	8. *mi tɛl i.*
4. *ai tɛl ɪm.*	9. *mi tɛl am.*
5. *a tɛl ɪm.*	

According to Allsopp, varieties 1–3 were characteristic of middle-class usage; 4–7, of the lower-middle and urban working classes; 8, of the bulk of the rural working class; 9, of old and illiterate (and predominantly Indian) rural labourers. Though this schema, as Cave (1970) has observed, is excessively rigid, and fails to allow for the flexibility of Guyanese speech as illustrated in the examples at the beginning of this chapter, it constitutes a useful guidepost to the labyrinth of Guyanese variation.

In his longer works, Allsopp sought to explore two areas in the speech of

[9] In fact, the African residue in creoles, and in particular in neighbouring Sranan, had already been amply recognised by Schuchardt (1914). There is no evidence that Cruikshank had encountered Schuchardt's work, however.

[10] Cruikshank treats this as an example of that good old creolist's standby, 'reduplication' – even though *semantic* reduplication using distinct morphs is very unlike morphological reduplication. For a better etymology tracing the Twi origins of the expression, see Cassidy 1960:63, or the entry under *se* in Cassidy and LePage 1967.

[11] Of course, numerous writers had pointed out this relationship anecdotally, but Allsopp's is the first specific matching of morphology with class level known to me. Similar observations for Jamaica seem not to have been made prior to Craig 1966.

the urban working class – the pronominal system and the system of tense and aspect. Allsopp's field methods were generally in advance of his time, and his observance of Labov's 'Principle of Accountability' – that the observer should list and quantify *all* variables in his data, not just those which happen to fit his analysis (Labov 1969) – is exemplary. The major weakness of his analysis is the absence of any theoretical framework adequate to deal with creole continuums; but then, none had been formulated when he wrote. Another (probably resulting from the first) was his assumption that if his informants constituted a homogeneous sample regionally (all were from the Greater Georgetown area), educationally (none had more than elementary schooling) and occupationally (all were in non-clerical occupations), then their dialect would in turn constitute a homogeneous object capable of unitary description. Such assumptions can produce plausible if often counter-factual results where (as in Sivertsen's study of Cockney [1960]) the material under analysis represents an end-of-dialect-chain phenomenon, and where, in consequence, the analyst can abstract a system of sorts by merely assembling the most non-standard constructions; there is nothing 'beyond Cockney, but like it' to which such constructions might more properly belong. However, there *is* something 'beyond the dialect of Georgetown, but like it' – to wit, the more creolised varieties of speech found in the rural areas which van Sertima too had ignored but which still vigorously persist and which cannot, except by arbitrary procedures, he divided from the 'rougher' types of Georgetown speech.

Allsopp's failure to take rural creole into account, and his consequent failure to relate non-standard structures in his data to the rural forms from which these urbanisms have developed, sharply reduces the explanatory power of his work, since there are many structures common in urban speech which can appear quite mystifying unless their origins are taken into account.[12] However, despite its limitations, his work remains an invaluable source of information on working-class Georgetown usage.

---

[12] See, for instance, Labov's (Labov et al. 1968 1:265–6) rather puzzled treatment of 'the quasi-modal *done*' in Black English, and compare it with the treatment of Guyanese *don* in Chapters 2 and 3 below; see also Carden's uncertainty as to the best analysis of Black English 'embedded questions' (Carden 1972), and the way the problem is resolved in Bickerton MS. Most striking, however, is the way in which failure to consider rural forms needlessly complicated Allsopp's analysis of '*is*-initial' sentences (Allsopp 1962:II, 251–4); he derives this structure from Gaelic initial *is* (which by no means always has the function of Guyanese *iz*) via a putative and apparently unattested variety of Irish English, and fails to mention that identical sentence-types with *a* instead of *iz* are common throughout rural Guyana. When equative *a* is replaced by *iz* in other contexts (cf. Bickerton 1973a, 1973b), replacement in this context naturally takes place also. Obviously there is no argument for deriving *a* from Gaelic, and if there were, one would

In contrast with the paucity of studies on Guyana, there have been a number of excellent recent studies of Jamaican Creole (e.g. Alleyne 1963; B. L. Bailey 1966, 1971; Cassidy 1960, 1966; Cassidy and LePage 1967; DeCamp 1961, 1971a; Lawton 1963; LePage and DeCamp 1960, to mention only some of the more significant). Resemblances between Guyanese and Jamaican speech are very numerous. It seems likely that the two have close genetic linkage,[13] and, synchronically, they share very many grammatical rules and lexical entries; the resemblance in sociolinguistic conditions is well illustrated by DeCamp (1961:82), who could have been describing Guyana when he wrote:

> Nearly all speakers of English in Jamaica could be arranged in a sort of linguistic continuum, ranging from the speech of the most backward peasant or labourer all the way to that of the well-educated urban professional. Each speaker represents not a single point but a span of this continuum, for he is usually able to adjust his speech upward or downward for some distance along it.

Since B. L. Bailey (1966) constitutes the most rigorous and the most comprehensive study of Jamaican Creole to date, it is worth examining in some detail. To the extent that it contains shortcomings, we may feel reasonably confident that these are not the fault of the author, but rather of certain basic assumptions about language which until very recently have been shared by a large majority of linguists: shared, one might add, with such a degree of faith that even where known facts contradicted them, the assumptions were preferred to the facts. For instance, Bailey herself is fully aware of the situation described by DeCamp. She describes the typical Jamaican speaker as one who 'is likely to shift back and forth from creole to English or something closely approximating English within a single utterance, without ever being conscious of the shift', and notes correctly that 'most observers of language in Jamaica have encountered extreme difficulty in distinguishing between the various layers of the language structure, and indeed the lines of demarcation are very hard to draw' (1966:1). Yet despite this awareness, Bailey deliberately chooses to 'attempt to describe *one* of the systems which lie at the core of this co-structure [i.e. the Jamaican speech continuum], that is, the Creole syntax' (1966:2; emphasis in original).

---

still have to explain why structures with extraposed equatives should be quite common among creoles, some of which can hardly have had contact with Gaelic bilinguals (for instance, Wilson [1962] derives a similar form in Crioulo from Portuguese).

[13] During the middle and latter part of the eighteenth century, the Dutch encouraged English planters from the islands with well-seasoned slaves to establish themselves in Guyana. Some came from Barbados, others from Jamaica, presumably bringing about a merger between Caribbean creoles and Sranan (see Appendix III).

It is not clear from the above passage exactly how many 'coexistent systems' are conceived of as constituting the 'co-structure'. It would appear that only two are envisaged, for, leaving aside one or two 'geographical variants', any morph which is not a 'morpheme borrowed from English' is described as a 'free morpheme variant' (1966:138–40). However, the distinction between these categories is far from being a clear one; in many cases, there seem no good grounds for assigning an item to one category rather than another, and in some it could even be argued that assignments should be reversed. For example, *Jaan a waak* and *Jaan waakin* 'John is walking' are treated as free variants, and therefore of presumably equal status in the creole system, even though the second is closer to English than the first, and probably (if Guyanese experience is anything to go by) co-occurs with far fewer creole features than the first does. Yet *dida waak* 'was walking', a form at least as remote from English as *waakin* (and clearly related to the avowedly creole *a waak*), is classed as 'English interference'. Similarly, while *it* is treated as a free variant with *i* (the more creole third-person-neuter pronoun), *shi* is regarded as 'English interference' alongside *im* 'she'; and while *a* is described as a free variant with *mi* 'I', *ai*, of which *a* is simply the reduced form, is also attributed to 'English interference'. This difficulty in apportioning items to their appropriate systems is inevitable, since not only are there forms which span both the putative 'systems', but also 'intermediate' forms which cannot properly be assigned to either.

The existence of such 'intermediate' forms might seem to suggest a means by which Beryl Bailey's approach could be salvaged. There is no *a priori* reason why 'co-existent systems' should constitute pairs rather than triples, and indeed Tsuzaki (1971) has proposed three or even four such systems for Hawaii. However, we can show that it is not so much the number of systems in a 'co-structure' as their presumed invariance and discreteness which makes the co-existent model inappropriate for analysing creole continua.

Let us take the nine variants of *I told him* as described by Allsopp (1958a; see p. 9 above). Since there are three variables under each node in the common derivation, one might suggest that there are, basically, these three systems:

	1st pers. sing. pro. (subj.)	*tell* + past	3rd pers. sing. pro. (obj.)
System I	*ai*	tɔuld	(h)ɪm
System II	*a*	toːl	*i*
System III	*mi*	tɛl	*am*

The outputs listed by Allsopp and not directly generated by any of these systems would then be presumed to derive from some random mixing process.

Unfortunately there are a number of things wrong with this suggestion. In the first place, the direct, unmixed output of System II is itself of highly doubtful grammaticality – certainly less acceptable than the 'mixed' forms *a tɛl i* or *mi tɛl i*. Moreover, a random mixing process applied to the three systems would produce a possible twenty-four such 'mixed' outputs, each with theoretically equal status and privilege of occurrence. There would therefore be no way of explaining why only the outputs listed by Allsopp occur with any degree of frequency, while the majority of the twenty-four never occur at all.

One could attempt to resolve the problem by removing the invariance condition on systems. Thus Weinreich, Labov and Herzog, while endorsing co-existent systems in principle, observe that they cannot account for all the variation perceived in everyday speech, and that 'variable element[s] within the system' must be provided for (1968:166–7). If we remove the invariance condition, we could have:

	1st pers. sing. pro. (subj.)	*tell* + past	3rd pers. sing. pro. (obj.)
System I	*ai*	*tɔuld* *to:ld* *to:l*	*(h)ɪm*
System II	*ai* *a*	*tɛl*	*ɪm* *i*
System III	*mi*	*tɛl*	*i* *am*

On the face of things, this might represent a considerable improvement. All, and only all, the forms listed by Allsopp are now derivable. Moreover, it is no longer necessary to introduce any form of 'mixing' in order to derive them. Indeed, some variables can be generated by straightforward morphophonemic rules operating *within* systems; these would account for the alternation of *tɔuld/to:ld/to:l* and *ai/a*, though they would be rather less plausible as an explanation of *ɪm/i* or *i/am*.

However, even this solution is far from satisfactory. For instance, System III would permit alternation of *i* and *am* as object-pronoun, but in fact there are very few speakers who alternate these two items. In other words, a native speaker, if forced to divide the continuum into discrete systems, would most probably assign these two items to two different ones, and he would certainly have solid linguistic grounds for doing this. *Am* and *i* are not simply variant ways of expressing the category '3rd person singular masculine object pronoun'; *am* represents all genders but is invariant as regards case, whereas *i*, generally opposed to *shi* and *it* in objective case, can also occur as subject or in the possessive case.

Furthermore, if we compare Systems II and III, we find that the forms *i* and *tɛl* occur in both; that is, only the *mi/a* opposition divides the two systems. Yet many speakers alternate between *mi* and *a* (as compared with the tiny percentage who alternate *i* and *am*). Thus a boundary within the system appears greater than the boundary which divides the system from others. Admittedly, boundaries could be readjusted to give, say:

System II	*ai*	*tɛl*	ɪ*m*
	a		*i*
	mi		
System III	*mi*	*tɛ l*	*am*

but this would merely produce a new set of problems. For, while there do exist speakers who alternate all three forms of the first-person-singular pronoun, there are some within this range who would use *mi* only or *ai/a* only, just as there are some who would use ɪ*m* only or *i* only. Moreover, the number who do alternate between ɪ*m* and *i* (a variation *within* a system) is probably no greater than the number who alternate *tɛl* and *to:l* (a variation *across* systems). Thus, no matter which way the continuum is divided, we end up with things together which should be separated, and things separated which should be together; and if this is the case where only a handful of items is concerned, how much more must it be true when every variable in the continuum has to be taken into account!

But there is a further objection which applies indiscriminately to all 'co-existent' interpretations. It is that, while few members of the Guyanese community actively produce *all* of Allsopp's outputs, the vast majority *understand* all of them, i.e. there is virtually no-one who does not know that *ai tɔuld hɪm* and *mi tɛl am* 'mean the same thing' (apart from connotations of class or context). Thus, while a co-existent systems model might (subject to the limitations described above) approximate to a model of *speaker* competence, it could not possibly serve as a model of *hearer* competence.

The evidence above can only confirm our intention of describing the Guyanese continuum as a single, if non-homogeneous, unit. Unfortunately, this decision will force us to differ in our mode of analysis from Labov, since he clearly recognises the existence of distinct systems within languages: 'Clearly Spanish, French, Navaho and English are different systems. But is Black English a different system from the surrounding white dialects? My answer would be yes, based on the following definition of a system: a set of rules or relations in equilibrium, which jointly carry out a given function' (1971b:57).

Let us see what the consequences of this position are for the analysis of variation. One of these, perhaps the gravest, is the isolation of a given system from varieties that neighbour it and, perhaps, have a great deal in common with it. If we look at our last model for Guyanese variation, we see that System II has three variables *ai, a* and *mi*. If these are genuinely variables within a discrete system, then we must assume that all speakers within that system share them (even if, for some reason, not all speakers produce all of them in the data available to us) and that, in consequence, a single rule for their use is all that a grammar of the system would require. However, we will observe that these three variables do not all occur with the same degree of frequency; and, if in addition we were to find their frequencies covaried with particular environments in which they were found, it would seem logical to write a 'variable rule' which would list a hierarchy of constraints for each variable. By Labov's definition cited above, such a rule would simply constitute one of a 'set of rules or relations in equilibrium', i.e. in a long-enduring if not perpetual stasis.

However, if we consider System II in the light of Systems I and III, an entirely different interpretation becomes possible. We note that one of II's variables is an invariant for III (*mi*) while another is an invariant for I (*ai*). We have already noted that even among speakers in II there are some who use only *mi*, and some who only use *a/ai* – sub-groups, in other words, who are already approximating to the outputs of the neighbour systems. It would seem reasonable enough even without further motivation to assume that System II, far from being in equilibrium, represented no more than an intermediate phase between Systems III and I. In fact, there is very strong motivation for assuming this.

It is correctly observed by Weinreich, Labov and Herzog (1968:155) that 'The problem of accounting for the geographical transition of dialects across a territory thus appears to be symmetrical with the problem of accounting for the transition of dialects through time in one community.' The same authors further state that 'all change involves variability and heterogeneity', and that 'The generalization of linguistic change through linguistic structure is neither uniform nor instantaneous; it involves the covariation of associated changes over substantial periods of time, and is reflected in the diffusion of isoglosses over areas of geographical space' (1968:188). In other words, linguistic variation is the synchronic aspect of linguistic change, and linguistic change is the diachronic aspect of linguistic variation. Thus if we are confronted with a situation in which speakers can be divided into three groups, one of which uses a feature F_1 only, one of which uses a feature F_2 only, and one of which alternates F_1 and F_2, then we are quite justified in assuming, in the absence of contrary evidence, that one feature represents an 'earlier' stage, one a 'later' stage of the language, and the third, the inevitable stage of transition between them – inevitable, because it is impossible for any population of speakers to change even a single feature simultaneously and overnight.

Are we justified in assuming' that this state of affairs is what underlies Guyanese variation? In Chapter 2, we will have occasion to compare the most deviant form of the Guyanese verbal system with that of Sranan as described by Voorhoeve (1957), and we will be able to show very close similarities between the two – similarities far closer than any that exist between the Guyanese extreme and standard English. Sranan was formed during the brief occupation of Surinam by the British from 1650 to 1667 (Rens 1953) and has undergone relatively little structural change since that period (Voorhoeve 1961). As it appears probable that Sranan was spoken in Guyana during the eighteenth-century Dutch occupation,[14] and probably merged with the contemporary Jamaican and Barbadian creoles brought in by British-owned slaves later in that century (see Appendix III), it would seem reasonable to suppose that the extreme creole varieties in modern Guyana represent survivals from a relatively early stage in creole development, and that, if Guyana had not come under pressure from standard English, all Guyanese speech, rather than a relatively small proportion of it, would closely approximate contemporary Sranan. Equally, had this pressure from English been more strongly and evenly applied, all Guyanese speech might have evolved into a variety of English differing from the standard variety no more, say, than Black English differs from White English in New York. If the latter situation had occurred, no-one would be able to dispute that the changes required to convert the original, Sranan-like creole into a merely marginally deviant brand of English were just as much diachronic changes as were those which converted Latin into Spanish, or Anglo-Saxon into Middle English.

---

[14] At least one nineteenth-century source claimed the existence of a 'Dutch creole' in Guyana (Dance 1881). However, the criticisms of Schuchardt (1914) leave no doubt that this was in reality Sranan or something very close to it. It is worth noting that inhabitants of Surinam (irrespective of race) and their language are today consistently referred to by working-class Guyanese informants as 'Dutch'.

However, and through a series of purely extralinguistic accidents,[15] the actual situation in Guyana went to neither of these extremes – or rather, both extremes operated, but on different sections of the population. Uneducated rural Indo-Guyanese were barely touched by standard English, while educated urban Afro-Guyanese were highly exposed to it; the remainder of the population, strung out between these extremes, advanced, at an uneven pace and not without sidesteps and hesitations, in the direction of the superordinate language. It would follow from this analysis that a synchronic cut across the Guyanese community is indistinguishable from a diachronic cut across a century and a half of linguistic development, and that therefore a grammar of the whole Guyanese continuum should be indistinguishable from the diachronic grammar that *could* have been written if *all* Guyanese had moved as close to standard English as *some* of them have. Thus the Guyanese continuum, far from being a quagmire of anomalies designed to bedevil the descriptivist, reveals itself as an unusual, though perhaps not unique, case of the preservation of diachronic changes in a synchronic state, and therefore an unrivalled natural laboratory for the study of linguistic change processes which can normally only be inferred from written materials.

This state of affairs has one further consequence. There can be no question that, in the study of linguistic variation, the greatest contribution to date has been that of William Labov; and yet the present work will be seen to diverge from Labovian practice in certain respects. Such divergence was not undertaken lightly, but it seems inescapable considering the facts involved. These are, briefly, that while on many linguistic items all of Labov's informants showed variable behaviour, there is no single item on which all my Guyanese informants showed variable behaviour. A moment's thought will show why this should be so. Although no-one should suppose that early nineteenth-century creole was free from internal variation, collections of Guyanese proverbs such as Speirs 1902, Abrams 1970, etc. suggest it may have been rather more homogeneous than the speech of contemporary Guyanese. To the extent that this older creole is preserved in country districts, there will be, for any given grammatical environment, speakers who

---

[15] The main factor differentiating Guyana from other Caribbean communities is the extent and nature of Indian immigration. The relatively small size of its permanently inhabited area and the absence of serious obstacles to communication would probably have brought about a more rapid and general decreolisation such as has affected Barbados, had it not been for the existence of a large, conservative and fairly unassimilated bloc located principally in rural areas. For fuller details of the social, political and economic mechanisms underlying the unusually wide span of the Guyanese continuum, see Appendix III.

in that environment use the creole form only, as well as speakers who alternate between creole and English forms or who, in some cases, use intermediate forms which properly belong to neither. Thus, no matter what the general status of 'variable rules' (and enough has been written on this topic in Bickerton 1971a, 1973c; Labov 1969, 1972; Sankoff MS.; Cedergren and Sankoff MS., etc. to make it unnecessary to return to that topic here), they would be quite inappropriate for the Guyanese situation, since they would simply obscure the considerable amount of invariant patterning that is to be found there.

The existence of invariant or partly invariant speakers within the wider variability of the continuum as a whole dictates a further difference from the Labovian approach. Labov's work has unfailingly centred on the social group rather than the individual as the primary object of investigation, and he has argued convincingly (1966) that in some communities the speech of the former is more consistent than that of the latter. However, it does not appear as if any unambiguous social lines divide 'variable' from 'invariant' speakers in Guyana – indeed, they hardly could, since among the latter there are vanishingly few whose output is invariant for *all* features. Thus, to take a group of any kind – whether a primary one or a broader class stratum – as one's unit of study for any single feature would submerge speakers who were invariant on *that particular* feature, just as would any attempt to divide the continuum into 'co-existent systems' on purely linguistic grounds; and, by submerging them, one would also segment and obscure the ongoing change processes which constitute perhaps the most interesting and important aspect of the Guyanese continuum. For no approach which sorts the continuum into discrete sub-systems can answer the critical question: where did these sub-systems come from? – how did they originate, and how do they relate to one another? In a 'co-existent' approach, each sub-system must be treated as a given, with a consequent loss of explanatory power.

It could be argued that any other approach must of necessity throw us back on the idiolect, which, whether interpreted broadly (e.g. Hockett 1958) or narrowly (e.g. Bloch 1948) has been shown by Labov to be an inadequate unit for analysis. But this is not so, since our motives in looking at individual outputs are quite different from those of earlier investigators. The latter hoped that such outputs would yield systems that would be both self-consistent and valid – save for minor detail – for the entire communities to which their producers belonged. The present study contains no such expectations, and is solely concerned with the ways in which grammars of individuals relate to the polylectal grammar of the community. In fact, these individual grammars are simply the building-blocks out of which the grammar of the community is constructed.

The defenders of a variable-rule schema might finally fall back on the following line of defence: they could argue that, despite our admitting that grammars should be neutral as between speaker and hearer, we have placed far too much weight on what speakers actually do. To do so would be a little inconsistent in view of the fact that the 'quantitative paradigm' (Sankoff MS., Cedergren and Sankoff MS.) has systematically ignored the hearer; however, it could be claimed that the hearer's ability to understand everything in the continuum represents a truer measure of competence than do limitations on the speaker's capacity to produce everything, that the latter are accidental, or 'performance features', and that therefore a variable rule showing, e.g. the relative frequencies of occurrence of *mi*, *a* and *ai* could more adequately reflect communal competence than any more atomised picture based on things people actually say.

Since this basic argument (if not its precise conclusion) could also be put by linguists who would emphatically reject the quantitative approach, it must be taken very seriously. In the first place, the weight attached here to actual outputs derives not from any metatheoretical bias, but simply from the nature of the situation under study. As is shown in Appendix I, the investigator of a creole continuum simply cannot rely on, or even make sense out of, what informants tell him. He is thus obliged, in the first instance at least, to induce rules from outputs. However, the rules he induces from outputs, given that he does this accurately, may be presumed under Occam's razor to be identical with the rules internalised by hearers and understanders of those outputs, even if those hearers and understanders never produce equivalent outputs themselves. In other words, if we describe all the rules necessary to yield all the outputs judged grammatical, we will have described the competence of that community's ideal (and sometimes real) hearer (whether we shall have done so optimally is, of course, an empirical question in any given case). The grammar that results will therefore still be neutral as between speaker and hearer; to suppose differently would be to perpetuate the structuralist confusion of discovery procedures with grammars.

As regards the specifically 'quantitativist' element in the argument, one can only say that it would prove quite impossible to write a Guyanese grammar with variable rules. All variable rules that have so far been proposed have had as their constraints features of the segments immediately preceding or immediately following the variable, whether these features were phonological or (as in Labov 1969) grammatical categories such as Pronoun, Adjective etc. There is no evidence whatsoever that (except for a minority of cases, which will be specified in the text) the markers of tense and aspect to be dealt with in this study are affected in any way by their immediate environments, or by anything other than the set of systematic rules which the chapters which follow will seek to describe and justify.

It may be questioned whether a grammar such as is proposed here may justly be called 'generative', but since so few generativists have attempted to handle variable data (Klima 1964 and DeCamp 1971a are two noteworthy exceptions) it is still far from clear what a generative grammar of variation would look like. Klima showed how certain structures characteristic of non-standard English dialects could be derived from a grammar of English by adding to the core grammar a small number of late rules and/or by varying the order of transformations. Such a procedure, however, presumes the existence of a large common stock of phrase-structure rules and transformations, which cannot be presumed in the Guyanese situation. Yet even DeCamp's approach can be shown to depend on presumptions of this kind. He himself sees its success as depending to a large measure on the extent to which syntactic differences between creole and English can be dealt with on the phonological level, as Labov (1969) dealt with copula deletion in Black English, and states that '[Labov's] conclusions seem to be equally applicable to copula-deletion in Jamaican English' (1971a:362).[16] Moreover, and despite his overt recognition of Jamaica as a 'post-creole continuum', his formalism, like that of Klima, is designed to generate discrete dialects, and dialects, moreover, which have a very *ad hoc* flavour: H[igh], M[iddle] and L[ow] for the phonology, but U[pper] M[iddle], L[ower] M[iddle], E[state] L[abourer] and P[easant] F[armer] for part of the semantics. But while more recent work by Carden (1970, 1972) does take into account variation by individuals, the nature of Carden's informants – educated speakers of standard English – means that he has not had to develop a formalism of a kind that could handle the very wide differences, deep as well as surface, which divide Guyanese speakers. Thus no existing formulation of a synchronic generative grammar can offer much assistance with the problems confronting us; and diachronic formulations, insightful as they may be on certain aspects of linguistic change, have hitherto been, as Kiparsky (1971:577) states, 'aimed at developing a theory of change that could hook up to the existing

---

[16] In fact they cannot be. As shown in Bickerton 1973a, the Guyanese copula situation is quite a complex one, though no different from Jamaica's (cf. B. L. Bailey 1966).

synchronic theory',[17] and therefore indifferent to the consequences of individual variation.

However, and despite position statements such as that of Chomsky (1965:3), there is no reason to believe that the inapplicability of existing generative theory to the Guyanese Creole continuum indicates any necessary, as opposed to merely accidental, limitation on that theory in general. Indeed, the reverse ought to be the case. In so far as that theory claims to be a universal one, it must be able to account for linguistic data of every kind; the argument that our present data are not of a kind with which theory must deal will be discussed in Appendix I. Generative attempts to deal with creole data have so far fallen between two stools; they have either assumed, with DeCamp, that creole rules could somehow be grafted onto English rules, or, with Beryl Bailey, that a creole could be described as a separate language without reference to its related superstrate. However, at least two other approaches are possible within the framework of generative theory.[18]

One, proposed in Bickerton 1973a, but owing much to the approach to phonology of Chomsky and Halle 1968, is essentially recapitulatory. Basing itself on the assumption that the range of synchronic Guyanese variation stems from, and reflects, a natural development from an historic creole to standard English, it takes as its point of departure the deep structure of that creole and then describes stages intervening between the extremes of the system by successively adding to, subtracting from and adapting the original set of rules. This is, in a sense, simply standing the Labov–DeCamp approach on its head, and though there are some clear advantages in so doing – real diachronic processes are presumably being re-enacted, one avoids the artificiality of adding to the grammar rules that often merely reverse English rules, and so on – it could be argued that it misses at least one important truth about English-based pidgins and creoles generally: that they *are*, in some meaningful sense, all English (rather than an array of non-Indo-European languages on which a largely English lexicon has been clumsily grafted) and that one ought, therefore, to be able to describe them, together

---

[17] Note that Kiparsky still accepts without question something which is by no means self-evident, i.e. that diachronic theories must depend on synchronic ones. He merely wishes to have better synchronic theories to depend on.

[18] A third might be suggested by Silverstein's (1972) ingenious treatment of Chinook jargon, i.e. distinct bases yielding a range of intermediate surface forms. As such, it is in effect little more than a more sophisticated version of the 'co-existent systems' model. Such a model may indeed apply during the early stages of pidgin formation; it would, however, be wholly inapplicable to an integral community of native speakers.

with English, in what Carden (1972) has described as a 'unified analysis'.

There is a good deal of evidence to support such a position: for instance, the widely attested fact that a number of what might seem to be characteristically creole forms are found elsewhere within pan-English – in non-standard dialects, in maturational development, and in types of performance error to which any speaker of English might on occasion be liable.[19] That a 'unified analysis' will work at least in part for Guyanese Creole, and can, moreover, indicate significant relationships between widely differing varieties of English, is shown in Bickerton MS. However, it is still an empirical question how far this approach can be pushed back, and in how many areas of the grammar. While there is much, even in the variety of Guyanese Creole most distinct from English, that could still be readily incorporated in a pan-English grammar, there are also elements (often, probably, derived from the Kwa group of languages in West Africa) which it would be hard to incorporate therein without severe distortion of the data. Nowhere, perhaps, are such elements as conspicuous as they are in the Guyanese tense-aspect system, as we shall see in Chapter 2.

Our present choice of field, then, will tend to stress the 'recapitulatory' rather than the 'unified' aspect of the present study. It is hoped, however, that the overall pattern will not be too much distorted thereby. Change-processes are the same in this as in other areas of the grammar, and the remoteness from English of the 'semantic cut-up' which underlies the extreme creole tense-aspect system does not, as I shall try to show, mean that there is any 'structural break' between varieties that directly realise such a system and others which realise the English one. Rather, there is a constant succession of restructurings of the original system, across the continuum, yielding a very gradual transmission in terms of surface forms between the

---

[19] Note that it is not being argued that creoles *derive* from such sources; treatments which would derive them from obscure English regional dialects or from 'baby-talk' or general linguistic incapacity are, one hopes, now so unequivocally dead that one can surely point to such resemblances without giving aid and comfort to linguistic backwoodsmen. It does not seem unreasonable to suppose that there are certain variants which the overall structure of a language would tend to encourage, just as there are others which it would reject. It is also worth noting that wherever resemblances to African syntactic structures are claimed, these generally turn out to have a common source so abstract that it would serve for African and English grammars alike. Compare, for instance, G. Lakoff's (1968) treatment of English instrumentals with Williamson's (1965) analysis of similar structures in Ijo; compare the overall similarity between Kwa 'verb-chains' and the prelexical derivations of generative semantics; note also the analysis of *mek* sentences (superficially a calque on Yoruba) in Bickerton 1971b.

two extremes. In the chapters that follow, we shall try to trace these restructurings, and in so doing, perhaps, gain insights into linguistic change-processes which, in other languages, cannot be observed, but can only be inferred from written records.

2 The basilectal verb-phrase

The first problem in dealing with a continuum is how to segment it for purposes of analysis. Ideally, one would like to deal with it all at once, but that is impossible. We have to begin by somehow isolating the basilect: that segment of the continuum which we assume is somehow 'furthest from' English and which is also 'earlier' than other segments.[1] There are, as I shall show, empirical tests with which we can check such assumptions, once the putative basilect has been isolated, but we have to isolate something before such tests can be made.

We will begin by assuming that speakers who use features such as the tense-aspect markers *bin, bina, a, don, doz* etc. – features which are not found in any acrolectal speaker – may be basilectal speakers, and that the features mentioned may be basilectal markers. If our assumption is correct, we will find that those speakers who use such features most frequently will use acrolectal features seldom, if at all; and that, conversely, those speakers who use acrolectal features with high frequency will use basilectal features infrequently, if at all.

Tables 2.1 and 2.2 show that the raw data satisfy our assumption. Table 2.1 shows the output for sixteen heavy users of basilectal items.[2] Table 2.2 shows the output for ten heavy users of non-basilectal items.

[1] The term *basilect* was originally used by Stewart (1965). In the chapters that follow, *basilect* will be used to refer to that variety of Guyanese Creole most distinct from English, *acrolect* to refer to educated Guyanese English (a variety which differs from other standard varieties of the language only in a few phonological details and a handful of lexical items), and *mesolect* to refer to all intermediate varieties. Since the term mesolect covers a broad range, it will be convenient from time to time to refer to the *lower mesolect* (that part of the mesolect closest to the basilect), the *upper mesolect* (that part of the mesolect closest to the acrolect), and the *mid-mesolect* (that part of the mesolect roughly equidistant, in terms of rule-changes, from basilect and acrolect). It should be strongly emphasised that the entities thus referred to represent sectors of a continuum and should in no circumstances be reified as discrete objects (in the way that languages and dialects are traditionally reified). They are named in this way solely for convenience of reference; they blend into one another in such a way that no non-arbitrary division is possible. For further discussion of the issues involved, see Bickerton 1973b on the terms *lect* and *isolect*, as well as the modified (and somewhat improved) account in Bickerton 1973c.

[2] Eight of the twenty numbers in the left-hand column of Table 2.1 represent four speakers each of whom was recorded by different interviewers on different occasions.

TABLE 2.1   Basilectal outputs

Speaker	-s	-ed	(be)	-ing	doz	don	bina	bin	a
2				3	1	1		1	21
9			1	2	21	7	2	3	128
15			1	1	7	3	1		26
24							1		18
25				1		1	1		31
27		2	8	2	2	2		4	42
28					14	5		4	55
118							2	3	28
129							2	4	16
137		1	2	3	3	1	7	6	9
148	2		1				1	4	22
168		1	6	1	5	3			44
170				1	8	2		1	11
172				1	2	9			15
176					12	6		1	39
178				1	6	3		5	56
186		1	13	10	1		2		38
188					9	3	9	9	94
198				1	8		2	10	15
219				1	1		5	1	24
Total	2	5	32	28	100	46	35	56	732
Total standard forms: 67					Total non-standard forms: 969				

NOTE: -s = 3rd pers. sing. non-past -s; -ed = past morphemes for all verbs except *have* and *be*; (be) = all forms of verb, inflected or otherwise; -ing = verbal, adjectival and nominal forms, but excluding *going to* or equivalents.

TABLE 2.2   Non-basilectal outputs

Speaker	-s	-ed	(be)	-ing	doz	don	bina	bin	a
92	11	18	44	17					
93	5	31	39	18					
94	7	17	47	23					
117	2	10	49	30	4				2
122	2	29	76	26					
125	1	19	36	62	9			2	
196	2	24	74	39	7			2	13
226	3	26	46	8					
236	3	10	46	59	2			2	
241	5	23	58	32					
Total	41	207	515	314	22			6	15
Total standard forms: 1077					Total non-standard forms: 43				

NOTE: Categories as in Table 2.1.

We observe that, in Table 2.1, the four non-basilectal items account for only 6.4% of the tokens in the table; while of these four items, the two that are most clearly acrolectal [3] – i.e. -s and -ed – account for only 0.5%. But even this statement does not show the full extent of the disparity between the two halves of the table. For instance, of the 67 non-basilectal tokens, over two-thirds – 47 – are produced by only two speakers (2/186 and 27/168). These two are none other than the two 'deviant' speakers discussed at length in Bickerton 1971a, where the mixture of levels in their output is related to factors in their character and personal experience.

Table 2.2, on the other hand, shows an almost diametrically opposed tendency. Here, it is the putative basilectal tokens which contribute only 3.8% of the total. Moreover, three of the five basilectal types contribute only 0.5%, and six out of the ten speakers produce no basilectal forms at all. The disparity between the two tables is illustrated in Table 2.3 – chi-squared or any other tests of significance would surely be superfluous!

TABLE 2.3   Comparison of Tables 2.1 and 2.2

	Standard forms	Non-standard forms	Total
Table 2.1	67	969	1036
Table 2.2	1077	43	1120
Total	1144	1012	2156

The question of interpretation now arises. Are we to assume that all the non-standard forms are truly basilectal? We note that, even in Table 2.1, four out of five such forms have token-counts of 100 or less, contrasting not only with the massive count for *a*, but also with the more uniformly high figures for standard forms in Table 2.2. Some of the questions raised by this apparent disparity will be answered when we come to discuss the grammatical functions of basilectal markers and how they differ from non-basilectal forms. However, we note that, for *bin* and *bina*, not only is the total low, but for several speakers there is no occurrence of one or the other (some-

---

Nos. 2, 9, 27 and 28 represent the four speakers as originally interviewed by Arnold Persaud; nos. 186, 188, 168 and 178 (in that order) represent the same four speakers as interviewed by myself. Implications of this and other reinterviewing will be discussed in Chapter 5.

[3] Both -*ing* (phonologically [in]) and some forms of the verb *to be* (in particular *iz*, *waz*) are introduced into the continuum at a fairly early phase of development, although they do not become fully established until a mid-mesolectal level has been reached. The past morpheme is not introduced before the latter level and occurs only sporadically at that level. Third-person -*s* is one of the last standard features to be acquired, and this is also the case in Black English (Labov et al. 1968, Wolfram 1969, Fasold 1972).

times, of either) marker. How can we say that items of such rare and sporadic occurrence form an integral part of the basilectal system?

In fact, while many Guyanese speakers use these markers, none uses them with high frequency, simply because contexts for their use are rare in ordinary discourse.

Note that the proportion (91:6) of their tokens in Table 2.1 to their tokens in Table 2.2 is almost identical with the proportion (1077:67) of the tokens of standard forms in Table 2.2 to their tokens in Table 2.1. This tends to confirm that we are dealing simply with the contrast between rare and common forms, rather than with forms which are marginal at any stage of the grammar.

However, we are left with the question of how to determine which of our markers are truly basilectal, if we cannot do this on the basis of raw figures alone. I shall suggest that comparison with other segments of the continuum is one way. If a form is commoner among typical basilectal than among typical mesolectal speakers, then we can conclude without hesitation that that form is basilectal; however, if we should find the reverse relationship, we would be entitled to assume, even if the form were commoner among basilectal speakers than other putative basilectal forms, that it was not genuinely basilectal.

With the four markers *don, bina, bin* and *a*, we find that use in the basilect is far commoner than elsewhere. With *doz*, however, the second relationship is found. Even though, in Table 2.1, *doz* is more frequent than *don, bin* or *bina*, we see from Table 3.1 that the typical mesolectal speaker uses *doz* much more frequently than the typical basilectal speaker does. We shall see also that there are good grammatical reasons why this should be so. We shall conclude, therefore, that *doz*, although frequently used by basilectal speakers, is not an integral part of the basilectal grammar.

This leaves us with a system which contains *don, bin, bina, a* and of course the stem form of the verb. These constitute what, following Voorhoeve's (1957) analysis of the Sranan verbal system, will be called the 'realis' sub-system of the Guyanese verb. This sub-system will now be examined in some detail before we proceed to the examination of the 'irrealis' sub-system.

The stem form

It has been often claimed for creole and especially pidgin languages that they 'have no tense system' or 'use an invariant form of the verb in all contexts'. As we have seen, this claim could hardly be made for even the basilectal level of Guyanese Creole. However, it is undoubtedly true that the stem form exceeds in frequency any of the marked forms. There are two principal reasons for this; first, it has several different and quite distinct functions; second, surface stem forms often result from marker deletion.

The stem form of the verb is identical with the stem form of its English cognate (phonological representation apart, and where such cognates exist) apart from a handful of exceptions. Three of these exceptions have stem forms derived from English strong past forms: *lef* 'to leave', *los* 'to lose', *brok* 'to break'. One has a stem form derived from an English weak past: *marid* 'to marry'. Three are rather more complex. The English verb 'to get' is the source of two distinct Guyanese verbs, *get* 'to obtain' and *gat* 'to have, possess' (for a more distinct distinction see Bickerton 1971a:479–80). English 'to do' yields four distinct Guyanese forms: a main verb *du* of similar meaning; a main verb *don* 'to finish'; a completive aspect marker *don*; an iterative aspect marker *doz*. There is, however, no trace of '*do*-support' except at the acrolectal level. English 'to go' yields three distinct forms: a main verb *go* of similar meaning; an irrealis aspect marker *go*; a specialised completive aspect form, unique to this verb, *gaan*, whose use may best be shown by the following sentence:

> 2.1 *yu na go si mi, mi go komaut, mi go gaan* (148/24/191) [4] 'You won't see me, I'm leaving, I'll have gone.'

It is, in other words, equivalent to *don go*, which seems in consequence seldom or never to occur; thus, while *i go a tong* 'he went to town' is devoid of presuppositions as to the person's present whereabouts, *i gaan a tong* presupposes that he has not yet returned.

The functions of the stem form in the Guyanese system depend on the stative–non-stative distinction. In its commonest function, with non-statives, it signifies 'unmarked past' – that is, a (usually) single action that happened at a moment in the past that may or may not be specified but should not predate any action simultaneously under discussion.

Thus the stem contrasts both with 'past-before-pasts' and with continuative–iterative forms. Since the latter, in narrative, are used for the speaker's generalisations and comments, the English relationship is reversed: instead of a morphologically marked past tense and unmarked non-past, we have a morphologically unmarked past and marked non-past. This relationship can best be exemplified by quoting a longish narrative passage:

----

[4] All cited sentences actually produced by informants will be marked, as this one, with the informant's survey number and the line and page number of the transcribed recording, in that order.

2.2 Well a-we *get up*, a-we *wake up*, L—— *run out*. Me *wake up* them pikni and so, all of them *hold on* 'pon me. Well all a-we *de* – a-we *de* – a-we *say* 'Oh God, a what *go happen* now with this – trouble?' Well, a-we *stand* for a time. A-we *frighten* because you [i.e. L——] *left* the house and *go 'way* and a-we *left* in the house. Well a-we *de* till morning. When morning *meet*, well, a-we *get up*, a-we *make* little tea and so, *eat* and so, not *eat* properly – # # You *a always get* this thing in you mind steady stand, how you *go eat* properly? You *not eat* – you *a eat* you little food but you *not feel* satisfy. # # Well one night more we *hear* drum a knock again. Well that night me just *go* and me and L——, a-we two *sit down* . . . (28/9–19/28).

The earlier section of the passage is not – as it would be in standard English – a description of usual or frequently occurring events: it deals with the incidents of a particular night. Then in the section separated by the boundary markers # #, the narrator pauses for a moment to make some general remarks about this whole period of her life (during the Guyanese racial 'disturbances' of 1964). In the last section, the description of another night's events is begun.

In the first and third sections, practically every verb denotes a past single action and is therefore in the stem form. In the second section, every verb is morphologically marked, one with the irrealis *go*, the others with *a*. The absence of surface *a* with the negated verbs comes about because the phonological shape of the negative particle is *na* and an obligatory rule assimilates consecutive low vowels.

With stative verbs, however, the stem form signifies non-past. Thus we have sentences such as the following:

2.3 *mi na no wai dem a du dis ting* (5/25/3) 'I don't know why they are doing this.'
2.4 *di rais wok get mo iizia fi du bika trakta a plau am* (9/21/9) 'Rice farming becomes easier to do because tractors do the ploughing.'
2.5 *nau fram wa mi ekspiirians, yu si, piipl a jelas dem iitsh an ada* (221/2/276) 'Now from what I've experienced, you see, people get envious of one another.'
2.6 *wi a pak am op hai laik haus an wi kaal di plees karyaan* (168/6/215) 'We pile it up as high as a house and we call the place the threshing-floor.'

Here, the stative verbs *no, get, ekspiirians, kaal* are non-past and carry no marker of tense or aspect, while the non-statives *du, plau, pak*, which are equally non-past, are all preceded by continuative–iterative *a*. *Jelas* in 2.5 is not the counter-example it might seem; it is true that in the Guyanese basilect, 'adjectives' are in fact stative verbs, but (as shown in Bickerton 1973a) they will take *a* when a *process* rather than a *state* is indicated. With this exception, the co-occurrence of statives and continuative markers is as unacceptable as it is in English:

> 2.7 **mi a no da* *'I am knowing that.'
> 2.8 **dem a gat wan kyar* *'They are having [sc. possessing] a car.'

At this point it should be noted that the stative–non-stative distinction in Guyanese Creole is a semantic one entirely: that is to say, it is not the case that specific lexical items are marked unambiguously [+ stative] or [− stative], rather that these categories apply to propositions irrespective of their lexical content. For instance, in the next two examples, though the surface verb is identical in each, the first sentence contains a stative proposition and the second a non-stative one:

> 2.9 *tu an tu mek fo* 'Two and two make four.'
> 2.10 *dem mek i stap* 'They made him stop.'

Since 2.9 has a stative sense, *mek* here follows the rule for stative verbs (stem-only for non-past). But 2.10 has a non-stative meaning, and in it, *mek* must therefore follow the non-stative rule (stem-only for simple past). Note that one must either arbitrarily list *mek*1 [+ stative] and *mek*2 [− stative] in the lexicon, or one must admit that the syntactic component can somehow 'read' semantic information, i.e. that semantics is generative rather than interpretative.

A third common source of stem forms arises from what, on one interpretation, we would have to regard as a system of deletion rules applying in the following environments:

(a) After passivisation. Guyanese Creole has two forms of the passive. One, which applies where the object of the active sentence is non-animate, results from subject–object inversion, followed by obligatory agent- and aspect-marker-deletion:

> 2.11 *den yu a dok am* (172/2/221) 'Then you flood it [the ricefield].'
> 2.12 *yu laan nau lef wid di rais dok* (175/24/225) 'Your land is now left with the rice flooded.'
> 2.13 **yu lan nau lef wid di rais a dok.*
> 2.14 **yu lan nau a lef wid di rais dok.*
> 2.15 *mi a kompliit mi raisfiil* (188/12/245) 'I prepare my ricefield.'
> 2.16 *wen dis raisfiil kompliit nau awi a haalaut dis plaant* (188/14/245) 'When this ricefield is prepared, now, we fetch out these plants.'
> 2.17 **wen dis raisfiil a kompliit nau . . .*

As with the stative–non-stative distinction (examples 2.9, 2.10), passive formation often results in a given verb having the same surface form in both past and non-past contexts:

2.18 *som de inglish laan* (149/30/192) 'On some days, English is taught.'

2.19 *dis man laan am fu dans an sing* (67/8/68) 'This man taught her to dance and sing.'

The other Guyanese passive, which applies usually when the object of the active sentence is animate, though sometimes when it is not,[5] inverts subject and object and deletes agent, but replaces aspect markers (or zero, if there are none) with *get*:

2.20 *bai, yu get stab!* (121/20/154) 'Boy, you've been stabbed!'

2.21 *wel plenti get biitop, haatit an ting* (9/5/10) 'Well a lot were beaten up, wounded and so on.'

(b) In temporal clauses.

2.22 *wel wen yu kom yu go get dis bai go opn di do* (146/11/188) 'Well when you arrive you'll get this boy to open the door.'

2.23 *wen yu go satide yu a dra yu sevn shilin moni an yu a kom hoom, yu a go di shap, yu a bai lil gudz an yu a kom an yu a meenteen yu chiren-dem* (222/30–1/276) 'When you went on Saturdays you'd draw your seven shillings pay and come home, go to the shop, buy a few things and come back and maintain your children.'

(c) In conditional clauses.

2.24 *bot if reen faal, yu a go neks de* (9/1/8), 'But if it rains, you go on the following day.'

2.25 *if di piipl-dem kom fi du eniting dem a go pipeer demsef* (188/1/247) 'If the people come to do anything, they're going to prepare themselves.'

(d) Before modals.

2.26 *yu gatu hosl fu go kot rais somtaim, so yu a hosl fu get moni fu bai op rashin* (28/4–5/29) 'You have to hurry to go and cut rice sometimes, so you rush to get money to buy food with.'

2.27 *wen di weda drai i a go gud* [Int.: *bot wen it reen nau?*] *i kyaan go bika i a faal dong* (129/6–7/178) 'When the weather's dry he can go all right. [But when it rains?] He can't go because he keeps falling down.'

---

[5] It may well be that originally the intransitive stem form functioned as a passive in all contexts, and that *get* in any context was a subsequent innovation or borrowing. Unfortunately, there will not be space here to fully analyse the passive, the use of so-called 'verb chains' or 'serial verbs', and several other extremely interesting but not directly relevant aspects of verb-phrase construction.

However, an alternative to the 'deletion' analysis is suggested by the fact that while continuatives and iteratives are deleted, completives are not:

2.28 *wen i don plau, put yu laan fi sook wan-tu de* (172/18/221) 'When it's been ploughed, let your land flood for a day or two.'

2.29 *wen i plau, put yu laan fi sook wan-tu de* 'When it's *being* ploughed, let your land flood for a day or two.'

2.30 *wen mi bin yong, yu no hau awi yuus tu wok* (119/24/150) 'You know how we used to work when I was young.'

2.31 **wen mi yong, yu no hau awi yuus tu wok.*

2.32 *'if mi bin no' a wan afta-blo* [Guyanese proverb, quoted Abrams 1970:13] '[The thought] "If only I'd known" is an "after-blow" [i.e. rubs salt in the wound, adds insult to injury].'

2.33 ***if mi no a wan afta-blo.*

2.34 *injan piipl bin kyaan waak baut in jaajtong* (22/30/21) 'Indians couldn't walk about in Georgetown.'

2.35 *injan piipl kyaan waak baut in jaajtong* 'Indians *can't* walk about in Georgetown.'

It would appear that the factor common to all these deletion-environments is stativisation. Passives are always statives in English (perhaps universally) as is indicated by a number of English sentences which are ambiguous as between 'passive' and 'copula-plus-adjective' interpretations: 'he was/seemed annoyed/interested/surprised' etc. Modals are not only statives in themselves, but also stativise the the verbs they precede, as can be seen from:

2.36 John told Bill to leave.
2.37 *John told Bill to be able to leave.
2.38 *John told Bill to have to leave.

As for temporal and conditional clauses, the restriction on deletion when completives are present indicates that such clauses must carry the sense of 'whenever, on any occasion on which . . .' for deletion to take place. In other words, these clauses too must be regarded as stative, since it is implied that the consequent state or action in the main clause will *always* apply if the condition in the subordinate clause is realised. The superior economy of a generative-semantic explanation should here be apparent. Any syntax-first grammar would have to generate sentences with marked aspect and then add a deletion rule that would separately specify all four of the above environments. A semantics-first grammar, however, can take advantage of the separately motivated rule that deletes (or perhaps better, fails to generate) continuative and iterative markers where there is a [+ stative] semantic marker in the derivation of any S. Since such a marker is part of the semantic specification of modals, since it can be assumed to underlie the 'ifs' and 'whens' of 'always-applicable' conditionals and temporals, and since it can be claimed to be present wherever the passive transformation operates,[6] no further apparatus would be required to generate the grammatical (and exclude the ungrammatical) sentences above; the main stative rule would simply apply across the board.

But whatever its derivational history, the non-appearance of continuative and iterative markers in the environments described is a further cause of the neutralisation of past and non-past in basilectal Guyanese Creole surface forms, and thus seems to lend further support to 'all-purpose stem-form' theories of creole structure. The situation is compounded by a development we shall have occasion to deal with at a later stage: the gradual disappearance of non-standard aspect markers in the mesolect. However, the reality of the 'deletion' phenomenon in the basilect can best be shown by quoting a longish passage from a truly basilectal speaker, showing the alternation of marked and unmarked verb forms. In this extract, each finite verb is italicised, and the reason for 'deletion' shown in parentheses after it (T = temporal clause, C = conditional clause, S = V[+ stative], M = modal):

2.39 When this rice *grow out* (T) about half an inch you *a carry* am and you *a throw* am. You *a throw* am upon this ricefield. But upon this time you *got* (M) to watchman am, *let* (M) bird and thing not eat am, and you *got* (M) for regulate you water. Well when you *see* (T) this plant come little good size, you *start* (M) complete you ricefield, but awe not *does get* [7] cow plenty-plenty. If you *get* (C, S) one and me *get* (C, S) one, you *a lend* me you one and me one *make* (S) one pair, then me *a complete* me ricefield. (188/6–12/245).

a

As we have seen, *a* is the commonest basilectal marker. Speaker 9's 128 tokens, for example, occur within a text of less than 2,500 words. As Zipf's Law would indicate, this frequency is related to the number of semantic roles it plays.

[6] For instance, one test for stativity in English is complementation of command verbs, e.g. 'I told him to leave' versus *'I told him to know'. Compare 'I advised John to leave Mary' with *'I advised Mary to be left by John.'

[7] At first sight, *does get* looks like a flat violation of the rule that prevents co-occurrence of stative verbs and [− punctual] markers. However, basilectal creole lacks adverbs of indefinite time such as 'sometimes', 'often', 'usually' etc. These therefore have to be replaced by pre-verbal markers or other devices. The clause here should be glossed: 'But we very often don't have very many cows.'

In her analysis of Jamaican Creole, B. L. Bailey (1966:46) treats *a* as a purely continuative marker, equivalent to English *be + -ing*. In Guyana, *a* does indeed have this function; however, if we look at 2.39, we will see that none of the *a*-verbs could be translated in this way. The speaker is in fact referring to a series of actions repeated at intervals. Moreover, since her account deals with rice-growing 'in the old days', that series is one which must be regarded as completed. In other words, *a* marks both continuative and iterative verb phrases, and (for truly basilectal speakers at least) it does this irrespective of whether temporal reference is past or non-past. We may therefore distinguish four functions of *a*:

(a) Continuative non-past.

> 2.40 *i se we yu a go wid bondl* (9/6/11) 'He said, "Where are you going with that bundle?" '
>
> 2.41 *mi a kom back haptanuun* (179/14/230) 'I'm coming back in the afternoon.'

(b) Continuative past.

> 2.42 *di kuliman bin prapa fraikn di blakman – evribadi a wach aut de an nait fu si wa go hapn* (27/28/25) 'The Indians were really afraid of the Negroes – everybody was watching out to see what would happen.'
>
> 2.43 *a beg mi a beg dis bai nau se le i ker aut wan baks fu mi bika mi son na de hoom* (148/21/189) 'I was literally begging this boy to carry out a box for me because my son isn't home.'

(c) Iterative non-past.

> 2.44 *dem na laan awi notn gud* [Int.: *wai?*] *dem a gyaf an na laan awi notn* (149, 152/6–7/192) 'They don't teach us anything properly. [Why?] They gossip and don't teach us anything.'
>
> 2.45 *evri de mi a ron a raisfiil* (137/29/182) 'Every day I hurry to the ricefield.'

(d) Iterative past.

> 2.46 *dis a hapn an dat a hapn aal abaut a wizma, makenzi an so, bot awi – awi na bin gat no distoobans a bushlat nat ataal* (8/21–3/6) 'This happened and that happened all around at Wismar, Mackenzie and so on, but we – we hadn't any disturbance in Bushlot at all.'
>
> 2.47 *evribadi bin gatu wach aut an evribadi a de aal abaut a rood, striit, dam* (28/1–2/28) 'Everyone had to be on the watch and everyone used to be all over the place, on roads, streets, dams.'

One of the strongest rules in basilectal Guyanese Creole is that which restricts the use of *a* to non-stative verbs (cf. Bickerton 1973a). One seldom if ever encounters sentences such as **mi a no*, **dem a waan* 'I am knowing',

'They are wanting' (but see discussion of Example 2.59 below). However, there are two apparent counter-examples which must be mentioned here. The first concerns the use of *a* with 'predicate adjectives' (which are in fact surface stative verbs in Guyanese basilect, as shown in Bickerton 1973b). Here (as is also shown in the cited paper) *a* reverses the polarity of the items it governs, converting e.g. [+ stative] *redi* 'to be ready' into [− stative] *redi* 'to *get* ready'. The second is exemplified in 2.47, where *a* is used with what most speakers would treat as a [+ stative] item, the locative verb *de*. Since *de* characteristically indicates temporary as opposed to permanent states (*i de a haus* 'He is at home' as opposed to *i a fulaman* 'He is a Moslem'), it may be that some speakers interpret its marker [− durative] as being fully equivalent to [− stative]. For instance, while only six occurrences of *a* + *de* are to be found in texts by the twenty-eight speakers of the Bushlot sub-sample, five of the six are produced by a single speaker (28). This would seem to indicate that 28 has allotted to *de* a semantic marking different from that allotted it by other local residents.

Another source of problems is the relationship between *a* and *doz*, which will be discussed in Chapter 3.

bin

In dealing with the stem form, we saw that the 'meaning' of this form was related to stativity − that stem + [+ stative] signified 'non-past', while stem + [− stative] signified 'past'. The 'meaning' of *bin* is similarly affected by the stative–non-stative opposition. With statives, *bin* indicates a simple past:

2.48 *dem bin gat wan lil haus* (9/26/10) 'They had a little house.'
2.49 *o gaad man ayu bin kyan kil awi laas nait* (178/29/244) 'Oh God, man, you could have killed us last night.'

For this reason, we find that speakers in general − and, indeed, the majority of individual speakers − use *bin* far more frequently with statives than with non-statives. This can be seen if we analyse the outputs of the heaviest *bin*-users in Table 2.1; we will note that only one speaker, 9/188, uses *bin* oftenest with non-statives, and that, significantly, in both her speech events.

The function of *bin* with non-statives is rather less clear. By analogy with its stative functions, one would expect it to indicate a time anterior to that indicated by the stem form. Since stem + [− stative] indicates 'past', *bin* would therefore have to indicate some kind of 'past-before-past' or pluperfect form, and indeed in many cases this is exactly what it does:

TABLE 2.4   Frequency of *bin* with statives and non-statives

| Speaker | bin | |
	+Stative	−Stative
9	1	2
27	3	1
28	4	–
118	3	–
129	4	–
137	4	2
148	3	1
178	5	–
188	4	5
198	8	2
Total	39	13

2.50 *wan taim J——— son se i bina – weda kom o go se dem blak piipl bin stap i kya fi biit am an ting* (9/23–4/10) 'Once J———'s son said he was – that either coming or going those black people had stopped his car in order to beat him up or something.'

2.51 *dem bin gatu get we an kom dis said, lef di plees an get we, bikaz terabl ting bin hapn wid dem chiren* (188/8–9/246) 'They had to get away and come over here, leave the place and get away, because terrible things had happened to their children.'

In other cases, however, such an interpretation is at best doubtful:

2.52 *di plan waz dis, da awi bin set op som dromz* (16/17/16) 'The plan was this, that we [had?] set up some drums.'

Note that this speaker is not purely basilectal (*waz, som dromz*) and may therefore be an inaccurate guide to basilectal usage. On the other hand, some clearly basilectal speakers use *bin* in contexts where a 'past-before-past' interpretation is barely possible. Sometimes simple completion seems to be indicated:

2.53 *dis fut bin swel he si di tu a saiz* (185/26/236) 'This foot has swelled up, compare the size of the two.'

Sometimes a past that is merely very remote, rather than a 'past-before-past', is being referred to:

2.54 *wen mi bin smaal laik a dem pikni dis den mi bin faal a trensh* (198/2/262) 'When I was as small as these children, I fell in a canal.'

Since *bin* + [− stative] occurs so infrequently, it may well be that different speakers have internalised marginally different rules for its use; however, later in this chapter we will consider a possible explanation that would account for all these examples.

bina

If *bin* occurs oftenest with statives, the reverse is true of *bina*. Of the 87 tokens that occur in our samples of basilectal speech, 70 are with non-statives. However, since *bina* is simply a combination of *bin + a*, and *a* is rejected by statives, it is the co-occurrence of *bina* with *any* statives, rather than the frequency of its occurrence with non-statives, that requires explanation.

With non-statives, *bina*, like *bin*, often conveys a sense of 'past-before-past', plus of course continuity:

> 2.55 *mi bina tel I——, mi se, bifo i lef, yu no, i go pe – i go pe som rent* (135/27/181) 'I kept telling I——, I said, before he left, you know, that he would – he would [have to] pay some rent.'

More frequent are sentences in which the *– a* segment of *bina* carries its iterative rather than its continuative sense; the only difference between these sentences and sentences such as 2.46 and 2.47 above (where repeated past actions are indicated by *a* alone) is that in the former the speaker wishes to assert that the time-phase in which the action(s) occurred is definitively terminated:

> 2.56 *baut fo taim mi bina tek autsaida triitment* (185/22/236) 'I've had "outside treatment" about four times.' [By 'outside treatment', the speaker subsequently specifies that she means treatment by an 'outside doctor', i.e. one not attached to a hospital; the whole point of her narrative is that she is no longer undergoing this treatment but is attending a local hospital as an outpatient.]
>
> 2.57 *wan blakman an i waif bina liv abak* (9/26/10) 'A Negro and his wife used to live inland.' [The whole point of this story is that, as a result of the 'disturbances', they live there no longer.]

A third function of *bina* more closely resembles one which in standard English is carried out by the past continuous tense, i.e. that of indicating an action of some duration, within the span of which a briefer or instantaneous action occurs (e.g. 'When John arrived, Bill was eating lunch' etc.):

> 2.58 *wan nait awi bina kom fram raisfiil, wen awi miit goolingroov ton, soja blak awi de wi dem taachlait* (15/32/16) 'One night we were coming from the ricefield, when we reached Goldengrove intersection, soldiers with electric torches stopped us there.'

One may well ask why, in the light of examples 2.42 and 2.43, *awi a kom* could not have been used here. While in all verbal systems there is some 'fuzziness' and consequent overlap, and while one would not risk completely ruling out *a* in this context, it could be suggested that 2.58 refers to a specific past time (*wan nait*) as opposed to the less definite past of 2.42, and to a remote past time as opposed to the more recent past of 2.43. The clearest distinction between *bina* and *a* can be seen when each occurs in a subordinate clause, as in the following examples:

2.59 *mi tel am wa mi a du* 'I told him what I was doing.'
2.60 *mi tel am wa mi bina du* 'I told him what I had been doing.

Of the seventeen cases of *bina* + [+ stative], at least one arises because (as noted in connection with examples 2.9, 2.10) semantic markers apply to nodes in derivations rather than to individual lexical items. This example is worth quoting at some length, since it illustrates one way in which the exigencies of discourse can affect otherwise categorical rules. Here the interviewer is interrogating a somewhat awkward informant about Kali Mai Puja, an Indian religious ceremony:

2.61 Int.: You can give an account how it [the ceremony] used to happen inside Albion [a sugar estate] really? Was it really inside Albion? Long days ago?
  252: You mean Albion?
  Int.: Uh-huh, inside Albion when them had the logies [ranges of huts used for housing indentured labourers] and thing.
  252: [Offended – logies are very 'low'] No, we never been in logie.
  Int.: No, I mean this Kali, was it inside there?
  252: Of course you not get different – different people in different – different – ahm . . .
  253: [Cuts in impatiently to interpret for his friend] He *bina want* for know if you been had this Puja, Kali Puja in here.
  252: Yes, but now he dismember with different members (246, 252, 253/1–7/334).

Here 253 has to incorporate two things: first, that it is what the interviewer originally wanted, not what 252 may have thought he wanted, that is really at issue; second, that the interviewer has been unsuccessfully requesting this information for some time, and is still requesting it. The first requires some sort of past, the second some sort of continuative; *bina* represents the only comprehensive solution.

A few instances of *bina* + [+ stative] occur because, as we saw while discussing *a*, speakers are unevenly divided on the question whether *de* is a stative or a non-stative verb. Speaker 148 is of the latter opinion:

2.62 *wel di plees bina de veekant* (148/27/188) 'Well, the place used to be vacant.'

At least one instance can be written off as performance error, as shown by its utterer's self-correction:

2.63 *evriting bina chiip – evriting bin chiip* (198/19/261) 'Everything was cheap.'

However, the bulk of *bina* + [+ stative] tokens occur in a batch of samples from the Port Mourant area of Berbice, collected by a student interviewer whose basilectal competence may have been eroded by contact with standard English. This interviewer used *bina* with a sub-class of stative verb, and promptly secured an 'echo effect' (Bickerton and Escalante 1970:266):

2.64 Int.: *lang taim piipl bina baad o gud?*
219: *no, lang taim piipl bina ova gud, tumoch gud* (199, 219/1–2/272)
'Were people in the old days good or bad?' 'No, in the old days people were very good, extremely good.'

An almost identical echo, though this time with a slight hesitation, is secured from Speaker 220. However, a third speaker, 222, produces four tokens of *bina* + 'adjectival' verb in a single sentence, without any stimulus from the interviewer, and this leaves open the possibility that the form may be a regional phenomenon of limited distribution rather than a mere performance error and its echoes.

don

So far, we have avoided any consideration of performance features, such as differential distribution of markers by type of discourse, even where such features were both statistically significant and of some interest to the analyst of extended discourse.[8] In the case of *don*, however, certain performance features virtually force themselves on our notice, and may provide a clue to the only significant difference between the basilectal Guyanese and Sranan verbal systems, to be discussed later in the present chapter.

In the Bushlot sub-sample (details of which are given in Bickerton 1971a) the proportion of speech on rice-growing to speech on the 'disturbances' is one of roughly three to two. However, of the twenty-six occurrences of *don*

---

[8] For instance, process-descriptions generally contain many *a* tokens and few if any *bin* ones. Conversely, accounts of past experience will contain more *bin* and relatively little *a*. Formal narrative (e.g. folk-tales) may often contain very few or no pre-verbal markers; since many linguists base their analysis on folk-tales, this fact has helped spread the 'one-verb-form-only, tense-determined-by-context' myth about pidgins and creoles.

found in this sub-sample, no less than twenty-three take place in 'rice-growing' texts, as against only three in 'disturbances' texts. Moreover, the only other dense concentration of *don* tokens (31) is found in a further sub-sample of Berbician speakers ($N = 7$) who also described the process of rice-growing. Without these texts, the incidence of *don* would have been so low that it could conceivably have been overlooked in analysis.

Don is unique in that it alone of Guyanese verbal markers can occur clause-finally; in this it resembles Neo-Melanesian equivalent *pinis*, as well as Hawaiian Creole equivalent *pau*.

> 2.65 *wen yu beel am don so yu si i a drai* (172/6/221) 'When you've finished draining it, then you'll see it getting dry.'
> 2.66 *wen mi kuk don, mi a hosl fiid op mi pikni* (176/5/226) 'When I've finished cooking, I hurry and feed my child.'

Post-clausal *don* is frequently associated with repetition patterns in discourse similar to those described for Saramaccan by Grimes and Glock (1970):

> 2.67 *mashop di plees, den wen di plees mashop don, yu tek aaf di aksn* (11/16/13) 'Break up the ground, then when the ground is completely broken up, you take the oxen off it.'

However, *don* with identical function is also used pre-verbally:

> 2.68 *wen awi don levl op dis biari, awi bos rais an bring am an shai am pan di laan* (171/26/219) 'When we've finished levelling this nursery bed, we sprout the rice and bring it and sow it broadcast on the land.'
> 2.69 *wen dem don plau dem chip* (28/3/30) 'When they've finished ploughing, they harrow.'

There is a good deal of evidence to indicate that clause-final *don* represents an older layer of the creole system than pre-verbal *don*. We have already noted Neo-Melanesian extra-clausal markers; these are treated by Sankoff and Laberge (1973) as typical of pidgin rather than creole development, and indeed they point to a parallel shift of one such marker (*baimbai*, reducing to *bai*) from sentence-initial to immediate pre-verbal position as being a concomitant of the current creolisation of Neo-Melanesian. We also observe an uneven distribution of finals and pre-verbals as between the Bushlot and Corentyne sub-samples, as shown in Table 2.5. It is widely assumed in Guyana, and with some justification, that the Corentyne in East Berbice represents a more archaic type of speech than does West Berbice, where Bushlot is located; certainly, those Bushlot speakers (such as 9 and 28) who do use post-clausal *don* are among the most basilectal in the village. *Don* also seems to be found in all West African English-based pidgins and cre-

TABLE 2.5 Distribution of *don* by area and sentence-type

	don		
	Pre-verbal	Clause-final	Total
Bushlot	19	7	26
Corentyne	7	24	31
Total	26	31	57

oles, such as Krio and Weskos; if it is correct (as has been suggested by Hancock 1969, summarising much previous work) that Caribbean anglo-creoles in general originated in West Africa, then this would be a further argument for its age.

However, some contrary evidence has to be taken into account. We have assumed hitherto that Surinam creoles such as Sranan and Saramaccan represented an earlier stage of Guyanese Creole; however, there is no mention of either *don* or any functional equivalent in the published literature on Sranan, while in Grimes and Glock's study of Saramaccan narrative, the repetition-triggering device is shown to be a morpheme *di*, occurring clause-initially, glossed as 'With reference to . . .', and apparently bearing no relation whatsoever to *don* (1970:409). Moreover, *don* is not found in Quow (1877) nor in Guyanese proverbs, the two most reliable sources for nineteenth-century Guyanese speech.

Leaving aside this question for the moment, we can speedily dispose of any suggestion that *don* could be merely a variant form of completive *bin*; while in sentences such as 2.69, *don* could freely be moved to clause-final position, *bin* could not substitute in either position:

2.70 *wen dem plau don, dem chip.*
2.71 **wen dem bin plau, dem chip.*
2.72 ***wen dem plau bin, dem chip.*

Moreover, most informants will accept the following distinctions:

2.73 *mi bin gat wan dag* 'I had a dog' [but some time ago, and I may not still have one].
2.74 *mi don gat wan dag* 'I have a dog' [still, and therefore don't need another one].
2.75 *mi bin se da* 'I said that' [once, but might not wish to repeat it].
2.76 *mi don se da* 'I said that' [and I stick by it].

Thus the Guyanese basilect distinguishes two types of 'completiveness' – a kind which marks a past state of affairs as no longer necessarily obtaining (*bin*) and a kind which marks such a state as being either a necessary preliminary to a succeeding state, or as persisting unchanged into the present (*don*). It could be argued that English makes a similar distinction with *have/had* + past participle. However, what is rendered by the English perfect cannot necessarily be translated by *don*, just as the English pluperfect cannot always be translated by *bin*; conversely, Guyanese *don*-completive may require to be translated by English simple present, simple past, perfect or perfect + *finish* + V*ing*, just as *bin*-completive may require to be translated by English simple past, perfect or pluperfect.

Having considered the realis system of the basilect, we can now turn to the irrealis system. This may be taken as including all states and actions which have not actually occurred, whether these are expressed by future or conditional tenses or by modals. As the irrealis system is considerably less complex than the realis, and subject to correspondingly less change in the decreolisation process, we shall deal with it rather more briefly.

Quow (1877) and proverbs have *sa* as their principal irrealis marker, covering both futurative and conditional uses. However, Speakers 28, 135 and 137 (all women, incidentally) were the only ones who used *sa*, and even they yielded only five tokens; all three more frequently used the irrealis marker currently used by all other basilectal speakers in our sample, i.e. *go*, and there is apparently no distinction in meaning between the two:

2.77 *wel if di ded kom aal awi sa tek ded rait he* (28/21/28) 'Well if death comes, all of us will die right here.'
2.78 *den yu go kaal fu boot an so yu a go a kriik* (28/11/29) 'Then you will call for a boat and that's how you go up the creek.'
2.79 *hi sa pe di rent tu* (135/26/181) 'He will pay the rent too.'
2.80 *fraidi awi go mek* (135/18/181) 'We'll make [some] on Friday.'

In addition to the pure futures of 2.79 and 2.80, *go* serves to convey unrealised conditions:

2.81 *wen awi he dem ting-dem dis, awi tu staat mek prepareeshn se wen dem blak man go atak awi, awi go no wa fu du* (6/3–4/4) 'When we heard these things, we, too, began to make preparations so that when those Negroes attacked us, we would know what to do.'
2.82 *if eni blak man fi kom in awi vilij fi mek eni trobl, dem go nak dis drom* (9/19–20/10) 'If any Negro should come into our village to make trouble, they would beat this drum.'

(Note the – for Guyana – very rare use of *fi* as an alternative conditional; though this form is common in Jamaica (cf. B. L. Bailey 1966:45), 2.82 is the only recorded context I have for its occurrence). However, when a condition is counter-factual as well as unrealised, *bin* + *go* can be used:

2.83 *i wuda tek awi lil taim but awi bin go kom aut seef* (242/19/322) 'It would have taken us a little time but we would have come out all right.'

Modals present the greatest area of similarity with standard English. It is unlikely that there is any speaker who lacks *kyan* 'can' or *mos* 'must'. It is true that both have variant forms: *eebl*, possibly more ancient than *kyan*, and *mosi*, derived presumably from 'must have' but not always used with a perfective sense. However, *kyan* and *mos*, when they do occur, are used in no ways that differ from their English uses (except that they follow rather than precede tense-aspect markers), and indeed they serve to introduce into Guyanese Creole the English verb-negation rule.

A note on basilectal negation must be made here, since (as we shall see in later chapters) changes in negation that come about in the mesolect serve as levers for more widespread changes in the tense-aspect system. The creole negation rule is that the negative particle *na* (presumably introduced under a higher predicate node) is moved into a position immediately between the grammatical subject and the negated verb phrase, irrespective of whether question or statement is involved, or of whether the verb phrase is simple or complex:

2.84 *hu na iit rengk kyan go in* (248/2/327) 'Those who have not eaten unclean foods can go in.'
2.85 *yu na taak tu di man neks de?* (127/8/153) 'Didn't you talk to the man next day?'
2.86 *noobadi na bina sliip a dem haus* (26/14/25) 'Nobody used to sleep at home.'

It seems likely that, when *kyan* and *mos* were first introduced, they followed this same negative rule, traces of which remain in the speech of some informants:

2.87 *bod an ting na mos pik am* (9/29/7) 'Birds and such mustn't eat it.'
2.88 *hu na kyan afood it* (2/2/6) 'Those who cannot afford it.'

However, even for these speakers, the negative rule with *kyan* and *mos* has become variable, so that alongside the last two examples we find:

2.89 *wen reen faal, mosn kech wata* (9/25/8) 'When it rains, it mustn't get wet.'
2.90 *yu kyaan go intafeer wid awi* (186/13/241) 'You can't go and interfere with us.'

(Negative *kyaan* is differentiated from *kyan* by a combination of greater vowel-length, heavier stress and higher tone.) In later chapters we shall see

how the English negative-placement rule (inserting the negative particle immediately after the first morpheme in the verb phrase, irrespective of sub-
ject-position) gradually spreads to other areas from this point of origin
among the modals.

We have now outlined the structure of the basilectal tense-aspect system.
Before turning to examine how this system has gradually developed through
mesolectal stages in the direction of the acrolect, we should really raise the
question: where exactly does the basilectal system come from?

On the face of things, there are three possibilities:

(a) The basilectal system represents a simplification of the English tense
system.

(b) It represents the transference, with or without simplification, of some
African system or systems.

(c) It represents some kind of lowest-common-denominator of the contributing systems, European and African – either a mixture of elements
from the two, or the recovery of some 'deep', 'basic', quasi-universal system
that would underlie both.

The question of creole origins is a vexed one which has been pursued for
several decades with little enough in the way of concrete and generally accepted results (cf. Alleyne 1971; Comhaire-Sylvain 1936; Hall 1958, 1966;
Taylor 1959, 1960, 1963; Thompson 1961; Turner 1949; Weinreich 1958;
Whinnom 1965, 1971, to mention but a few), and little purpose can be
served by involving oneself in controversies such as those of monogenesis
versus polygenesis, or European versus African genetic affiliation. However,
we may be able to provide certain facts which will prove useful to future
students of creole origins.

The first hypothesis has perhaps been the most widely held in the past;
deriving from Bloomfield's original pronouncement (1933:472) and maintained unaltered by at least some generativists (e.g. Naro 1970), it underlies
much of Hall's work, and was at one time partially endorsed for Guyana's
linguistically closest neighbour, Jamaica, by DeCamp (1964:228).[9] Furthermore, C.-J. Bailey's theory of linguistic change can be interpreted as mean-

---

[9] In fairness to DeCamp, one must point out that he has since explicitly rejected simplification as a valid account of creole origins. However, since his previous position might
still seem plausible enough to be defended by others, it may be worth quoting:

I would much prefer to indicate this multistructural aspect of a creole language at a
higher level of abstraction: to say for example that Jamaican Creole consists of English
(in a somewhat archaic and provincial form), which has undergone certain structural
simplifications, and to which have been added certain structural complexities from an

ing that creoles decreolise merely by adding superstrate rules (Bailey 1974); this would imply that, however it might be derived, the 'aboriginal' grammar of an anglo-creole would be equivalent to a simplified ('unmarked') grammar of English.

The most radical possible simplification of English, or any other, grammar would involve using only a single (presumably, the stem) form of the verb in all circumstances, and using adverbs and/or other periphrastic devices to convey tense and aspect wherever context failed to make them unambiguous. It has often been claimed (most recently in Tsuzaki 1971 and Labov MS.) that pidgins are characterised by, or at least originate with, this type of structure, even though no well-described pidgin seems entirely devoid of tense-aspect markers, and it could well be argued that 'tenselessness' is characteristic only of the earliest stages of second-language learning (irrespective of whether the language learnt is a pidgin, a creole or a 'developed' language). Clearly, however, no level of Guyanese Creole exhibits structure of this kind.

A less radical simplification would be to select some, but not all, of the parameters that determine the English system. For the realis section of that system, there are effectively three such parameters – ± past, ± continuative, ± perfective – the eight possible combinations of which exhaust the English realis set:

– P – C – Pf	walk
+ P – C – Pf	walked
– P + C – Pf	is walking
+ P + C – Pf	was walking
– P – C + Pf	has walked
+ P – C + Pf	had walked
– P + C + Pf	has been walking
+ P + C + Pf	had been walking

Since the only thing that looks like a perfective in the Guyanese basilect is *don*, and since *don* has such a narrow range of use, it might seem reasonable to begin with the hypothesis that only the first two parameters were selected. This would yield only four possible combinations:

Footnote 9 continued

alien linguistic system. That this probably mirrors the historical facts is not the point here. I contend that this is the most efficient description for synchronic purposes.

From the present study, however, it appears highly unlikely that simplification followed by piecemeal addition either 'mirrors the historical facts' or provides the best hypothesis for synchronic description.

	Stative	Non-stative
− P − C	Ø	a
+ P − C	bin	Ø
− P + C	–	a
+ P + C	–	a

Two things should be noticed about this very inadequate representation of the Guyanese basilectal system. First, it has been necessary to introduce the basic stative–non-stative distinction, a distinction which plays no part (at least, no overt part) in the English system, and therefore cannot in any sense represent a simplification of that system. Second, even with this degree of adaptation, we have failed to include all the Guyanese forms; even if we dismiss *don* as marginal and/or recently acquired, we have to ask what has become of *bin* before non-statives and of *bina*.

Let us consider what would be the simplest possible way of accounting for the basilectal system. First let us assume that there is a semantic marker, ± anterior. For stative verbs, [− anterior] would mean 'now', i.e. that the state of liking, knowing, wanting or whatever, though it might have commenced in the past, would still be in existence at the present moment. For the same verbs, [− anterior] would mean simply 'not now, no longer', i.e. a terminated state. These are precisely the 'meanings' of Ø and *bin* with statives, and these markers are the only ones that can normally accompany statives.

For non-statives, however, the same distinctions would not apply. Let us assume a second semantic marker, ± punctual. To ask whether a stative is [+ punctual] or [− punctual] makes no kind of sense, since states have by definition an extended duration. The distinction, however, is meaningful for non-statives: [+ punctual] would imply a single action, [− punctual] an extended or repeated one. If we speak about a single, non-extended action, it can hardly be taking place in the immediate present (unless we are giving a running commentary, a rather unusual type of speech event!). However, it does not follow that because an action is [+ past] it must therefore be [+ anterior], provided that our point of reference is *another action or actions* rather than *the present moment*. A [+ past] action can then be [− anterior] in that the past action was the last to occur, or the last of its kind to occur, or the second of two in which the speaker is interested. Likewise, a [+ anterior] action does not have to be a 'past-before-past', since it could be regarded as both related and prior to a state of affairs at present in existence. The latter point helps to account for sentences such as the following:

2.91 *hau awi dis bina wok dem na eebl fi wok bikaz dem gro saaf* (188/3/246)
 'They can't work like we worked because they've grown soft.'

as well as examples such as 2.53 and 2.54. If the Guyanese stem form with
non-statives operated exactly like the English simple past, there would be no
way of explaining why *bina wok* rather than *wok* is used here. But as we
have already observed, the latter form cannot refer to the earlier of two actions simultaneously under discussion, and here the process of growing soft
and the state of being unable to work well are pre-dated by the referent of
bina wok. The latter is therefore [+ anterior], and a form containing *bin*
must be used, irrespective of English grammatical conventions.

If we assume that ± anterior, ± punctual are the relevant parameters for
the basilectal system, rather than ± past, ± continuative, ± perfective, we
get the following neat, comprehensive and economical picture:

Stative			Non-stative
		+ Pt	Ø
Ø	− A	− Pt	*a*
		+ Pt	*bin*
bin	+ A	− Pt	*bina*

This still does not include the marginal *don*, but it accounts for many things
that would otherwise be puzzling, such as the fourfold merger of past and
non-past, continuous and iterative in *a*, and the fact that the same forms
(Ø and *bin*) seemed to have quite different functions when used with statives and non-statives.

However, this system clearly bears little or no relation to the system of
English, and to insist on regarding it as a simplification of the latter seems to
be merely perverse − particularly in view of the fact, frequently noted in this
text, that any Guyanese tense form may take several different English trans-
lations, depending on its immediate context, while any English form may
similarly require different Guyanese equivalents. The relationship between
the two systems (at the cost of some oversimplification) is graphically dis-
played in Fig. 2.1, which gives emphasis to the point that no single English
tense or even group of tenses has a single distinct Guyanese equivalent.

At this stage, it may be instructive to compare the Guyanese system with
some related ones. Krio, Weskos (Cameroons Pidgin), Jamaican Creole and
Sranan are four varieties of creole English quite similar to Guyanese Creole
and probably genetically related to it. For Krio, Weskos and Sranan there
are published studies of the tense-aspect system (Jones 1968, Todd 1973,

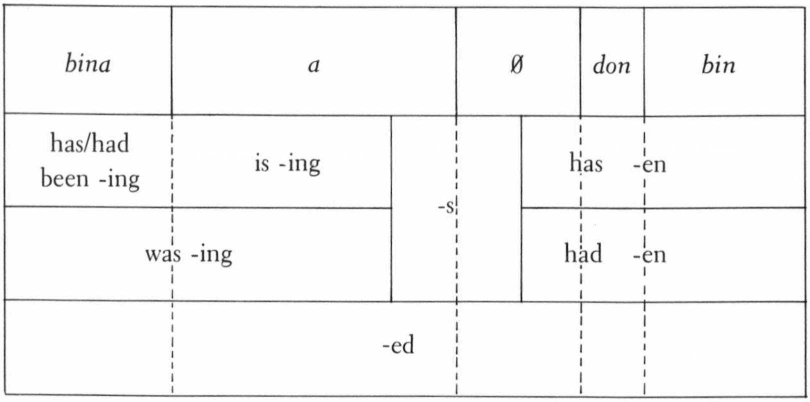

bina	*a*	*∅*	*don*	*bin*
has/had been -ing	is -ing		has -en	
was -ing		-s	had -en	
	-ed			

Fig. 2.1. Approximate relationship between GC and SE markers of tense and aspect

Voorhoeve 1957 respectively); while there is no specific study of this system for Jamaican Creole, the latter is otherwise better documented than almost any other anglo-creole.

According to Jones (1968:87) the realis system of Krio can be expressed in the following paradigm:

> *a bin rait* = I wrote
> *a de rait* = I am writing
> *a bin de rait* = I was writing
> *a don rait* = I have written
> *a bin don rait* = I had written
> *a bin don de rait* = I had been writing

Oddly, Jones neither shows any means for expressing habitual or iterative aspect, nor mentions the stem form, except to note (p. 87) that 'there is an unmarked past in Krio, often used when there is another time indicator in the utterance'.

Several things must strike us about this analysis. In the first place, with one exception, the phonological form of the pre-verbal markers is identical with that of the Guyanese ones. That exception is more apparent than real. Continuative markers in some relevant creoles are: Krio *de*, Weskos *di*, Sranan *e*, Jamaican Creole *da* or *a*, Gullah *duh*. All these (including Krio) have *de* as a locative verb. Even in Guyana, *de* can be used with statives to indicate a temporary state:

> 2.92 *shi mosi de baad mek shi tek i* (41/33/35) 'She must have been hard up to marry him.'

It would seem reasonable to suppose that all these variant forms derive from a single etymon, but that, in all varieties except Krio, subsequent splitting between locative and continuative functions has taken place.[10]

The second thing we may note is the greater combinative power of Krio markers – or to be more precise, of one particular marker, *don*. In Guyana, no combined forms with *don* have as yet turned up either in recordings or in elicitations from informants; they may exist, but if they do, they are remarkably rare. Moreover, as we have seen, the meanings of *don*-combination structures in Krio are ones which are rendered, in Guyana, by *bin* or *bin* + continuative alone.

The third point is the one-to-one relationship which Jones states between Krio and English structures. One's immediate reaction is to doubt the validity of any such analysis, in the light of the considerable overlaps we have seen in the Guyanese system, and in the face of the apparent anomaly that a system that has been in contact with English for hundreds of years should be less like English than a system that has had close contact with African languages throughout its existence. However, one speedily realises that if *don*, as a quasi-perfective, has indeed been admitted into combination with other markers, the result may well have been to make the Krio system more closely resemble English – if, perhaps, not quite as closely as Jones's analysis makes it appear.

This suggestion is borne out by a rather fuller treatment of the Weskos system by Todd (1973). Todd observes a restriction on the co-occurrence of statives with continuative or habitual markers identical to the restriction we observed for the Guyanese basilect; she does not, however, note any further differences between statives and non-statives, and, as with Jones, there is no clear treatment of the stem form. The Weskos realis paradigm as she states it, barring minor phonological detail, is identical to that given by Jones for Krio: [11]

---

[10] This possibility is all the more interesting in the light of recent suggestions that continuatives in general may originally derive from locatives; cf. Ross 1969.

[11] Some of the phonological differences seem to be artefacts of analysis rather than features of the data. For example, *don* is transliterated as *dɔŋ*, the final segment being justified by the following rather curious explanation:

> /dɔŋ/ has several common pronunciations, /dɔŋ/, /dɔn/ and /dɔ̃/. I have regularized the pronunciation to /dɔŋ/ which is among the commonest forms especially since /dɔŋ/ frequently precedes the motion verbs /go/ and /kɔm/ with their initial velars (1973:14, note 6).

I have here taken the liberty of adjusting Todd's orthography to conform with that used generally in the present study.

> *i chop* (*i* = he, *chop* = eat)
> *i bin chop*
> *i di chop*
> *i bin di chop*
> *i don chop*
> *i bin don chop*
> *i bin don di chop*

Todd wisely does not attempt one-to-one glosses for these paradigm forms, but the glosses given in exemplary material suggest a picture somewhat closer to ours than Jones's. True, the stem form is glossed as non-past, but the examples are all stative. *Di* is shown to be iterative as well as continuative. At least one *bin* example suggests our ± anterior analysis rather than the 'remote past' explanation Todd herself puts forward:

> 2.93 A: *bot a neva siam* 'But I haven't seen him yet.' B: *mi, a bin siam nau nau so* 'I've seen him just this minute.'

Three out of the four *bin di* examples are glossed with English simple pasts. It seems likely that a more thorough analysis would show the Weskos system to be even closer to the Guyanese than Todd's work would suggest.

In at least one respect, however, it would still differ. The combinatory possibilities of *don* seem to be identical in Weskos and Krio. It is particularly interesting that neither author attests the forms **don di* or **don de*. This suggests an interesting difference between *don*-forms and the English perfective. Either of the starred forms would have to be glossed as, roughly, 'have been . . . ing', a form which implies that the action described need not be a complete one. Their absence, then, may derive from the fact that *don* is a 'true' completive which can only be predicated of actions no longer continuing and not expected to be resumed. However, only empirical study can resolve this point.[12]

One final point about Krio and Weskos must be made. Jones's claim that Krio unmarked past is usually linked with the appearance of an adverbial time-marker, quoted above, is a hardy perennial in pidgin and creole studies, and is reinforced by Todd (1971) when in reviewing Schneider's (1966)

---

[12] Since writing the above, I have received reports of *don de* forms from St Kitts and Belize, as well as of *bin* (phonetically [mɪ]) *don, bin don de*, and even *don bin de*. One informant, however, suggests that (a) the latter form is simply synonymous with *bin don de*, and (b) that it is characteristic of second-language learners (i.e. native speakers of Black Carib, Maya, Spanish etc.) of Belize Creole and of children, which suggests that some kind of grammatical restructuring is taking place. However, it is obvious that far more research into Caribbean verbal structure is needed before anything definite can be said on this and similar issues.

acceptance of an unmarked past in Weskos, she claims that stem-only can only indicate past if there is explicit time-marking either adverbially or by *bin* occurring in the initial sentence of a narrative. Whatever the facts about Krio and Weskos (and it is worth noting that Igbo, an indigenous language neighbouring the latter, has a 'subsequential tense' that behaves much as, according to Todd, Weskos stem does [Carrell 1970:68]), none of these claims are valid for the Guyanese basilect. On the one hand, explicit 'past' – or, in our terms, [+ anterior] – markers repeatedly occur alongside fully explicit adverbial time-markers:

> 2.94 *lang taim deez de we awi bin du rais wok* (24/12/23) 'Those were the old days when we did rice work.'
>
> 2.95 *wel lang taim deez yu bina get mo rais an mo prafit* (25/14/24) 'Well in the old days you used to get more rice and more profit.'

On the other hand, narratives of past events almost invariably begin without any explicit time-marking – unless, as sometimes happens, the rules as already stated require such marking. In example 2.2, for instance, we noted how the transition between non-past generalising comment and past narrative was effected with no other marker than the suppression of [− punctual] *a*. A typical narrative introduction is 2.96:

> 2.96 *dis tu fren liv neks neeba. wan bina goolsmit an wan bina kaumaina. wel dis wan goolsmit an di kaumaina se wel ting baad* (67/10–12/68) 'There were these two friends who lived next door to one another. One was a goldsmith and one was a cowherd. Well, this goldsmith and this cowherd said, "Well, things are bad." '

Though there are two [+ anterior] markers, these do not affect the initial verb of the discourse, but are there simply because the equative copula *a* is [+ stative] – *wan a goolsmit* would have presupposed that the goldsmith was not a figure in a story but a person known to the narrator whom one might run into at any moment. The two earliest non-statives *liv* and *se*, however, remain unmarked.

That the Jones–Todd analysis may be faulty even for the varieties they discuss is suggested by Agheyisi's (1971) analysis of 'West African Pidgin English' – in effect, the Nigerian kind, although the author claims (contrary to, e.g. Mafeni 1970) that this represents merely part of a dialect continuum embracing Krio and Weskos. Agheyisi states bluntly that 'action verbs, such as *kot* "cut", *tek* "take", *silip* "sleep" etc., generally express Past Tense whenever they occur in a sentence as the only verbal constituent of the Verb Phrase – that is, without any of the pre-verbal Tense or As-

pect particles', while 'stative verbs, such as *get* "have", *no* "know", are
characteristically associated with the Non-Past Tense when they are not
preceded by any of the Tense or Aspect particles' (1971:133). One's confidence in this analysis is raised by the fact that Agheyisi is virtually the only
writer who has spotted the consequences the above facts must have in the
differential functions of *bin: 'bin* is interpreted as Remote Past, if the verbal
is Active rather than Stative; but ambiguously as simple or Remote Past if
the verbal is Stative' (1971:134). If the foregoing points are correct, then
there is a much greater degree of similarity between African pidgins and
creoles and Guyanese Creole than the work of Jones and Todd would
suggest.

We must now examine the Sranan paradigm as set forth by Voorhoeve
(1957:383):

		Tempus		
		Past	Present	
	Realis	ben-	[zero]	Completive
Mode	Irrealis	ben-sa	sa-	
	Realis	ben-e	e-	Non-completive
	Irrealis	ben-sa-e	sa-e	

The resemblance to the Guyanese system is striking. If we take *ben* and *e* to
be merely phonological variants of *bin* and *a*, then at least five of the eight
Sranan forms are still to be found in Guyana. A sixth, *ben-sa*, has its
Guyanese equivalent *bin sa* alternating with the *bin go* of 2.83 (and with an
identical meaning of *would have* + past participle) in the stories and poems
of Quow (1877), so that we may reasonably assume it to have been characteristic of nineteenth-century Guyanese Creole. Of the remaining two,
ben-sa-e and *sa-e*, Voorhoeve himself remarks that they 'seem to occur
only rarely. We did not observe them in the recorded material, but found
them due to questions put to the informants' (1957:375 note 4).

In Guyana, equivalent forms – *bin sa a* and *sa a* – have neither been
recorded nor elicited. However, there is an assimilation rule in Guyanese
phonology which merges contiguous low vowels; this rule, which gives us
na from *na + a* and *da* from *da + a* (thus contributing its share of 'unmarked
verbs' and 'zero copulas' to creole folklore), would automatically reduce *bin
sa a* to *bin sa* and *sa a* to *sa*, thus causing a merger of punctual and non-
punctual irrealis forms.

The closest similarity between the two systems lies in the realis forms.
Here, the only crucial difference from our Guyanese analysis concerns the

stem form. In fact, internal confusions and contradictions in Voorhoeve's analysis suggest that the difference may be more apparent than real.

Voorhoeve first states (contrary to the implications of his own paradigm) that 'the unprefixed form represents a perfect or an imperfect past tense (*mi waka*, I have walked, I walked)' (1957:376). Subsequently, he notes the different functions of the stem with statives and non-statives, and tries to account for them:

> It is understandable that it is the verbs like *nati* (to be wet), *nen* (to be called), *abi* (to have), *de* (to be) etc., where the unprefixed form agrees with the occidental present, while the unprefixed form of verbs like *waka* (to walk) agrees with the occidental perfect. This is because the former in our language only indicate a state of being and express a completive meaning. As our present tense of these verbs has a completive meaning, we find that the unprefixed form of these verbs in Sranan corresponds to our present tense. For verbs like *waka* on the contrary our present does possess a non-completive meaning and for this reason we find the verbal forms prefixed by *e-* to correspond to our present tense. (1957:379)

Though this paragraph is perplexingly worded – it is hard to see in what sense 'he has a job' is more completive than 'he walks to his job' – Voorhoeve here seems to have the correct stative–non-stative distinction almost within his grasp. Unfortunately in subsequent work he loses it again. Referring once more to *mi waka*, now glossed only as 'I have walked', he comments: 'The last example given can create confusion because one often interprets this perfect tense as a past tense. However, by comparison with verbs such as *nati* and *lobi* it is clear that the completive aspect (absence of *e-*) creates this impression with verbs like *waka*, because their English equivalents have only completive meaning in the perfect tense' (1962:40).

The unreality of this statement is made evident by Voorhoeve himself; in the long Sranan text which follows this last analysis (1962:57ff.), not a single non-stative stem form is glossed by the English perfect – every one is glossed by the simple past! Meanwhile, the text itself bears out the Guyanese analysis in sentences such as the following:

> 2.97 *mi ler a wroko, ma fos – fos dati, mi ben-g a wan apotek* 'I learnt the work, but before – before that, I went to a pharmacy' (1962:65).

This sentence illustrates very clearly the relationship between creole and English ways of handling past events: even where one occurred prior to another, both can be handled by the English simple past, but (unless the actions are sequent ones in a narrative) creole will normally give the

[−anterior] one the stem form, and the [+anterior] one the marked-past form.

This similarity between Sranan and the Guyanese basilect is hardly surprising, considering their proximity and historical connections. However, according to Voorhoeve, Sranan lacks one feature which Guyanese Creole shares with the African pidgins and creoles, i.e. *don*.

It is, of course, possible that *don* exists in Sranan as a very rare or marginal form; as pointed out above, its frequency in Guyanese recordings would have been very low if no process-descriptions had been included, and Voorhoeve's main sources are narrative. However, there is good reason to suppose that Voorhoeve has been accurate in this respect.

As noted above, the tokens of *don* are more numerous, and its powers of combination wider, in African pidgins and creoles than they are in Guyanese Creole. This statement is probably true for most of the Caribbean, in so far as there are no attestations of **ben don a* or **ben don* from Jamaica (but see note 12 above). This would suggest that *don* initiated as an innovation in Africa, possibly as a calque on a form in some as-yet undetermined indigenous language, and was subsequently transmitted to the New World – since, according to wave theory, a rule is most widely generalised at its point of origin, most narrowly constrained at the periphery of its spread (C.-J. Bailey 1974, Bickerton 1973c). A plausible agency for such transmission would be the many thousands of Africans who came to the West Indies after the suppression of slavery either as free immigrants or persons rescued from slavers bound for Cuba or Brazil; since, at the most conservative estimates, African pidgins date back to the late eighteenth century, it seems almost certain that some of these immigrants would control an anglo-pidgin. However, since few if any such immigrants reached Surinam, Sranan would not have been affected by African innovations.

A further claim of wave theory is that the form in which a rule is found at the periphery of its diffusion represents the original form the rule had at its point of origin. Within Guyana, this periphery would presumably be represented by those Indian speakers whose contact with Africans is minimal, i.e. elderly speakers in rural areas, particularly women.[13] Unfortunately, full details are not available for the Corentyne sub-sample. In the Bushlot sub-

[13] Until fairly recently, Indo-Guyanese have been reluctant to send their daughters to school; of the five female Bushlot post-*don* users, three had had no formal education at all. The fear of contact between Indian girls and young African males (the Indian stereotype of black sexuality depressingly copies the European one) was the most powerful factor in this reluctance.

sample, however, the differences between pre-*don* and post-*don* speakers are striking. There are six speakers who use only pre-*don* and six who use either both structures or post-*don* only. The average age of pre-*don* speakers is 40, that of post-*don* speakers, 53. Pre-*don* speakers have had, on average, nine years of school; post-*don* speakers, two and a half years only. Five out of six pre-*don* speakers are male; five out of six post-*don* speakers are female. We may therefore feel entitled to conclude, pending hard evidence to the contrary, that the peripheral-diffusion form of the *don*-rule is insertion in clause-final position only. If the predictions of wave theory are correct, then at some as-yet undetermined date one of the West African pidgins or creoles added the *don*-rule to its grammar in this form, subsequently modified the rule to permit pre-verbal insertion, then dropped clause-final insertion and generalised the rule to permit tense-aspect combination. The overall process would be as in Table 2.6.

TABLE 2.6   Diffusion of *don*-rule

Time 0 (1800?)	post-clausal insertion	—	—
	(WAP)	Afro-GC	Indo-GC
Time 1 (1840?)	variable post- pre- insertion	post-clausal insertion	—
	(WAP)	Afro-GC	Indo-GC
Time 2 (1880?)	pre-verbal insertion	variable post- pre- insertion	post-clausal insertion
	(WAP)	Afro-GC	Indo-GC
Time 3 (1920?)	tense-aspect combination	pre-verbal insertion	variable post- pre- insertion
	(WAP)	Afro-GC	Indo-GC

NOTE: All times conjectural. WAP = West African pidgin or creole; Afro-GC = Guyanese Creole as spoken by Africans; Indo-GC = Guyanese Creole as spoken by Indians.

We would then assume that further generalisation of the rule in GC would be blocked by the decreolisation process: we shall return to this question in more detail in Chapter 5.

For the initial stage in the process, there is much support in a phenomenon so widespread as to be arguably, in some sense, a 'natural' one. We have already referred to clause-final markers of similar function and meaning in Neo-Melanesian (*pinis*) and Hawaiian Creole (*pau*). To these we should add Sango *awe* (Samarin 1967a:158) meaning literally 'it is finished', and Mauritian Creole *fin* (Richardson 1963:10) from French *fini*. Richardson relates this form to forms of identical function and meaning in Swahili (*kwisha*) and Malagasy (*efa*), thus providing additional evidence for our suggestion that *don* may in the first instance have been a calque on some African form. It is worth noting that in Guyana, *don* as main verb always has the meaning of 'finish':

> 2.98 *wen mi wan don den mi a ker am a yu* (188/12/245) 'When mine is finished I bring it to you.'
> 2.99 A: *wat a klak awi a kom bak?*
> B: *wel a da mi na no. wen awi go don de.* (178, 180/14/229) 'What time are we coming back?' 'That's what I don't know. Whenever we've finished there.'

Don exists in Jamaica both pre-verbally and clause-finally; indeed, in some respects the Jamaican Creole verbal system matches the Guyanese as closely as that of Sranan does. There is a marker of some kind of pastness, *ben* – often reduced to *en* – and a continuous aspect marker *a* (*da* in some areas), which will combine as in Guyanese Creole. However, B. L. Bailey (1966:45) claims that 'if there is no tense indicator, the verb lacks time reference, and one must rely on context for that information'. This is certainly true of verbs prefixed by *a*, as we have seen; however, it is questionable whether it would be true of Jamaican stem forms, and indeed in most of Bailey's own examples, the latter is glossed by an English preterit when the verb is [− stative], by a non-past when it is [+ stative]. In fact, there is not as yet any study of the Jamaican verb which is sufficiently detailed to use for comparative purposes; the most one can say at present is that such a study may well show a degree of similarity stronger than has so far appeared.[14]

---

[14] Of the very little comparative work that has so far been carried out on Caribbean anglo-creoles, the most one can say is that the methods used have been calculated to obscure rather than reveal correspondences. The first and most ambitious attempt in this direction was Le Page's linguistic survey of the Caribbean (Le Page 1957–8), which relied heavily on postal questionnaires. Unfortunately, if one mails a questionnaire into a lectal continuum, there is no way of knowing exactly what one is getting back. Six of Le Page's entries for Guyana (then British Guiana) are: *maaga* 'thin', *mi a iit* 'I am eating', *he di dronk* 'he was drunk', *is wen* 'when', *de tuu kyats* 'the two cats', *banana flour* 'banana flour' (1957–8:61–2; I reproduce the somewhat inconsistent orthography of the original). While it is true that all of these forms may occur in Guyana, it is quite certain that there is no Guyanese who would spontaneously use all of them while maintaining the same style level, and unlikely that there is any Guyanese who would use all of them, period. The first two are basilectal, the second two mesolectal, the third two acrolectal. The result of such work can only be to give a completely distorted picture of Guyanese Creole, particularly when, as here, it is compared with other creoles for some of which basilectal forms are consistently given. For instance, 'banana flour' is given as

However, no comparative work within anglo-creoles, or even outside them (for work by Taylor [1956, 1963 etc.], Thompson [1961] and others indicates that some of the similarities noted extend to French- and Por-tuguese-based creoles), can really answer the question: where did the Guyanese tense-aspect system originate? Of the two hypotheses that remain open to us, that of African derivation might appear the most concrete and the easiest to settle empirically. However, the creolist who would attempt this will find himself faced with severe difficulties.

The first is simply the problem of determining the field of provenience. The catchment area for slaves for the New World stretched from Senegal to Angola, and embraced, at the most conservative estimate, several distinct language families and several hundred distinct languages. Many of these languages are still undescribed; where descriptions exist, they differ so much both in quality and theoretical assumptions that comparison is far from easy, while differences in analysis affect even the better-described languages. To take only one example, there are two recent descriptions of Yoruba by linguists who are also native speakers (Bamgbose 1966, Ogunbowale 1970). Ogunbowale treats the pre-verbal markers *n*, *a máa* and *máa ń* as all being continuative, and *ti* and *ti máa ń* as both indicating a 'fixed end' (sc. completive?) aspect (1970:51). Bamgbose, however, distinguishes between *n* (continuative) and *a máa*, *máa ń* (habitual), as well as between *ti* (perfective unmarked) and *ti máa ń* (perfective habitual) (1966:90–4). The first dis-agreement is critical for our purposes; if Ogunbowale is correct, it suggests that Yoruba may conflate iterative and continuative functions just as the Guyanese basilect does, whereas if Bamgbose is correct, Yoruba would more resemble the Guyanese mesolect after *a/das* splitting had taken place (see Chapter 3).[15] Multiply such problems by the number of possible language sources, and one can see why it is virtually impossible to either confirm or exclude any given source in the present state of our knowledge.

Quite apart from such difficulties, many linguists would argue that to search for the source of any creole system amongst African languages is in it-self a futile undertaking. Not only is the possibility of purely coincidental

kongkonte for Jamaica, but *kongote* is passively known to, if not used by, a vast majority of Guyanese. Any future comparative work in the Caribbean *must* ensure that equiva-lent levels are compared in all cases.

[15] There exists, of course, the possibility that both are right, for different varieties of Yoruba – a language known to contain considerable dialect variation. Should this prove to be the case, it would provide further evidence that there is no difference between changes in creoles and changes in 'natural' languages, and that the student of the latter has much to learn from the dynamics of the creole continuum.

similarity a high one; it is a widely attested historical fact that slaves in any given area in the New World were drawn from a large number of different African language areas (see, for example, Le Page and DeCamp 1960; de Granda 1968, 1969, etc.). Seldom if ever could speakers of any one language have formed even a temporary majority, so that the chances of such a group imposing its own system on others seems small indeed. However, it could still be argued that contact between several distinct African systems could have produced some kind of lowest-common-denominator of those systems.

Clearly some characteristics of verbal systems are so general that it would be absurd to use them as criteria. Probably a large majority of the world's languages distinguish in some way or other between continuative and non-continuative actions, or between some kind of past and non-past. It may well be that African systems differ from Indo-European ones in that their past–non-past distinction is measured from one action to another (as with our suggested ± anterior feature) rather than from the speaker's immediate present. For example, Arnott observes of Fula that its general past tense

> very often refers to past time in relation to the time of utterance, but it also refers frequently to time that is past *in relation to some other time* implied by the context or indicated by a time-word, or to the time of some action indicated by other verbs. It may thus correspond to a variety of tenses in English – simple past, present perfect, pluperfect (especially in indirect speech) or even future perfect. (1970:262; emphasis in original)

However, the distinction between the two forms of reference is frequently a vague and uncertain one. Two rather more specific characteristics of the Guyanese Creole system (and doubtless others) are (a) a single form that is neutral to both the continuative–iterative and past–non-past oppositions and (b) a stative–non-stative distinction that has specific consequences in the shape of varying time-reference for identical formal items.

The first feature seems to be quite widely distributed among the Kwa languages. One of the earliest studies of the Akan sub-group (Christaller 1875:102) describes the continuative form as indicating an 'action, state or quality without regard to the beginning or ending of it, either in the time present to the speaker, or in the past time'. According to Carrell (1970:31), the auxiliary *nà* in Igbo has both progressive and habitual functions. Ogunbowale (1970:54) says of Yoruba that 'the continuous aspect may be used to express an action permanently characterising the subject, i.e. describing a habitual or recurrent action'. The pre-verbal marker *è* in Nupe indicates actions that were frequentative in the past or are continuous in the present (N. V. Smith 1969:118).

There is also some evidence for the second feature. Westermann (1930:116) says of Ewe that 'the aorist (a stem form) indicates a past action, so that it is the form peculiar to narrative', but adds that 'the aorist also indicates an action completed in the past, but the consequence or result of which is a condition of the present, and is therefore generally expressed by the present in English'. This definition is a little confusing, but it is clarified by Westermann's examples, all of which include statives such as 'agree', 'like', 'believe', 'think', 'stand', 'possess' etc., e.g.:

> 2.100 *mexɔe se*, literally 'I have accepted and heard it,' i.e. 'I believe it.'
> 2.101 *menyâ nú*, literally 'I have come to know something,' i.e. 'I know something.'

According to Smith, the stem form in Nupe can express either past actions or present states (1969:117).

However, such evidence is far from conclusive, and counter-evidence (such as the apparent distinction between iterative and continuative in Ewe, or the relationship between the Twi stem and non-past or iterative actions) could as easily be adduced. Furthermore, it should be obvious that at the level of abstractness we have now reached, the 'Africanist' hypothesis and the 'language-universals' hypothesis (cf. especially Kay and Sankoff MS., Traugott 1973) become virtually indistinguishable from one another. We simply lack sufficient knowledge both about the actual languages involved in the process and about the nature of, and constraints upon, linguistic change and inter-influence in general. The most one can do is make suggestions which one hopes may be of use to future investigators.[16] Meanwhile, it is obviously of the highest importance to analyse as thoroughly as possible any change processes which *can* be directly observed. The next two chapters will therefore be devoted to tracing the changes which occur to the basilectal system as described above, and which serve to link it to the system of standard English.

[16] While the Guyanese evidence does not permit us to go beyond this point, it seems worth mentioning that my current and still incomplete study of Hawaiian Pidgin/Creole does provide strong evidence for a language-universals hypothesis – but as applied to *creoles* rather than *pidgins*. This evidence is so rich and complex that it would be quite impossible to summarise here, unfortunately.

3   From basilect to mesolect

In the last chapter, we had for tactical reasons to segment the continuum and describe the basilectal tense-aspect system as if it constituted some clearly demarcated, homogeneous and integral object. From all that has been written so far, however, it should be clear that to take this description as more than a tactical device, as somehow consituting a true picture of any state of linguistic affairs, would be incorrect. There probably are some Guyanese speakers whose productive capacity – as opposed to their receptive capacity – falls within the limits already described: 28/178, for example, who failed to style-shift at all during a conversation with the author in which everyone else present was style-shifting to some degree. However, there can be no doubt that such speakers are both very few and diminishing in number.

We may better regard the basilect as a phase through which some creole-speakers pass (as the language itself has passed through it), or as something which constitutes only a part of the competence of most synchronic speakers – a very large part for some, a much smaller one for others. We must beware in particular of suggesting that, at some time in the past, what is now the basilect was the 'pure', 'genuine' and only creole, miraculously free from variation, quite different in kind from the degenerate modern mix of the continuum caused by 'interference from English'. The amount of variation in any given language may vary from epoch to epoch, but is always present in some degree, and continually shifts its locus; if the feature that is variable today was often invariant yesterday, it is equally often true that today's invariant was yesterday's variable. We should therefore view the development from basilect to mesolect not as the breakdown of some balanced organism, but merely as a phase in a development process that has been going on from the moment that Guyanese Creole or its antecedent pidgin originated – a phase which differs from previous phases only in that, unlike them, it is accessible to direct observation.

The main changes that take place in this basilect-to-mesolect phase may be summarised as follows: *doz* develops from a marginal to a central position in the grammar, acquiring a more precise function as it does so; the characteristic basilectal markers disappear and are replaced by other forms; *-ing* forms make their appearance, but with only sporadic accompanying *be; go* as irrealis marker is replaced by *gon* which develops as a pure future, with modals fulfilling conditional-type functions; extensive changes take place in verbal negation; English-type past morphemes begin to appear, at first in sharply limited environments.

doz

In considering *doz*, we have first of all to ask whether we are dealing with one item or two. This question arises because, for the majority of basilectal speakers who use it, the phonological shape of *doz* is [das] (sometimes [dʌs]). Moreover, this difference in shape correlates fairly closely with an apparent difference in function. To complicate the matter still further, [das]-speakers are invariably of Indian descent; Africans produce only [dʌz].

The argument for two items, *das* and *doz*, would go as follows: *das*, as we shall shortly see, is used without specific time reference, whereas *doz* is usually applied to series of actions that have continued up to the present. To some extent, then, *das* resembles *a*. In the last chapter, it was noted that a variant form of *a*, i.e. *da*, still exists in certain areas of Jamaica, and may therefore have existed in Guyana also. *Das* – the argument would go – could then simply be a variant form of *da*, having only a coincidental connection with the mesolectal *doz*.

However, *das* may be much more plausibly explained. Most Indo-Guyanese originated in Hindi-speaking areas of India, and Hindi, alone of Indian languages, is still widely, if diminishingly, spoken by the older generation. Hindi has no voiced sibilant, except in Urdu loans, and no low back vowel. It seems likely, then, that [das] is simply the original reflex of *doz* as learnt by monolingual Hindi-speakers from African plantation workers in the nineteenth century, and preserved unchanged (even after voiced sibilants and low back vowels had been acquired in other environments) owing to subsequent diminished contact between members of the two races.

Presumably, *doz* derives from periphrastic Early Modern English *does*, a feature preserved until a much later date in some regional dialects.[1] While *does* may have served as a phonological model, however, we should not assume that there is any necessary resemblance in meaning or grammatical function between it and *doz*, any more than exists between English *been*,

---

[1] The history of the rise and fall of periphrastic-*do* constructions in English should be a rich field for the student of variation. A wealth of interesting data have recently been collected in the monumental work by Visser (1969).

limited to the copula and passives, and creole *bin* or *ben*. *Doz* does not alternate with *do*, but remains invariant regardless of person and number; loss of *doz* as an aspect marker invariably precedes acquisition of English 'support' *do/does*. Moreover – except for sporadic interference in speakers with a very wide style range, e.g. example C2 in Chapter 1 – *doz* is never negated with following *n(t)*; *na doz* is the normal form of negation for [das]-speakers, and *doon(t)* for [dʌz]-speakers. 'Counter-negative' *doz* – as in English 'But he *does* speak Tibetan!' – is non-existent.

Doz was presumably adopted by at least some African speakers prior to the start of Indian immigration into Guyana in the mid-nineteenth century. Its apparent absence from Sranan and the African pidgins and creoles suggests that it was a purely Caribbean innovation. There is some doubt as to whether there are Guyanese who have no *doz* at all, or merely a number to whom it is marginal; no clear pattern emerges from those who do not actually use it in recordings (for instance, in Bushlot, five non-users are females over forty, but three are males under thirty-five). However, we would be justified in at least assuming that the *doz*-rule has only recently been acquired by speakers of mainly basilectal varieties.

The most likely possibility is that *doz* entered Guyana through Barbadian immigrants. *Doz* has long been established in Barbados (Collymore 1965) and was presumably spread from there to Trinidad, where its use is widespread (Solomon 1966). Until recently it had not been attested in any other anglo-creole; there is no mention of it in the extensive literature on Jamaican Creole, for instance. However, there was also no mention of it in the almost equally extensive literature on Gullah until Cunningham (1970), though its frequency in the Sea Islands is noted in that work and confirmed in more recent fieldwork by John Rickford and William Stewart (personal communications); also, according to Rickford (personal communication), Karl Reisman has recently discovered several occurrences in his data from Antigua. It therefore seems possible that *doz* is much more widespread than had been supposed, and has either been missed or ignored by previous analysts.[2]

However, the question that most directly concerns us is whether, given

---

[2] This possibility is all the more likely in view of the traditional approaches to creoles discussed in Chapter 1. Any linguist trying to isolate the 'real creole system' would inevitably – once he found that *doz* replaced a 'more creole' form – dismiss it as a clear case of 'interference from English'. But when one stops to consider that anglo-creoles without exception owe their very existence to 'interference from English', traditional approaches become even harder to comprehend.

that Indian immigrants restructured *doz* phonologically, they may not also have restructured its grammatical function. This seems unlikely for at least two reasons. As we saw in the previous chapter, speakers who are predominantly Indian maintain a tense-aspect system which differs only in very minor detail from systems used by speakers of purely African origin, and certainly no more than such systems differ among themselves. Moreover, while there is a clear explanation in Hindi phonology for the appearance of [das], Hindi verbal syntax, with its distinction between past and non-past in both perfect and imperfect tenses, contains no precedent for the characteristic lack of a past–non-past distinction in Indian handling of *doz*:

3.1 *an kakadilo wi das go haid an wan a dem das go pik liif an bring it, and das kom saach fu mi* (210/18–19/268) 'And in "cockadillo" [a child's game] we go and hide and one of them goes and picks a leaf and brings it, and then comes and looks for me.'

3.2 *yes, tiich, wi no. wi gon get – wi das aalweez get fram yu aal* (183/1/236) 'Yes, Teach, we know. We're going to receive – we always receive [something] from you.'

3.3 *lang taim wen awi bina plant rais ova kriik awi das gatu plau wid kau* (15/11/15) 'In the old days when we used to plant rice over the creek, we used to have to plough with oxen.'

3.4 *an wan taim dag bin bait mi tu an mi granmoda bin ker mi a haspital a mi moda an wen mi kom hoom piipl das kom si mi an so* (210/26 – 7/268) 'And once a dog bit me too and my grandmother took me to hospital with my mother, and when I came home people used to come and see me and so on.'

Even at this stage, *doz* is clearly limited to iterative ('habitual') expressions, and never occurs in continuative ones. As an iterative, it still alternates with *a*:

3.5 *dem a mash it wid kau an i get saaf an den wi awi a plant it. wi das plant* (186/17/237) 'They broke it [the ground] up with oxen and it got soft and then we planted it. We planted it.'

3.6 *so – wa awi a wok a lenora fu? wel di wok na pe awi a aiflok so awi das gafu go we a lenora go wok* (119/26–7/150) 'So why did we work at Lenora [Estate]? Well the work didn't pay us at Uitvlugt [Estate] so we used to have to go away to Lenora to work.'

3.7 *evri de mi a ron a raisfiil* (137/29/182) 'Every day I hurry to the ricefield.'

3.8 *aagas rais das bos* (137/4/183) 'Rice ripens in August.'

But for continuatives, *a* remains unchanged:

3.9 *dem a kom jis nau maan* (133/12/182) 'They're coming right now, man.'

3.10 **dem das kom jis nau maan.*

Doz–a alternation is anything but static. If we take speakers who have both forms, and who use at least one of them at least five times (to remove distortions through low sample size) we find a steady rise in the percentage of *doz*-tokens, as shown in Table 3.1. If we examine this table, we will note

TABLE 3.1   Distribution of *doz* relative to *a*

Speaker	*doz*	*a*	Total	% *doz*
186	1	38	39	2
219	1	24	25	4
2	1	21	22	5
222	1	20	21	5
27	2	42	44	5
248	2	32	34	6
134	1	12	13	8
188	9	94	103	9
168	5	44	49	10
172	2	15	17	12
178	8	56	64	12
10	2	13	15	13
119	1	6	7	14
9	21	128	149	15
12	1	5	6	18
28	14	55	69	20
15	7	26	33	21
198	4	15	19	21
176	11	39	50	22
165	2	7	9	22
137	3	9	12	25
175	6	12	18	33
196	6	11	17	35
8	4	6	10	40
170	8	11	19	42
221	4	5	9	44
131	7	7	14	50
5	5	5	10	50
210	16	2	18	89
224	9	1	10	90
99	23	1	24	96
183	42	1	43	98

some striking facts. Among the more basilectal speakers (in the upper half of the table) the rise is extremely gradual – twenty out of the thirty-two speakers are concentrated in the span between 2% and 22%. The rise then becomes much more rapid: there are only eight speakers in the span between 23% and 50%. Then there is a gap between 50% and 89%. Finally, four speakers are found between 89% and 98%.

The configuration of these results is rather different from the 'S-curve' which has been found in variable data by Labov, C.-J. Bailey and myself (Bailey 1974) and therefore requires some explanation. In the classic S-curve, when the percentages of a variable are assessed for a number of speakers, and then expressed in terms of a graph as in Fig. 3.1, the line join-

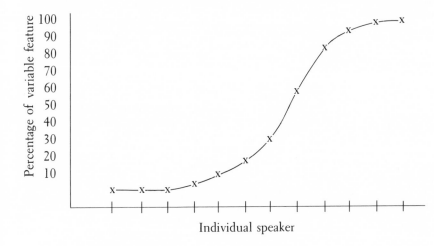

Fig. 3.1. Classic S-curve

ing the speakers' positions on the graph will resemble a flattened S. Such a curve may be taken as representing a change passing fairly rapidly through a population. The low percentages are those of speakers who are in the process of acquiring a new feature; the high percentages are those of speakers who have almost fully acquired this new feature and are in process of getting rid of its antecedent; these two groups between them account for the bulk of speakers involved in the change. The reason for relatively few speakers being found among the middle percentages is that, at a certain stage of development, grammatical reinterpretation takes place; some speakers have a grammar that rewrites a given feature as '*a*, with *b* as a possible variant', others have one that rewrites the same feature as '*b*, with *a* as a possible variant', and while performance factors tend to blur the distinction between the two groups, few if any speakers are found who have the two variables in balance.

However, in Table 3.1 and Fig. 3.2 we are dealing with two categories, not one: [+ iterative], in which *doz* and *a* are variables, and [− iterative] ([+ continuative]), in which *a* is, in the beginning, invariant. The 100% mark for *doz* is therefore in reality the 50% mark in Fig. 3.2. Speakers who

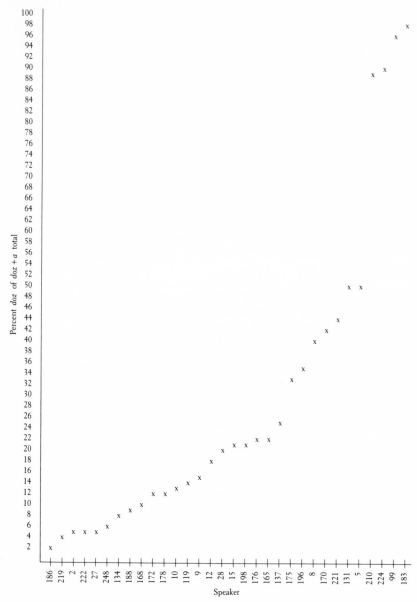

Fig. 3.2. Distribution of *doz* percentages

are approaching or have reached this mark, such as 221, 131 and 5, have something not far short of a categorical instruction to use only *doz* in [+ iterative] structures and only *a* in [+ continuative] structures – certainly, all 221's and 131's *doz-* and *a*-tokens fall into these categories, while 5 has only a single *a*-token in a [+ iterative] structure.

However, while *doz*-establishment has been moving to completion, another change, which we shall shortly analyse in more detail, has already begun: the replacement of [+ continuative] *a* by *-ing*. It would appear that completion of the *doz*-change coincides fairly precisely with the 'flip-flop' phase of the *-ing*-change, i.e. that in which an '*a* with variant *-ing*' grammar gives place to an '*-ing* with variant *a*' one. Thus, instead of all the *doz*-change-completing speakers being found in the 40–50% range of Fig. 3.2 – as would have happened if *a* had remained unreplaced – some are found in the 90–100% range.

The restriction of *doz*'s time-reference to non-past is less easy to document. At or around the time of *doz*-acquisition, *yuus-tu* is also acquired; at least sixteen out of the twenty-eight Bushlot speakers have it, for example. *Yuus-tu* is never used with non-past reference, but with past reference it seems at first to be merely an occasional variant for *doz*:

> 3.11 *dem das plant dem faam an ting an dem das yuus-tu stan de* (9/27/10) 'They used to cultivate their farm and so on, and they used to stay there.'
>
> 3.12 *yuz* [= yu doz] *get lilbit lilbit wata an yu das plant am de. mi aja yuus-tu du it* (11/14/12) 'You used to get a little water and plant it there. My father used to do it.' [3]

Sentences like this are characteristic of Indian speakers, but the use of *doz* for past events is by no means confined to them. Here is 196, an African:

> 3.13 *an i get ting, a doon no wat iz it bot i mek it az a dringk an i geev mi, a miin, tu dringk. an a dringk i gubi. a miin a doz go de nau an ageen an a doz vizit dem* (196/1–3/255) 'And he got something, I don't know what it was but he made a drink out of it and gave it me, I mean, to drink. And I drank from his calabash. I mean I used to go there now and again and visit them.'

---

[3] Z, the reduced form of *doz*, is very common in rapid speech among Africans. It could well have contributed to the failure to perceive *doz* referred to above, since observers may have either failed to hear it or attributed it to reduction of *iz*. Its occurrence among Indian speakers, as here, is much rarer; note, however, that when it does happen, the voiceless sibilant of *das* may become voiced through regular assimilation processes.

Speaker 196, it is true, is unusual in that he has close Indian friends with whom, in fact, he was picnicking when this recording was made. It could be that his grammar has been influenced by them. However, another speaker, 209, showed no sign of such influence, and indeed was a Barbadian by birth, having come to Guyana at the age of seventeen. Yet, though his grammar is much 'higher' than that of 196, he still uses *doz* when speaking about his youth in Barbados:

> 3.14 Well my grandmother was a midwife nurse and she does work with that gentleman. (209/12–13/267)
>
> 3.15 This boy – he was a little sickly and sometimes he does go and play with he sister boy. (209/22/266)

Speakers such as these suggest that our theory about the original, Afro-creole function of *doz* is correct; that it was a tenseless iterative and not (as claimed for Trinidad [Solomon 1966], and Gullah [Stewart, personal communication]) a marker of non-past tense, and that this function was transmitted unchanged to Indian speakers. However, one has to admit that, among *doz*-users who have lost *a*, a majority of *doz*-tokens refer to non-past iterative series only. It may well be that growing contact with standard *does* serves to reduce and finally eliminate past reference, but it would require further study to resolve this point adequately.

What one can be certain of is that *doz* is *always* an iterative or habitual marker and *never* a simple marker of non-past tense – in Guyana, if not elsewhere. The main stative rule applies to it just as to its predecessor *a*, and in consequence it seldom or never appears before modals or stative verbs or in conditional or temporal ('whenever'-type) clauses. Once again, as in example 2.39, we will examine an extended passage by a heavy *doz*-user to see how this rule operates:

> 3.16 And before he finish drinking this quarter [sc. small bottle of rum] he *does* go 'long bad [sc. make trouble]. I *does* look at he and I *does* come out. I *does* meet friend and I *does* drink a lot. I *does* ride my cycle and go home and, you know, a lot of people *does* give me se I don't drink rum [sc. people regard me as a non-drinker]. If they come in here now and they see me in front this rum in this shop they *does* say, 'Boy, you surprise me boy, you *does* drink!' I *does* go straight home ride, I take my drink. If I want me meals me say and I *does* relax home. Nobody know if I drink or not. But you see most of them in the Scheme [sc. housing estate], when you see they drink a quarter, they want the public to know they drink. They begin rev-up and go 'long so people *does* say them is drinkman [sc. drunks]. He saying people *does* jealous him for what he

say he account *does* be – four hundred dollar per year for drinking (99/28/116–5/117).

For this speaker, as for others at the mid-mesolectal level, the main stative rule is unweakened, and, apart from some uncertainty over the verb *say* and some types of dependent clause (e.g. 'to know they drink' in lines 10–11 of the above example) there are no absences of *doz* which that rule would not warrant. The same is even true of a speaker such as 41, who controls the acrolect but whose range extends well down into the mesolect:

> 3.17 Then what you *does* talk, what you *does* talk when you and the girls get together? (41/23/180)
> 3.18 Oh, that is how he *does* work? Ahm, but tell me when you carry the, ahm, the – how you *does* make this pocket? (41/7–8/181)
> 3.19 Well tell me what you and the children *does* do when the teacher stand up and gaff [sc. gossips]? (41/10–11/192)

Note that in every case, *doz* is excluded from the temporal clause.

However, while a speaker like 41 (who has no *doz* at all in her formal speech) may correctly apply the main stative rule in her lower ranges, the case is rather different when a speaker like 99, with *doz* firmly fixed in his vernacular, feels impelled to move in the direction of the acrolect. Speaker 99 is re-recorded in our data as 125 (cf. Bickerton 1973b). As 99, he uses *doz* twenty-three times in a text of about 700 words; as 125, he uses it only ten times in a text of over 3,000 words. In part, the difference is due to a different type of subject-matter, but other factors are involved, and we shall have to look at 125 on at least two more occasions – when we discuss the changes that take place between mesolect and acrolect (in Chapter 4) and when we examine what is implied by 'switching' phenomena (in Chapter 5).

For the present, we can say that the introduction of *doz* into the Guyanese system indicates a division of the [− punctual] category into two: [+ continuative] and [− continuative] ([− continuative, − punctual] = [+ iterative]). Subsequently, a straightforward past–non-past time distinction is gradually introduced, with [+ iterative, + past] reference being covered by *yuus-tu* or other forms, and *doz* becoming restricted to [+ iterative, − past] reference.

did

One very characteristic strategy of the decreolisation process is the replacement of morphemes of non-standard appearance by others which, on the surface, look like – or at least, look more like – morphemes of standard English. However, grammatical rules are much slower to change; more often than not, new, 'English-looking' morphemes are simply slotted into place in creole structures – semantic as well as syntactic. A case which clearly illustrates this type of process is the replacement of *bin* by *did*.

Did doubtless derives from periphrastic English *did*, as *doz* derives from periphrastic *does*; however, as with *doz*, this phonological resemblance is the extent of their similarity. Support-*did* does not appear in questions, and (as we shall see when we deal with changes in negation) although $di(d)n(t)$ begins to appear in negative sentences, it is by no means necessarily as a negator of *did*. But most importantly from our standpoint, *did* never has its English 'counter-negative' sense – 'But I *did* remember to send one!' – nor functions as an equivalent of the -*ed* morpheme; it simply slots into the space in the grammar vacated by *bin*.

Since *bin* and *did* are items of far less frequent occurrence than *doz* and *a*, the changeover process is much harder to document; moreover, the distribution of *doz* is much wider than that of *did*, and its onset in the decreolisation process much earlier. None of the heavy *bin*-users in Table 2.1 has been recorded as using *did*, for example. In consequence, we find very few speakers who have both *bin* and *did*. However, such speakers use the two items interchangeably, whether they come from an all-Indian village in Berbice (as does 183) or from an all-African village in Demerara (as does 30):

> 3.20 *wi bin tretn, yu no, wi did fraikn laik kowad* (183/15/234) 'We were threatened, you know, we were frightened like cowards.'
> 3.21 *ai biliiv iz dats wai shi di sen* [4] (30/6/387) 'I believe that's why she sent [it].'
> 3.22 *an iz gud ting wen mi bin sen it da dei* (30/14/387) 'And it was a good thing when I sent it that day.'

Out of context, the last two examples might be taken as corresponding to simple English pasts with non-statives. However, they come from a conversation about tangled personal affairs in which events at different times are continually being compared and related to one another. The following example from the same conversation will illustrate this more clearly:

> 3.23 30: *bot a wa stori dis, wel a wa shi kom fu den?*
> 32: *si or neeborz an so aan an tu tro hint an so.*
> 30: *an di seem di de wen shi di kom an se shi din get cheenj an so mi tingk mi di len shi wan somting* (30, 32/25/386–3/387) 'But what kind of nonsense is this, what was it she came for, then?' 'To see her neighbours and so on and to throw out hints and that sort of

---

[4] In rapid and informal speech, *did* often reduces to *di*.

thing.' 'Just like the day she came and said she didn't have any change and so I think I lent her a bit.'

Here, two visits by the subject of the conversation are under discussion. The later in time, topic of 30's first utterance, is allotted the unmarked past; thus, when the earlier in time is compared in 30's second utterance, it has to be marked with *did*.

Sometimes, as with these instances, *did* + stem requires a simple past gloss; in others, as with *bin*, pluperfect is required:

3.24 *bai di taim mi moda travl op di maanin, bifo mesij kom bak shi di ded an de din sen bak no mesij an shi – de se de miit in taim fu di fyunaral* (125/17–18/169) 'By the time my mother travelled up in the morning, before a second message came, she [sc. the speaker's grandmother] had died and they didn't send another message, and she – they say they arrived in time for the funeral.'

(Note here that *din* negates, not a [+anterior] event, but one that, if affirmative, would have been allotted an unmarked verb.)

The effect is even more striking when [+ anterior] *did* is found alongside early-acquired English past forms. In 3.25, it is true, one such form (*had*) is also used exactly like *bin*; in 3.26, however, English 'strong' pasts are used in an English way:

3.25 And when she *go* home she *get* sick. She *stay* a long time before she *go* back to see what *had happen* to this seed she *did plant*. (101/29–30/119)

3.26 She *say* Miss T——, Miss T——, I tell you please to tell Bertie don't go in the house. And hear me – You *saw* Bertram in the house? She *said*, No, but I *hear* that he *did go* in. (43/11–12/50)

In the latter, 'I *heard* that he *had gone* in' would be the most likely English equivalent. However, discussion of 43's output anticipates Chapter 5, where we will return to this mixture of mesolectal and acrolectal forms.

Returning to the mid-mesolect, we can find all the functions of *bin* duplicated by *did*. There is the simple-past-with-stative function of 2.48, as given in a beautiful 'stylistic translation' by 30:

3.27 32: *di wan dat hi had waznt inof.*
30: *di wan wa i di get din inof?* (32, 30/25/389/–1/390)

There is the counter-factual–unrealised–condition function of 2.83, the punch-line of a story about a little boy who was told that 'lady does get baby' by burying 'a cent sweetie' in the ground; when he dug up the candy and found 'one set o' ants', he exclaimed indignantly:

> 3.28 *luk, if ayu wazn mi chiren a did step pan ayu langtaim, ye?*
> (162/6/204) 'Look, if you weren't my children, I'd have trodden on
> you long ago, you hear me?'

Still more striking, there are the allegedly verbatim remarks of a murderer to
an eye-witness of his crime:

> 3.29 'Tell the police what me *do*, or tell who you *want* – or tell the judge
> what me *did do*.' (87/10–11/95)

The murderer tells the witness to tell the police 'what me *do*' because that
will constitute a 'first telling', from which point the deed itself will be the
most recent relevant occurrence, therefore (− anterior). If, however, the
witness repeats his evidence at the trial, that will constitute a 'second telling';
there will then be two previous relevant occurrences, the first telling and the
deed itself, and since the deed is of course the earlier of the two, it must
now be marked [+ anterior].

Like *bin, did* is not limited to + stem occurrences; *did + a* never occurs,
but *did* + V*ing* is sometimes encountered. We shall return to this form after
discussing the *a/-ing* change. However, one important point about *did*
must be made here. We have suggested that *did* inherits the functions of
bin, but there is one point on which the two forms differ strikingly. As
shown in Table 2.4, the distribution of fifty-two *bin* occurrences in the
recordings with regard to the stative–non-stative distinction was thirty-nine
stative, thirteen non-stative: i.e. 75% of *bin*-occurrences were with statives. The figures for *did* exactly reverse this distribution. Of forty-eight occurrences, nine only are stative, a further three possibly interpretable as stative, and the remaining thirty-six clearly non-stative: i.e. 75% of
did-occurrences are with *non*-statives.

More than one factor may contribute to this state of affairs. As we shall
see in Chapter 4, *did* continues to be used by some speakers above the mid-
mesolectal level, and their use of *did* differs from that of truly mid-mesolectal speakers in several ways. For instance, such speakers have all acquired
had, so that one of the most propitious environments for *did* – before stative
gat – disappears. Further, as we shall see, the distinctively [+ anterior] character of *did* weakens shortly before its disappearance, so that it occurs a
number of times in simple-past non-stative environments. Thirdly, a
number of stative *bin*-occurrences precede 'adjectival verbs'; in the mid-
mesolect, these are reanalysed as predicate adjectives, and are never (at least
in our recordings) preceded by *did*.

All these factors combine to reduce the incidence of stative *did* and increase that of non-stative; however, a fourth may be still more critical. Some of the rules which most sharply differentiate the basilect from standard English are those which, on a formal level, equate non-past statives and past non-statives (giving both zero marking) as well as past statives and past-before-past non-statives (marking both with *bin*). These rules must yield at some stage before standard rules can be established, and it is at this level that they begin to weaken. Later we shall have occasion to look in greater detail at the mechanics of this change; for the moment, we need only note that, with increasing frequency, stative verbs are left unmarked even where there is clear [+ anterior] reference and even where non-statives have [+ anterior] marking – as shown, for example, in the following passage from a clearly mid-mesolectal speaker:

> 3.30 The letter, I believe is that's why she *did send*, she *feel* is Miss C—— get it, she didn't know is F——, but after she *done send* she *shame* because it was given to Miss C——, she *feel* is Miss C—— get it, if she only *know* was F—— had it she wunt a sent for it. (30/6–9/387)

ing

If we look back at Table 2.1, we will see that the *-ing* form is not entirely unknown to all basilectal speakers. True, it is far from common: if one subtracts the thirteen cases produced by 2/186, the heaviest *-ing* user in that table, the remaining fifteen speakers yield only a further fifteen occurrences among them. Of that fifteen, moreover, only two are examples of verbal *-ing*.

In the section that follows, it will be suggested that *-ing* forms are first acquired as nominals – independent lexical items which are not analysed by the speaker as resulting from any productive process. Subsequently, participial forms are acquired, and only then does the speaker begin to replace *a* with verbal *ing*. This suggestion conforms both with what we shall find when we examine past-tense acquisition, and with C.-J. Bailey's suggestion that changes in general initiate through the addition of lexical items rather than through direct acquisition of new rules as such (C.-J. Bailey 1970a).[5]

In Bushlot, there are five speakers who have participial *-ing* with or

---

[5] Bailey was in fact discussing phonological change. However, the general principles involved seem to apply equally well to syntactic change. A speaker seems to have to have acquired a number of examples of a new form simply as entries in his lexicon before he can generalise from them so as to set up a new rule. More evidence for this hypothesis will be advanced when we discuss the acquisition of *-ed* forms.

without nominal *-ing*, and six speakers who have only nominal *-ing*. On a four-class system, the first group has an average class level of 1.4 as against the second group's average of 3.0, while the first group has an average of nine years of education as opposed to the second group's six and a half. While the numbers involved are not large enough to make the matter conclusive, it seems reasonable to suppose that the simpler N*ing* like 9's

> 3.31 *if yu wan niit plantin nain badi a du wan eka* (9/9/8) 'If you want neat planting you have nine people to the acre.'

is acquired before the more complex participial *-ing* of 15's

> 3.32 *you seev fram getin dis win rais* (15/23/15) 'You're saved from getting this spindly rice.'

The relationship between participial and verbal *-ing* can be clarified by examining a comment on it in Cave 1970 (pp. 259–60):

> When someone says in GC: 'Wan sheep *ah graze*' we convert this into the RP: 'A sheep *is grazing*.' When, however, the person says in GC: 'Dah ah wan sheep *ah graze*' we convert this into the RP: 'That is a sheep *grazing*.' In the two structures, then, the person finds RP *is grazing* and RP *grazing* used for his single GC form *ah graze*. Hence in his attempts at speaking and writing standard language he produces 'A *sheep grazing*'; and his confusion is further confounded when, in attempting an even more complicated communication pattern, he comes up with 'That is a sheep is grazing.'

Cave's observations are pertinent but somewhat misleadingly worded in that they suggest a real, as well as a perceived, equivalence between V – NP – V*ing* and V – NP – *a* – V. It is natural enough for a speaker of standard English to gloss

> 3.33 *awi a si piipl a waak a rood* (178/20/244)

as 'We saw people walking on the road,' or

> 3.34 *auta tauzn yu a get wan hondrid, wan fifti ar wan siksti piipl a go.* (222/8/277)

as 'Out of a thousand, you'd get a hundred, a hundred and fifty or a hundred and sixty people going.' However, it is significant that one never encounters sentences such as

> 3.35 **a waak mek bai trang* 'Walking makes boys strong.' [6]
> 3.36 **i gi mi wan a taak bod* 'He gave me a talking bird.'

---

[6] The star on this example means, not that it is unacceptable, but that it is unacceptable with the meaning given. That it is the *unprefixed* form of the verb that is the Guyanese nominalisation can be shown by the correct translation of the sentence, which is '*It is walking that* makes boys strong.'

In other words $a + V$ does not function like V*ing* except where there exists the possibility that no nominalisation has taken place, i.e. where the complement of a verb (usually a sense-verb) can be interpreted as a sentence embedded without further structural change. This suspicion about the status of $a + V$ is confirmed by the existence of a parallel structure with *se* 'that':

> 3.37 *awi he se drom a nak* (26/21/25), not, as morph-for-morph translation would suggest, 'We heard that drums were beating,' but from context, clearly 'We heard drums beating.'

Thus the underlying structure of a sentence such as

> 3.38 *da a wan shiip a greez.*[7]

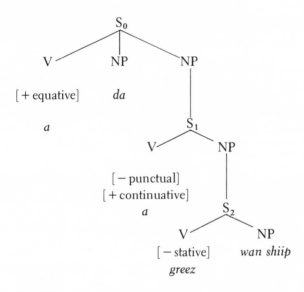

Fig. 3.3

is that shown in Fig. 3.3 and the requisite transformation:

SD: [V NP [V [V NP]]]
SC: 1   2   3   4   5   →   2 1 5 3 4

It is certainly worth noting that the standard-language 'error' contained in Cave's [*That is* [*a sheep is grazing*]] would simply represent the speaker's analysis of the complement as a finite rather than a non-finite structure.

---

[7] Cave's example is unusual in that, in the vast majority of cases, *da a* would be reduced to *da* by the adjacent-low-vowel rule. However, he is sociolinguistically correct in that the sentence could hardly be uttered except by a child describing a picture to an applied linguist, and in such a context, slow, careful speech would be the order of the day.

It seems likeliest, then, that $a + V$ is the equivalent of $be + Ving$ in all cases, and that non-finite *-ing* forms, participial as well as nominal, have to be acquired as novelties by the basilectal speaker. In this sense, they would represent additions to, rather than restructurings of, his verbal system. However, their repeated use, plus perception of their [+ continuative] feature, plus contact with users of verbal *-ing*, would pave the way for the introduction of $Ving$ as a variant of $a + V$.

At this stage, one might ask why $Ving$, rather than $be + Ving$, is so chosen, especially if our argument about finite versus non-finite verbs was correct. It is important here to realise that sentences such as 'That is a sheep is grazing' are only likely to occur in the context that Cave suggests, i.e. where a student is under pressure to produce his acrolectal extreme. At the stage where *-ing* replaces a, many speakers have not yet acquired *be*, and those who have are familiar only with *iz*, or at most, *iz* and *waz*; moreover, even *iz* at this stage is limited to a very narrow range of environments (cf. Bickerton 1973a, 1973b). It is true that *iz* first appears as a variant of equative a, but there is no reason to consider this the same item as [+ continuative] a; even if they could be proved to share a common etymon, their synchronic meanings and functions are quite distinct. It seems likeliest that [+ continuative] simply gets respelled as *-ing*, at the same time as a rule moving this feature to post-verbal position is acquired. No question of 'there being anything missing' would arise, and therefore to treat NP – $Ving$ finite structures as cases of 'zero copula' is quite unwarranted.

That non-verbal *-ing* and verbal *-ing* are originally quite distinct, and that the former is invariably acquired before the latter, is shown by the Bushlot sub-sample, sixteen of whom have *-ing* forms, while only four of the sixteen have $Ving$. Even at a much later stage, there is reason to believe that speakers may keep distinct underlying forms for nominals and verbals:

3.39 *dis bilding staat tu bil* (209/1/265) 'This building began to be built.'
3.40 *de bilin di bilding* (field notes, Matthews Ridge informant) 'They are building the building.' [8]

The way in which verbal *-ing* (and probably many other features too) is actually acquired is suggested in a conversation between 41, who one can say with some confidence completely lacks active $a +$ verb (she fails to produce it even once in a series of conversations in which she receives it eighty-

---

[8] Note the velar nasal in the nominal form. This indicates that develarisation of verbal forms does not come about through a general phonological process, but is limited to precisely these forms – which in turn provides further evidence that verbal and nominal forms are conceptually distinct.

nine times) and 137, who as we saw in Table 2.1 is a pretty basilectal speaker:

3.41 41: *we yu livin bifo yu kom he?*
137: *mi livin a sevntiwan* (41, 137/7/183) 'Where were you living before you came here?' 'I was living in Seventy-one [Village].'

Here, one would have expected *mi bina liv*, a form the speaker well knows, but instead she 'echoes' a form which she otherwise uses only non-verbally – 'farming and thing', 'training school' (137/18–21/184).

However, once *-ing* has been acquired as a permissible variant of *a*, the change moves to completion much more swiftly and smoothly than the *a/doz* change. As compared with the twenty-eight speakers who fulfilled the conditions for Table 3.1 (at least five tokens of at least one variable), only nine fulfil the same conditions for Table 3.2. On the other hand, as shown

TABLE 3.2   Percentage *-ing* for *a/-ing* alternators

Speaker	*a*	*-ing*	Total	% *-ing*
2	21	1	22	5
172	15	1	16	6
137	9	1	10	10
186	39	12	51	23
165	7	7	14	50
196	11	20	31	65
177	2	7	9	77
224	1	6	7	87
99	3	23	26	88
183	1	12	13	92

in Fig. 3.4, the distribution of tokens conforms much more closely to the classic S-curve. Indeed, conformity is probably even greater than Fig. 3.4 indicates, since 165 is not an individual, but a cover-term for participants in a bar-room conversation who could not be individually identified (and thus, though members of the same primary group, probably had differing outputs), and 196, as we have seen, was under the pull of contrary social influences. These exceptions apart, a span of fifty percentage points in the centre of Fig. 3.4 would be empty. Indeed, taken alone, the *a/-ing* change would constitute the strongest available evidence that there were at least two Guyanese 'co-existent systems' and that performance factors alone blurred the difference between them. Unfortunately for this explanation, few other changes are as abrupt, and few if any changes take place simultaneously with others: the isoglosses obstinately refuse to bundle. That this is so can be

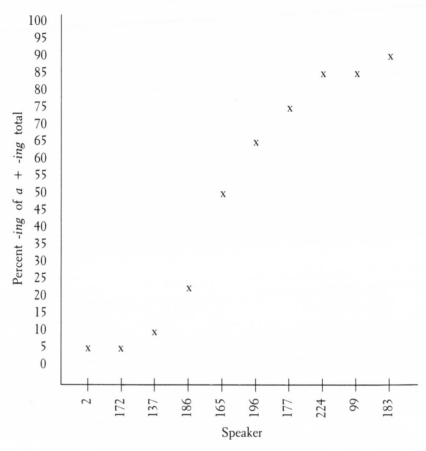

Fig. 3.4. S-curve for *a/-ing* change

shown if we take thirty speakers on whom we have substantial data (at least ten tokens of at least one of the features under examination) and show their outputs of *a, doz,* non-verbal *-ing* and verbal *-ing,* as in Table 3.3. On these features alone, speakers fall clearly into six groups: those with *a* only, those with *a* and *doz,* those with *a, doz* and non-verbal *-ing,* those with all four features, those with both *-ing* forms and *doz* only, and those with only *-ing* forms (note that the last two groups really belong in the mesolect-to-acrolect stage; they are included here for purposes of comparison). There is only one gap in the table (172's absence of N*ing*) but we may fairly conclude that this is an accidental gap due to 172's low sample size. With this exception, the

TABLE 3.3   Distribution of *a*, *doz*, N*ing* and V*ing*

Speaker	V*ing*	N*ing*	*doz*	*a*		
118				27		Group
129				12	*a*-only	I
148				19		
134			1	12		
168			5	43		
176			12	39	*doz* 16%	Group
188			9	94	*a* 84%	II
248			2	32		
219			1	23		
210			16	2		
178		1	8	56		
222		1	1	20	N*ing* 3%	Group
175		1	6	12	*doz* 19%	III
198		1	4	15	*a* 78%	
170		1	6	11		
172	1		2	15		
99	3	2	23	1	V*ing* 30%	
183	12	4	42	1	N*ing* 29%	Group
196	20	19	6	11	*doz* 31%	IV
223	4	14	2	3	*a* 10%	
242	35	34	2	6		
117	17	13	4			
125	44	18	10		V*ing* 54%	
41	24	5	39		N*ing* 26%	Group
209	11	2	5		*doz* 20%	V
227	31	19	1			
236	36	23	2			
107	17	8			V*ing* 60%	Group
108	21	16			N*ing* 40%	VI
169	14	12				

first four tiers of the table constitute a perfect implicational scale; presence of a feature in any column implies the presence of all features to the right, absence implies absence in all columns to the left. In the two lower tiers, these conditions are simply reversed. The average percentages of features in the different groups all grade smoothly and almost without exception, as shown in Table 3.4. One can only conclude that, while some changes may take place more abruptly than others, we are dealing with a true continuum rather than a mere overlapping of discrete systems.

We must next ascertain whether *-ing* inherits the lack of explicit time-

TABLE 3.4   Percentage-grading for *a*, *doz*, N*ing* and V*ing*

Feature	I	II	III	IV	V	VI
a	100	84	78	10	0	0
doz	0	16	19	31	20	0
N*ing*	0	0	3	29	26	40
V*ing*	0	0	0	30	54	60

reference which we noted as a feature of *a*. Let us examine the twelve speakers in Groups IV and V of Table 3.3. They produce between them 239 verbal *-ing* tokens of which we can discount 7 which are marked with *bin* or *did* (we shall deal with these forms later). Of the remaining 232, 159 have present reference and 73 have past reference. A total of 150 are *-ing*-only forms and 82 are marked with some part of the verb *to be*. Of the 159 present-reference verbs, 109, or 69%, are *-ing*-only; 50, or 31%, are marked with *be*. Of the 73 past-reference verbs, 41, or 56%, are *-ing*-only; 32, or 44%, are marked with *be*. From this, we might conclude that there was little difference between marking rates; that unmarked *-ing* began as a form used indifferently for past and non-past, that it then began to be marked for past tense, and that subsequently *be*-forms begin to make their appearance in non-past contexts also. However, closer examination of the data makes this conjecture slightly less plausible. Table 3.5 shows us that if we take the nine speakers in Groups IV and V who have V*ing* scores of over ten, and examine their output of *-ing* forms with past reference, we find that they fall into two sharply divided groups: one consisting of speakers who mark past-

TABLE 3.5   Analysis of V*ing* forms (Groups IV, V)

Speaker	+*iz*	$\emptyset$ non-past	+*waz*	$\emptyset$ past
183	5	4	0	2
117	4	5	1	7
209	2	5	1	3
236	4	7	4	18
41	1	21	0	0
Total	16	42	6	30
196	4	5	8	4
125	6	29	5	4
227	12	17	2	0
242	10	12	11	2
Total	32	63	26	10

reference *-ing* rarely if at all, and one consisting of speakers who mark past-reference *-ing* on a majority of occasions. Notice that this sharp change in the marking of past does not correlate with anything in the marking of non-past. If one leaves aside 41 [9] (who has no past-reference verbs anyway), speakers with little or no past-marking mark the non-past rather oftener than speakers who regularly mark past *-ing*. How is one to account for this phenomenon?

The difference probably lies in the quite different functions of past *waz* and non-past *iz*. The two items seem to be acquired at roughly the same time, but what little evidence there is (e.g. Table 4.1) would indicate that *iz* is perhaps the earlier of the two. Then when *-ing* is acquired, it is prefixed by *iz*, not as a non-past marker, but principally as a marker of emphasis or formality; the basic form remains *-ing* for past and non-past alike. Soon, however, a past–non-past distinction appears (we shall later discuss the evidence that this may be merely a facet of a general past–non-past distinction that comes into effect at this stage), and this distinction is marked by an overt past item *waz* as opposed to zero marking for non-past *-ing*. It is only at this stage that it begins to make any sense to speak of 'zero copula', and even here an alternative analysis may still be preferable; *iz* (plus *am* and *are*, which now begin to be acquired) are still probably better treated as optional stylistic variants than as tense-marking forms variably deleted.

In the meantime, is there any way in which this analysis could be empirically checked? If *iz* is a stylistic marker and is introduced at a stage prior to tense-distinction in *-ing* forms, we would expect to find that speakers who had not acquired *waz* or who had it only marginally would sometimes use *iz* with past reference. Although this phenomenon is rare, it does occur, and precisely with speakers such as those in the first half of Table 3.5:

> 3.42 Archimedes engine – well that *was* much faster, one Archimedes *would take* up this boat with the assistance of the men but it *was* still hard – but not *as* hard – because that Archimedes *pushing*, you understand? You get – for instance when you *rest* off the engine *is carrying* but when you *pulling* like that [sc. propelling the boat by means of paddles] and you *stop*, you *rest* off, the *boat* stop [laughs], so we *had* a great ease. [Int.: Yes, yes.] We *work* that for a couple years, then they *bring* Johnson outboard. (117/1–7/146)

[9] It is worth noting that 41, the nearest of these speakers to categorical *iz*-absence, is by far the best educated. Since education entails learning to categorise on an all-or-nothing basis, the output of an acrolectal speaker 'switching down' is often more categorical (at least in areas of the grammar that come under active scrutiny) than that of the mesolectal or basilectal speakers whom he strives to resemble.

It could, perhaps, be argued that the passage from 'for instance . . .' to the speaker's laughter constitutes a timeless interpolation, despite the *had* at the end of the sentence and the closing-off of the Archimedes epoch by the sentence that follows. However, in the following example no such explanation is possible:

> 3.43 Them particular things *lost* 'cause they *disappear* and he never *see is wanting* until he *get* it here. But they *didn't had* it. They *had* to send from England to get it. (209/18–20/265)

However, the converse – *waz* in non-past contexts – has never been recorded. Moreover, if *iz* is merely stylistic, one can see why acquisition of a past + *-ing* marker would have no observable effect on the frequency with which *iz* occurs; apart from, perhaps, slightly reducing its incidence by removing it from [+ past] environments. Even this detail accords with our findings in Table 3.5.

did + -ing

As mentioned above, *did* can co-occur with *-ing*. This form is fairly infrequent (there are only a half-dozen examples in our recordings), mainly because it has several other competitors (*yuus-tu*, *bin/been* + *-ing*) for the role vacated by *bina*. However, it is worth noting, since its existence marks an ordering of grammatical changes and indicates this order to be different from that of Jamaican Creole. For the latter, B. L. Bailey (1966:140) records *dida* but no *did -ing*. The form *dida*, however, is totally unknown in Guyana. Clearly we are here dealing with two changes:

(1) $a \rightarrow -in(g)$
(2) $bin/ben \rightarrow did$

The changes are ordered thus in the diachronic development of the Guyanese continuum, but for Jamaica, they must be reversed to give (2) – (1) ordering. Note that this analysis will remain unaffected even if *did* + *-ing* should be attested in Jamaica, but that, so far as one can see, it has no implications for any synchronic ordering of rules in either continuum, even assuming that rules for continua can have a specifically synchronic ordering.

bin/biin (± -ing)

We suggested earlier that *did* replaced *bin*, but this remark needs some qualification. *Bin* does not simply disappear; rather it undergoes a phonological change that makes it conform more closely to its probable etymon. As this change involves little more than a lengthening of the nucleus, and as these processes are not discrete but part of an articulatory continuum, it is not easy, in the Guyanese mesolect, any more than it is in rapid English speech, to distinguish [bɪn] from [biːn].

This is no problem in the basilect, where *bin* is uniquely represented as [bɪn], or in English, whether standard or sub-standard, where, whatever its surface manifestation, *been* has an invariant grammatical function. There would be little problem in the mesolect, apart from some inevitable fuzziness, if we could say that *bin* always stood for [+ anterior], while *biin* always stood for [+ perfect, α passive, − α continuative]. However, it is not possible to claim this, and the problem is compounded by the relative rarity of *bin/biin* occurrence, which gives insufficient evidence on which to base a reliable judgement. The most we can do is look at some doubtful sentences and try to suggest one or two factors that may be involved.

Let us begin with 183, a mesolectal speaker in a predominantly basilectal environment:

> 3.44 *abaut mont an a haaf a bin duin dat ting stedi* (183/12/233) 'I was doing that job continuously for about a month and a half.'
>
> 3.45 *dem das fain aut wat an we dem biin an we de go* (183/13/233) 'They used to find out what and where they had been and where they were going.'

The anglocentrist would analyse 3.44 as deriving from English 'I have been doing' by 'deletion' of *have* and certain phonological changes. However, the English structure presupposes an incomplete action (cf. *'I have been writing letters last night'), while context shows that 183 is speaking of events that took place several years earlier. Since his referent is an action that is [− punctual], [+ anterior], we may more accurately conclude that *a bin duin* is simply a relexification of *mi bina du*. Example 3.45, however, is much more susceptible to English derivation. One could argue that it comes from *bin de* by *de*-deletion, and it is true that *de* may begin to disappear at about the stage 183 has reached (cf. Bickerton 1973a, 1973b). However, the presence of *go* in the co-ordinate clause makes it seem likelier that the colloquial English perfect of *go* ('Have you been to Rome?' as opposed to *'Have you gone to Rome?') is the real source here. That the last two examples were uttered within seconds of one another says something about the flexibility of the grammar in this area and at this point in the continuum.

Another mid-mesolectal speaker, 99, has a still more indeterminate example:

> 3.46 *laas nait hool nait i biin du dis du da* (99/7/116) 'Last night all night long he was doing all sorts of things.'

Here, several signs are pointing in contrary directions. The phonological shape of the item indicates an English derivation; its co-occurrence with a stem form indicates a creole one. 'He has been doing' is impossible with 'last night', but *i bin du* is only possible with [+ anterior] reference, and here the context is unfavourable (see example B1 in Chapter 1, in which this example occurs). The subject's actions are not being related to subsequent actions, and both before and after this sentence, unmarked past is used to describe them. The only difference between 3.46 and its immediate neighbours is that it relates a series of actions rather than single ones. But this forms no part of the meaning of *bin*, and is more plausibly relatable to the [+ continuative] element in *been* – certainly 'he has been doing all kinds of things' would be a valid gloss, were it not for the definite-time markers.

However, even where *biin* seems to have been influenced by English, we should be wary of any explanation that requires deletion of *have*. There is evidence that most of the speakers discussed so far do not have *have* either as auxiliary or main verb, while for those who do have it, it is a marginal and rarely occurring item. Moreover, we shall later show evidence that *had* is acquired before *have*, as an individual item (or as past of *gat*) rather than *have* + past. It seems likely that *biin* gradually moves to something close to its English function *before have*-insertion begins. We shall return to this problem in Chapter 4; for the present one would merely suggest that even sentences such as

> 3.47 Because I saw her and she tell me 'bout what she been going to this one for. (43/7/41)

can be accounted for without appeal to '*have*-deletion'. Here, *had* rather than *have* is what is 'missing' and, in any case, the 'past-before-past' reference of the verb brings about an overlap between the polar systems: *shi bina go* would fit the semantic specification as readily as 'she had been going'. 'Deletion' arguments in creoles are generally counter-intuitive, first because they assume phonological processes which are often otherwise unmotivated, and second because they implicitly claim that speakers first put things in to make their utterances look more English, then take them out to give a quite contrary appearance – an intrinsically unlikely procedure, even in an area as complex as the mesolect has been shown to be.

don

This form persists into the mesolect, but is of fairly infrequent occurrence, and seems to disappear altogether well before the acrolect is reached. We suggested earlier that *don* could not root firmly in the grammar until it achieved combinability with other verbal markers, and that this stage had been cut off by the decreolisation process. A rather similar state of affairs appears to exist in U.S. Black English; according to Labov et al. (1968 I:265) it is a 'Southernism, widely used among whites, which we find in moderate frequency in our data', but which 'may be disappearing in the northern ghetto areas'. The same source claims that *done* is a 'perfective particle', but notes (as we have done) certain sentences which would not require perfective marking in standard English; the rather dubious conclusion is that 'It has a perfective meaning, and with it there is usually associated an intensive meaning. But there are occasions when the intensive sense occurs without a perfective sense, and then *done* is seen as perfectly appropriate' (ibid., p. 266).

It was suggested above (Chapter 1, note 12) that puzzling forms in decreolised lects could only satisfactorily be accounted for by appeal to less decreolised ones; there is no need to assume identity of sense or function between lects, but where a form exists in both, at least some plausible type of change-process must be invoked to account for any differences.

The following are three sentences found puzzling by Labov et al. (numbers in brackets represent the original numbering):

3.48 (263) After you knock the guy down, he done got the works, you know he gon' try to sneak you.
3.49 (264) After I done won all that money.
3.50 (265) 'Cause I'll be done put – stuck so many holes in him he'll wish he wouldna said it.

We note that two of these sentences contain *after* while a paraphrase with *after* could easily and adequately convey the meaning of the third. Let us now examine three sentences from the same Guyanese speaker – a predominantly basilectal one, but one who shows this and one or two other mesolectal features:

3.51 *When* you *done peel* the top straw you get other straw. (15/2/16)
3.52 *After* you *done mash* it afternoon time you heap it up. (15/6/16)
3.53 *After* you *finish cut* you draw out the straw. (15/27/15)

The semantic equivalence of *when . . . done* V, *after . . . done* V and *after . . . finish* V in these three sentences is unquestionable. Sentence 3.53 shows most clearly what the shared meaning is: the first of two actions has to be completed before the second can be begun. Indeed, all three sentences could be glossed 'When peeling/mashing/cutting is completed/is completely finished'. Sentence 3.52, however, comes closest in form to the Black English examples, as do mesolectal Guyanese uses such as that of the comedian who sometimes 'perform girl part':

> 3.54 But I does take great care that the stage door lock, 'cause I don't want no boy run in from the pit an' come telling me stupid, 'cause *after* I *done play* me part I gone back as Sam. (162/22–4/206)

Even where *after* is not inserted, the sense of 'necessary completion' is equally clear:

> 3.55 All right, child, let he talk, when he done talk, you can talk. (43/14/43)

With these examples in mind, it should be possible to account for all the uses of *don*, from its post-clausal one on down, as well as its standard and non-standard English equivalents, within a Carden-type 'unified analysis' (Carden 1972). An attempt to do this is made in Fig. 3.5 below. If to the

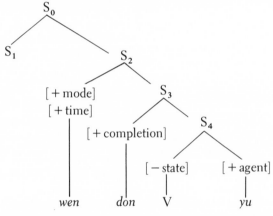

RULES

1. T_a: SD [P [P [P NP X]]]   SC 1 2 3 4 5 → 1 4 3 5 2
2. T_b: SD same   SC 1 2 3 4 5 → 1 4 2 3 5
3. T_c: SD same   SC 1 2 3 4 5 → 1 4 3 5
4. Lexical entry: [+ mode, + time, + completion] → *after*
5. Lexical change: [+ completion] → *finish*

STAGES   OUTPUTS
  I. Rule 1   *wen yu* V (X) *don*
 II. Rule 2   *wen yu don* V (X)
III. Rules 2, 4   *after yu don* V (X)
 IV. Rules 2, 4, 5   *after yu finish* V (X)
  V. Rules 3, 4   *after yu* V (X)

(For SE, add [+ completion] → [+ perfective]; with Rule 2 this yields: *when you have Ved* (X).)

Fig. 3.5

formalism expressed therein we add a rule that, where a sentence with a [+ completion] marker is not embedded in a higher sentence, [+ completion] can be rewritten 'completely', we can account for two sentences which Labov et al. found still more puzzling:

3.56 (266) I done about forget mosta those things.
3.57 (267) I forgot my hat! I done forgot my hat! I done forgot it!

Two very plausible glosses for these sentences would be, respectively, 'I've almost completely forgotten most of those things' and 'I completely forgot my hat!' They seem all the more plausible in the light of the fact that, while both sentences express states of affairs that anyone might need to express at one time or another, it is unlikely that the speakers of 3.56 or 3.57 would have either English *have* + *-en* in their grammar or 'completely' in their lexicon, at least for productive purposes.

That the meaning of *don* differs according to the kind of sentence in which it is found should come as no surprise to us, in view of the differences we noted between, on the one hand, sentences such as 2.68 and 2.69, and on the other, sentences such as 2.74 and 2.76, and of the more general evidence that meaning inheres in sentences (or rather, the propositions underlying sentences) rather than in lexical items. It is true that it would be absurd to gloss 2.74 as 'I completely have a dog', but we have already admitted that it would be unreasonable to expect complete identity of meaning between cognates in Black English and Guyanese Creole; the development from the earlier 'definitively, unalterably' to the later 'completely' is both a small one and of a type that seems highly plausible as between different but related varieties.

gon

This form looks, at first sight, like a reduced form of *going*. Such, indeed, may be its original derivation, but to suppose that creole speakers have an underlying *going* which morphophonemically reduces to *gon* is not in accord with all the available evidence.

In the first place, if *gon* were formed from *go* + *-ing*, we should expect it to appear at about the same time as V + *-ing* structures in general. Broadly speaking, this is the case, but there are a number of speakers, some quite basilectal in other respects, who have *gon* but no V*ing*: 5, 121, 168, 176, 220. Indeed, only one of these speakers (121) even has N*ing*.

Of course, the fact that they did not utter particular forms on particular occasions is no guarantee that they have grammars which do not include the missing forms. In the case of at least 5 and 168, I can say from unrecorded observation that they control more acrolectal levels and that, at these levels, V*ing* forms appear in their outputs. The point is that when operating at a basilectal level, these speakers saw fit to exclude V*ing* forms, but included *gon*. This exclusion can hardly have been accidental; all *gon*-users who also use V*ing* use the latter form several times oftener than *gon*. Thus we can only assume that speakers such as 5 or 168 regard *gon* and V*ing* as unrelated forms, the former suitable for basilectal use, the latter not.

A second counter-argument to a direct *going* derivation comes from the comparison of auxiliary and verbal *go*. When V*ing* is acquired, speakers regularly produce [goːɪn] or [goːɪŋ] as main verb, but the auxiliary form remains [gʌn] or [gɔn] (where it is not further reduced to [gʌ] or even [n]). One never encounters utterances such as

   3.58 *He [goːin] tell she.[10]

but one finds the same speaker regularly and indeed (at this level) without exception distinguishing between

   3.59 *doon ke it iz hu kleem, i gon say wel yu go an wok* (117/25/147) 'It didn't matter whose claim it was, he would say, "Well you go and work!" '

and

   3.60 *bikoz if de goin nau an de se len mi a tauzn ar tri tauzn di iist injan wud giv dem* (117/16/147) 'Because if they were going now and they said, "Lend me a thousand or three thousand," the East Indians would give it to them.'

It is true that English has morphophonemic rules which apply to the auxiliary but not to the main verb form, though it is doubtful if such rules ever apply as consistently as they do here. But there is the further point of what happens to *to*. Black English may reduce *going to* just as drastically as the Guyanese mesolect does (cf. Labov et al. 1968 I: 251–3; Fasold 1972) but there are at least intermediate stages of the *gonna* type which enable one to reconstruct the reduction process. No such intermediate stages exist in the Guyanese mesolect, and one reason for this is that *tu* is never inserted after *gon*. *Tu* itself is in the grammar of all *gon*-users; as was shown in Bickerton

---

[10] Such utterances may, of course, be produced by speakers who are acrolectal throughout. Perhaps equally relevant here is the fact that *goin* is never reduced to *gon* under any circumstances – an utterance such as **shi gon tu di maakit tumara* would be very puzzling to the hearer, as well as ungrammatical, since he would almost certainly interpret *gon* as a realisation of the completive *gaan*.

1971a, the *fu–tu* change, though a long-drawn-out one, begins with modals and quasi-modals of the type to which *go/gon* belongs. Certainly the five speakers who had *gon* but no V*ing* all used *tu* in that type of environment.

None of this evidence might seem conclusive in itself. However, it must be taken in conjunction with the fact that there is a much more natural explanation than the 'reduced-*going*' one: that *gon* is produced by a lowering and nasalisation of the nucleus in the basilectal marker *go*. At a subsequent stage, the output *gon* might be reinterpreted as a reduced form of *going*; in other words, the underlying representation could change from *go* to *going* without any necessary change in surface representation.

As the surface change is on a phonological continuum, one might expect it to be long-drawn-out, but this is not the case. Only twelve speakers alternate between *go* and *gon*. Yet the figures are (even allowing for small sample size) hardly characteristic of rapid change; as Fig. 3.6 shows, the familiar S-

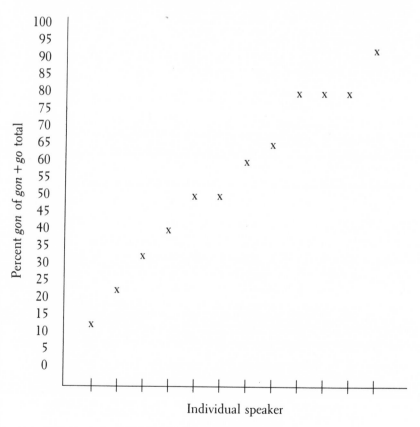

Fig. 3.6 Percentage *gon* of *gon/go* alternation

curve is almost reversed. However, a change which is phonologically vague may be sharpened by social factors. Table 3.6 shows a sharp contrast between the outputs of the five Africans and those of the seven Indians who alternate. Moreover, speakers who have invariant *go* are invariably Indian; mesolectal Africans who do not alternate have *gon* only.

If we examine the functions of *gon* we will find further evidence that it has nothing to do with *going to*. While irrealis markers *will* or *would* in standard English and *go* in basilectal creole can be used to indicate probable actions of some frequency in present or past time, English *going to* cannot be so used: while 'every morning he'll get up early' can be taken as a description of someone's usual habits, 'every morning he's going to get up early' can only be read as referring to someone's future intentions.

TABLE 3.6 Percentage *gon* (African v. Indian)

	go	*gon*	Total	% *gon*
Africans (N = 5)	8	33	41	80
Indians (N = 7)	52	25	77	32
Total	60	58	118	–

We saw that in basilectal creole, *go* had all these functions, and in fact *go* is the only form for these functions: not a single *go*-only speaker used either *will* or *would* in our recordings. This state of affairs is not noticeably affected by *gon*-acquisition. Of the five speakers who have *gon* but no V*ing*, not one uses *will* or *would*. However, the African *go/gon* alternators all have *would* and some have occasional *will* also. *Gon* then begins to alternate with *would* for past probables; an extended passage from 117 will illustrate this type of alternation:

> 3.61 You see a bottle of whisky wasn't nothing much to buy – I think was three dollars for a bottle of whisky, something of the kind – and the pork-knockers [sc. diamond prospectors] *would buy* the whisky and think nothing of it. When the boat left here and it reach its destination where the shop is, that whole night the men *would spree*. The shop owner *gon' spree*, they *gon' drink* whisky and brandy and so on, the whole night the pork-knockers *gon' spend*. They had dancehall and so on up there, piano-playing – yes, in those days so the men *would spend*, you *would drink* whisky and brandy the whole night. (117/22–30/146)

The next stage is the extension of *would* to 'future-in-the-past'; this is reached by 125, at least in his more formal speech, while he retains *gon* for probables, at least for present ones:

3.62 He told me they *would not give* workers allowance for cycle, that he *would see* we get transportation so that good enough. (125/30–1/174)

3.63 Now when they come to price it, this work bad. But the overseer *gon' tell* you that although the work bad, you meet the maximum [sc. are being paid at the highest possible rate]. (125/6–7/172)

Thus the scope of *gon* is gradually being narrowed to that of a pure future. However, this stage is not finally reached until *will* has become firmly established – a process which belongs to the mesolect-to-acrolect phase of development.

Negation

We now come to what is one of the most baffling developments in the mesolect: the proliferation of negative markers. In the basilect, and some way into the mesolect, the unique negative marker for all verbal forms (excluding post- modal -*n*) is *na*. Suddenly, however, and in rapid succession, the forms *en*, *doon*(*t*), *di*(*d*)*n*(*t*) and *neva* make their appearance, soon to be followed by sporadic *izn*(*t*), *wazn*(*t*), *wudn*(*t*) etc. This development is shown in Table 3.7, which takes the speakers from the first five groups of Table 3.3 – a representative spread across the basilect-to-mesolect span – and shows the distribution of all their negative forms, excluding only negated modals *kyaan*, *mosn* and *kudn*.

The new forms all derive in some sense from English forms, even though it is unclear whether *en* stems from *ain't*, or *haven't*, or is the joint product of both. However, as regards their meaning and function, there is certainly no systematic correspondence between these markers and their English equivalents, and apparently little consistency as between different mesolectal speakers (see Table 3.8). This lack of correspondence is connected with the fact that, though these forms may derive *diachronically* from English negative forms, they do not derive *synchronically* in the way that English forms derive. In (standard) generative grammars of English there must be rules of the type

3.64 Aux → Tense. . . .

3.65 Tense → *do* + Tense/ $\dfrac{\text{(NEG)}}{\text{(Q)}}$ ——V

But at this level of the Guyanese grammar there is no *do*; thus there can be no rule that would move *do* to the left of the subject NP, nor one that would insert NEG between *do* and V; there are, on the contrary, merely two dis-

TABLE 3.7   Verbal negation – basilect to mesolect

Speaker	*na*	*en*	*neva*	*doon*	*didn*	Other	Total
118	23						23
129	16						16
148	25	1					26
134	2						2
168	6						6
176	2						2
188	40						40
248	16		5	4	1		26
219	8						8
210	1						1
178	5						5
222	9		2				11
175	6						6
198	9						9
170	6						6
Boundary between Groups III and IV							
172	5						5
99	2		2	2		1	7
183	6			1	1	3	11
196	5	2		5	1	10	23
223	3			3	2	1	9
242	5	1	3	6	5	10	30
117		4	4	2	2	5	17
125	1	3	2	5	2	6	19
41	5	10		10			25
209	2	1	2	2	4	1	12
227				10	3	1	14
236	1	7	2	15	3	3	31
Total	209	29	22	65	24	41	390

NOTE: 'Other' includes *wudn, izn, wazn, nat, 'm nat, hadn* etc.

tinct and quite unrelated morphemes, [+ iterative] *doz* and [+ anterior] *did*, plus a negative-placement rule that inserts the negative particle *before* the verb-phrase, and question-formation rules that simply prepose WH-forms, and/or add intonation contours, to affirmative strings. If there is no *do*, the Guyanese speaker obviously cannot analyse *don't* into *do + not*; yet *doon(t)* is one of the two commonest forms of negation in the mesolect.

It might be argued that he could still analyse *dozn(t)* into *doz + nat*, or *di(d)n(t)* into *did + nat*. However, for the speaker whose vernacular lies in the mesolect or below it (as opposed to the acrolectal-vernacular speaker who can 'drop down' into the mesolect) these seem equally unlikely procedures. As noted in our original discussion of *doz*, *dozn(t)* hardly ever occurs

TABLE 3.8   Relationship of Guyanese mesolectal negatives to equivalents in English

Speaker	English equivalent					
	Did not	Had/ have not	Do not	Was/ were not	Am/are/ is not	Would not
164	en 3 neva 2 doon 3		doon 6	en 1	en 3	neva 1
186	na 9 neva 1 didn 1	na 2 en 3	na 14 doon 6		en 1 na 2	neva 1 wudn 1
192	en 2 didn 1	en 2	doon 1	didn 1 (+ -ing)	en 1 'snat 2	
165	na 3		na 5 en 1 doon 3		na 3	
162	neva 2 en 1 didn 4	havn 1	en 1 doon 5	didn 2 (+ -ing) wazn 1	en 1 'mnat 1	
196	na 2 neva 1 didn 1	na 1 en 1 havn 2	doon 5	wazn 4	en 1 'mnat 1 izn 2	wudn 1
209	neva 1 didn 4	neva 1	na 1 doon 2	na 1	en 1 'rnat 1	
236	en 4 neva 2 doon 3 didn 2	en 2 didn 1 havn 1	na 1 doon 12	en 1	nat 1	wudn 1
125	neva 1 didn 2	en 2 neva 1	doon 5	wazn 1	na 1 en 1 'r/'z/'mnat 3	wudn 2
30	na 3 neva 3 didn 8	na 1	na 1 en 3 doon 1	didn 1	na 2	wudn 1
43	en 4 didn 3	en 1 doon 1	en 7 doon 9	en 1 wazn 1	en 8 'snat 1	
117	neva 4 doon 1 didn 2	en 4 hadn 2	doon 1	wazn 3		
Total	neva 17 na 17 en 14 didn 28 doon 7	na 4 en 15 havn 4 hadn 2 neva 2 didn 1 doon 1	na 22 doon 56 en 12	na 1 en 3 didn 4 wazn 10	na 8 en 17 nat 1 (be)-nat 11	wudn 6 neva 2
Total	83	29	90	18 ·	37	8

TABLE 3.8   (*continued*)

Speaker	Did not	Had/ have not	Do not	Was/ were not	Am/are/ is not	Would not
			English equivalent			
Percentages						
na	33	8	42	2	15	100
didn	85	3		12		100
neva	80	10				10 100
en	23	24	20	5	28	100
doon	11	2	87			100
na	20	17	24	12	28	
didn	34	4		50		
neva	20	9				25
en	17	65	14	38	72	
doon	9	4	62			
	100	100[a]	100	100	100	25

[a] Percentages are based on the totals for each category *after* removal of negated *have* and *be* forms. Discrepancy is due to rounding.

among *doz*-users. When it is used, either of two possible explanations could account for it. It could be a straightforward hypercorrection (general absence of number-concord might be taken as evidence of this); or it could be a negation of [+ iterative], equivalent in meaning to 'don't usually'. The latter would account for its rarity, since doing something frequently (*doz*) or not doing it at all (*doon(t)*) are conditions much more commonly expressed. Often – probably oftener than not – it is not clear which explanation is valid:

> 3.66 If you go to people they doesn't got nothing to give you. (183/23/235)
> 3.67 You doesn't get up 'pon a morning for make tea? (242/16/324)

If the first analysis is correct, the form is marginal to the grammar; if the second, *dozn(t)* falls into the creole arena, and cannot be in any sense a negative of English *do/does*.

As regards *didn(t)*, we note first of all that its occurrence is much more frequent than that of *did*. In our recordings, there are ninety-five tokens of *didn(t)* produced by mesolectal speakers, as opposed to only forty-eight tokens of *did*. The relative rarity of *did* is understandable in the light of the rules governing its use; yet it is probably a universal of human language that any form is affirmed more frequently than it is negated. Can we conclude that *didn(t)* is not the negative form of *did*?

In discussing *did*, we observed that it followed very closely the rules for

bin, i.e. that it was a [+ anterior] rather than a [+ past] marker, and therefore indicated simple past for statives but remote- or past-before-past for
non-statives. Basilectal speakers who are just moving into the mesolect often
if not invariably use *didn*(*t*) in this way:

> 3.68 *if ai didn hia wat mai moda se, somtaim – taim laik dis ai du wikitnis*
> *an badnis* (186/1/241) 'If I hadn't paid heed to what my mother said,
> sometimes – at times like this I would have done evil things.'
> 3.69 Long years gone by they didn't have no certify midwife. (192/16/250)
> 3.70 *dis plees din oopen yet* (236/30/301) 'This place still hadn't been opened
> up.'
> 3.71 And the same the day when she did come and say she didn't get change
> (30/2/387 – for comment see Example 3.23 above).

However, the closer a speaker moves to the mid-mesolect, the greater the
likelihood that he will extend the use of *didn*(*t*) to [– anterior] as well as
[+ anterior] referents, given that they are [+ past]

> 3.72 Is yesterday the letter come but I didn't read it yet. (30/13/385)
> 3.73 I can't remember the year, I sorry that I didn't tick it down [sc. make a
> note of it]. (236/27/301)
> 3.74 *yu gat lok yu din pleein krikit* (162/7/206) 'Lucky for you you weren't
> playing cricket.'

The transition is rendered all the smoother because of the already existing
overlap in statives: a sentence such as

> 3.75 They didn't know where M—— go [sc. would] pick it up. (30/22/387)

would fit either a creole or an English interpretation, in contradistinction to
3.68, 3.70 (grammatical only in a creole framework) or 3.72, 3.73 (grammatical only in an English one).

We would thus be justified in concluding, first, that if *didn*(*t*) is initially
analysed as *did + not*, the *did* involved is not English *did*, and second, that
as *didn*(*t*) expands its area of meaning, any meaningful internal structure it
might have had for the speaker must disappear, since (as we shall see in the
next section) at this stage of development, [+ anterior] *did* begins to phase
out as *-ed* and 'strong' past morphemes phase in, but without, as yet, any
trace of *did*-support in questions, or, for that matter, of *did not* even in the
slowest and most careful speech.

Moreover, the fact that the grammarian can analyse low-mesolectal
didn(*t*) into [+ anterior] *did* and *nat* does not mean that the Guyanese
speaker so analyses it. Let us assume for the moment that Guyanese speakers
acquire all quasi-English negators (*doon*(*t*), *didn*(*t*), *dozn*(*t*), *en*, not to men-

tion *kyaan, mosn* and the rest of the negated modals) as indissoluble forms, monomorphemic sentence-negators which are in process of replacing *na*. This would mean that the negative-placement rule would not have to be changed. If we suppose that the forms can be analysed, we must then assume that the average mesolectal speaker has two negative-placement rules, one for *na* and *en* (pre-VP placement) and one for *n* (*t*) (post-Tense placement), and that they operate without any confusion: one never finds sentences such as

3.76 **mi an(t) go* 'I'm not going.'
3.77 **i na did go* 'He didn't go.'

If, however, the forms are treated as indissoluble negative alternants of *na*, pre-VP placement can be retained for all forms of sentence negation. It is not easy to see what kind of evidence (other than, perhaps, experimental) could settle this issue, but the latter position has parsimony on its side.

If this explanation is correct, it would account for the wide differences in the distribution of Guyanese negative forms and their English cognates, but it would still fail to provide a coherent picture of negation in the mesolect. In order to achieve this, let us first of all set aside the *be-, have-* and *would-* forms in Table 3.8, since these, without exception, concur with their normal English functions. Let us then assume that, earlier in mesolectal development, basilectal categories such as stative and non-stative, anterior and non-anterior, remained effective. Then, English categories would begin to appear and spread at the expense of the basilectal ones; or rather, to be more precise, the newly acquired negative forms would actually introduce and begin to define these categories, along with *had, was* and the earliest *-ed* forms which also begin to be acquired at about this time. In other words, rather than learning new rules and categories and then acquiring the morphological fillers for them, the speaker in a creole continuum characteristically acquires new morphemes and then makes adjustments to his existing rules and categories so as to provide distinctive environments for these morphemes. It is therefore hardly surprising that long after the new material has become firmly established, there should still be a mismatch between the creole and superstrate systems.

Table 3.9 represents an attempt to show this process at work. It is doubtful whether any table could fully capture the complexity of the process, and in attempting to show the very real regularities that underlie the superficial confusion of Table 3.8, some oversimplification has inevitably occurred. This affects principally the categories 'Did' and 'State', and two issues are in-

TABLE 3.9 Relationship of Guyanese mesolectal negatives to hypothetical mesolectal categories

Speaker	Category: Did	Eng + past	Have/be	State	Imp	Eng − past	
164		neva 2	en 4	doon 5 / en 3	doon 4		
186	na 1 / didn 1	na 7 / neva 1	na 5 / en 4	na 9 / doon 5	na 1	na 4 / doon 1	
192	didn 2	en 2	en 3	doon 1			
165		na 2	na 3	na 4 / en 1 / doon 2		na 2 / doon 2	
162	didn 3	neva 2 / didn 3	en 2	doon 3 / en 1		doon 3	
196	didn 1	na 2 / neva 1	en 2	doon 5			
209		didn 4 / neva 2	na 1 / en 1	doon 1		na 1 / doon 1	
236	didn 1	neva 2 / didn 2 / doon 1	en 3	na 1 / en 4 / doon 13	doon 1		
125	didn 2	neva 2	en 3 / na 1	doon 2	doon 2	doon 1	
30	didn 6	neva 3 / didn 3	na 2	na 5 / en 3 / doon 1			
43		didn 3	en 10	en 11 / doon 7	doon 1	doon 2	
117	didn 2	neva 4 / doon 1	en 4				
Subtotal	na 1 / didn 18	na 13 / neva 19 / didn 15 / en 2 / doon 2	na 12 / en 36	na 16 / en 23 / doon 47	na 1 / doon 8	na 7 / doon 9	
Total	19	51	48	86	9	16	
Percentage							
na	2	26	22	34	2	14	100
didn	54	46					100
neva		100					100
en		3	59	38			100
doon		2		72	12	13	100
na	5	26	25	20	11	44	
didn	95	30					
neva		38					
en		4	75	26			
doon		4		54	89	56	
	100	100	100	100	100	100	

NOTE: Categories: Did = V [+ anterior, ± stative]; Eng + past = V [− stative, − anterior, + past]; Have/be = all environments for English *have/be*, minus [+ anterior] ones; State = V [+ stative, ± past]; Imp = Imperative; Eng − past = V [− stative, − anterior, − past].

volved, one fairly trivial, the other of much more far-reaching importance. The first is that, because of the overlap noted in discussing 3.74, it is impossible to tell whether a mesolectal speaker who negates a stative verb with *didn* is applying the basilectal [+ anterior] rule or the English [+ past] one. The other concerns the different possible ways of handling past statives. These are obscured in Table 3.9, since all statives not negated by *did*, whether past or non-past, anterior or non-anterior in reference, are lumped together in the 'State' category. In fact, a number of past statives are negated by what might appear, at first sight, to be 'non-past' forms, e.g. *en* and *doon*. Puzzling as this phenomena may seem, however, it can be systematically accounted for within the framework shortly to be proposed.

Among other forms, one is easily dealt with. *Neva* occurs exclusively before non-statives and in contexts which would satisfy English simple past but not creole [+ anterior]. It is, in other words, acquired as an alternative to *na* where actions in the unmarked past are to be negated, and in Guyana it does not seem to spread outside such environments. *Didn*, on the other hand, is acquired as an alternative to *na bin(a)*. However, as a general past rule is acquired, *didn* begins to compete with *neva* as a simple-past marker. We know that these changes take place in the order given because while there are speakers who have *na* (165), *na/neva* (186, 196) or *neva* only (125, 164) in the 'Eng + past' category, there is none who has *na/didn*, or even *na/neva/didn*; the latter fact would indicate that *didn* is not acquired until *na* has been lost in this category, though it is not clear whether this is a necessary or an accidental condition on the change.

It should be emphasised here that the inevitable fuzziness which exists at the boundaries of all semantic categories in any system is a potent factor in making possible the transitions characteristic of the Guyanese continuum. For example, *neva*, for those who have no other marker for 'Eng + past', can usually be best glossed by English *didn't*:

> 3.78 I tell you that you never gone into the cinema. (164/28/208) (Context makes clear that only one occasion is referred to.)
> 3.79 Now he never take up this matter. (125/7/175)

However, as *didn* begins to be acquired in this category, *neva* tends more and more to be relegated to contexts in which it could be used in at least sub-standard English; for instance,

> · 3.80 Nobody never drown with me. (117/13/146)

where Guyanese concord would render ungrammatical standard English 'nobody ever drowned', while the fact that the speaker no longer works on river-boats would preclude 'nobody has never drowned' (and indeed, as we shall see in Chapter 4, the hold that this speaker and others like him have on *have* is tenuous in the extreme).

It appears likely that *en* is first acquired as a simple negator of the copula. It is hard to settle this point on synchronic evidence alone; *en* has become such an overt marker of ethnicity that one can be sure any Indian using it has or has had extensive relations with Africans at work or in private life or both. Hence data on *en*-acquisition by Indians is too scarce to be of use, while even Africans with a low-mesolectal vernacular are too exposed to higher lects to preserve *en*'s original environment uncontaminated by subsequent change.

However, twenty-two of the thirty-six *en*-occurrences in the 'Have/be' category are copula negations, while of the remaining fourteen, eleven relate to a single verb, *gat*:

3.81 *yu en gat di waata* (186/3/239) 'You haven't got the water.'
3.82 *a en gat di peepa* (192/14/250) 'I haven't got the certificate.'

It seems likely that *en* spreads from the copula to its close semantic neighbour, the verb of possession, and only subsequently and sporadically to other contexts where English has *have*; the marginality of *have* at this stage supports the analysis here.

Note that, with two exceptions, *en* occurs in categories other than 'Have/be' only where it also occurs in that category. Of those two exceptions, one, 165, is a composite of several speakers, probably with marginally differing outputs, while the other, 30, has few occasions for negating either copula or *got*. It therefore seems likeliest that *en* spreads from 'Have/be' to statives in general, rather than vice versa.

As a 'Have/be' negator, *en* is employed indifferently with past and non-past reference:

3.83 When they go at the venture [sc. prospecting] now sometimes they *en got* that money to pay. (117/18/147)
3.84 Well, they had, le'-me-see, mussy 'bout three or four, they *en got* nothing much. (177/24/148)
3.85 Anyway three or four months pass and me and R—— *en talking*. (164/4/210)
3.86 Boy, this auntieman [sc. homosexual] thing what you goin' on with *en* with me, you hear what I tell you? – done it! (164/24-5/209)

This tenseless character is retained as *en* spreads to statives generally:

3.87 And she say, 'I know you *en know* what is the contents of this letter.' (43/6-7/33)

> 3.88 When C—— was a little boy so, he came to spend couple days with me, and then you know the plenty – I *en have* time to bathe him the morning. (43/25–6/33)

It is worth noting that the immediate effect of this last development is to yield an output further from standard English than that of lower lects. The speaker who simply relexifies *bin* to *did* before [+ anterior] statives will produce sentences such as

> 3.89 I *didn't know* – is only now I hearing about he. (125/28/170)

rather than

> 3.90 Well we *en understand* because we were small. (236/31/300)

We should be wary of assuming that *en* acquires past reference with statives simply as a carryover from its role with stative *have* and *be*. This would hardly account for the occurrence of *en* with past non-statives:

> 3.91 We government en say nothing. (162/11/208)
> 3.92 I en grow [sc. grow up] on this coast. (192/13/251)

Still less would it account for similar behaviour by *doon*.

Doon is probably first acquired as an imperative, a function in which it has no competition from *en* or other mesolectal forms: **en do that*, as opposed to *na do that* or *doon do that*, is wholly ungrammatical at any level. Subsequently it becomes a variant in all environments in which *en* is found, except for *en*'s 'home ground' 'Have-be' (and in the upper mesolect, as we shall see in Chapter 4, it even encroaches on this). The precise relationship between *en* and *doon* is not easy to state. At first glance, one might suppose *doon* to be merely a more formal alternate, and no doubt this is so for many speakers. However, many others (of which 43, surreptitiously recorded in the bosom of her own family, is one) alternate the two forms with no trace of such a distinction. For instance, 43 negates *know* ten times, five times with *en*, and five times with *doon*; if stylistic factors are involved, these are too obscure to be perceived by the outsider, and indeed *doon* often occurs in contexts heavily laden with creole idiom and culture:

> 3.93 No, no, the husband, I don't know what happen to he, but like somebody handle he [sc. is working black magic on him], which means you got to say that because he can't keep no work, just as he progress and he meet it [sc. gets work], bam! – something happen, he have to get pelt out someplace. (43/30–2/32)

However, from our point of view the most interesting feature of *doon* is that it occurs not only in environments where English *don't* would fit:

3.94 You *don't use* it, you just throw it out. (209/27/267)

3.95 Well, who [sc. anyone who] *don't give* him nothing, they get cane that fall. (125/1/173)

but also with past statives:

3.96 But when I was a girl growing up there, I hear them talking this language [sc. Sranan], we *don't understand* it. They talking in the African twang, I *don't know* it. (236/26–8/300)

and even with non-statives, provided that their referent action is non-punctual:

3.97 Well sometime steamer *don't come* in here till eight, half-past eight. (236/11/303) (The steamer service referred to had been discontinued for over a year at the time of recording.)

3.98 At that time wages wasn't like this – you might go up to sixty cents, you *don't go* further. (117/7–8/145)

Since (as we saw in Table 3.8) *en* and *doon* between them account for 26% of negation in English-past-type environments, and since their users employ *didn* and *neva* in other past contexts, we can hardly account for these phenomena in terms of hypercorrection, or lack of knowledge of forms or of the correct use of forms. Fortunately, they can readily be accounted for in terms of the overall development of the system.

In discussing *did*, we suggested that the rules which distinguished statives from non-statives probably weakened at this stage. In fact, with the exception of the rule that inhibits co-occurrence of statives and continuatives (a rule which basilectal creole shares with English), they probably give way altogether. Such a collapse would constitute a simplification of the grammar, and would mean that statives would have to be marked in the same way as non-statives, i.e. either [+ punctual] or [− punctual], and, if the latter, either [+continuous] or [−continuous]. Since statives are non-punctual and continuatives are non-stative, they would have to be marked [− punctual, − continuous]. At this level, that combination of features should be spelled *doz*, but by the time the stative rules collapse, *doz* has become variable and, in particular, is disappearing from past environments. In fact, *doz* is very seldom found with statives, and the net result of any such rule-development as we have outlined would be the appearance of past statives with stem-only forms. As noted in the discussion of *did*, such forms begin to appear at precisely this stage. In consequence, *en*, which was introduced as negator of the two commonest statives, would potentially occur with all verbs marked [− punctual] once statives had been remarked in this way. Similarly *doon*, its alternant, could freely occur with any [− anterior] form irrespective of whether it was [+ past] or [− past], [+ stative] or [− stative], provided only that it was [− punctual].

On the basis of the foregoing analysis we can account for the data of Table 3.9 with only eight rules:

(1) Neg + V→*na* + V
(2) Neg + V[+ anterior]→*didn* + V
(3) Neg + V[− anterior, + past]→*neva* + V
(4) Neg + V[Cop, *gat*]→*en* + V
(5) Neg + V[Imp]→*doon* + V
(6) Neg + V[− punctual]→*en* + V
(7) Neg + V[+ past]→*didn* + V
(8) Neg + V[− punctual]→*doon* [Exc.: Cop, *gat*]

Possibly all these rules are known to all the speakers in Table 3.9, if by 'knowing a rule' we mean 'being aware that a rule is in use in the community' rather than 'using a rule productively oneself'.[11] It seems unlikely, however, that all rules are functionally operative for all speakers; for some, (1) is already inactive, while others may not yet have acquired (6), (7) or (8). Further, it is far from clear whether differences in output might arise from differential ordering of these rules, and whether 'ordering' should be interpreted as order of acquisition or rule-ordering in a synchronic grammar or both. It may well be that varying treatment of non-punctual pasts might arise through variations in the ordering of (6), (7) and (8).

-ed

Possibly the most striking difference between basilectal and acrolectal grammars concerns their respective functions for the verb-stem form of non-statives: a surface form which unambiguously relates to past referents in the basilect equally unambiguously relates to non-past ones in the acrolect. In consequence, while past referents are morphologically marked in the acrolect, non-past ones are morphologically marked (with *a*, *doz* or both) in the basilect and mesolect. These facts, which seem to be true of Caribbean creole English in general, have led Labov, following Solomon 1966, to claim that two distinct language-systems must be involved, and to endorse

[11] Generative grammarians, Chomsky in particular, frequently refer to competence as the speaker's 'knowledge of his language'. Unlike epistemologists, they seem to assume that the term 'knowledge' is quite transparent and unambiguous. We shall have cause to return to this issue in Chapter 5.

Solomon's belief that 'the passage of one system into the other could not be a gradual affair, since both items must give way at the same time.' (Labov 1971a:456).[12]

According to Solomon, the Trinidadian Creole paradigm could be expressed as

	Past	Non-past
Trin.	He give	He does give
SE	He gave	He gives

While the Trinidadian elements are certainly involved in Guyanese Creole, any such analysis would grossly oversimplify the Guyanese state of affairs. As we have seen, the mesolectal Guyanese speaker has *doz* for iterated actions (not always or necessarily non-past), *-ing* for continuous actions (not always or necessarily non-past), *did* for [+ anterior] past actions and states, and the stem form for non-past states, [− anterior] actions (roughly equivalent to English 'simple past' actions), and in a variety of contexts where underlying propositional statives preclude the generation of [− punctual] markers.

Thus, in both mesolect and basilect, there are stem forms with non-past in addition to stem forms with past reference, and marked forms with past in addition to marked forms with non-past reference; there is not, therefore, the simple opposition between mirror-image systems which was assumed as the basis for Labov's judgement. It follows that (excluding for the moment any semantic shifts which might be involved) all that is required for mesolect and acrolect to merge is a continuing decrease in the number of marked non-past forms and a continuing increase in the number of marked past forms.

The first part of the procedure is relatively uncomplicated, since it involves only loss of *doz*; the second is quite a different matter. In theory it would be possible to expand the range of *did* to cover non-anterior past actions. However, linguistic change does not seem to work in this way. From our study of negation, it would seem that, while a form that has once been acquired can spread to already existing environments, it cannot create environments that did not pre-exist; to create new environments, new forms have to be introduced.

Such a hypothesis is certainly borne out in the acquisition of English simple past tense. Until *neva* is acquired, the category of 'simple past' simply does not exist in Guyanese Creole. When it does exist, it begins by inheriting the zero marking of [− anterior, + punctual] verbs − at least in affirma-

---

[12] This conclusion is specifically challenged in Bickerton 1974.

tive utterances. The acquisition of the full range of English past-morpheme variants is a long, slow and tortuous process, which is not completed until the acrolect is reached. In this chapter we shall deal with its first phase only.

Our analysis of -*ing* showed that this form was not acquired through a productive rule; rather, that deverbalised -*ing* forms were added as simple vocabulary items before the suffix spread to verbs and became generally productive. Deverbalised forms play a large part in past-morpheme acquisition also; however, they are by no means the only factor involved.

The first affirmative English past forms to be acquired are *had* and *waz*: irregular forms apparently added to the lexicon without necessarily implying

TABLE 3.10   Early environments for -*ed* acquisition

	Environment					
Speaker	PP + syll	*start*	PP − syll	V + syll	V − syll	
100	0/0	1/4	0/2	0/1	0/5	
101	0/0	0/1	0/2	1/7	0/10	
121	3/0	0/3	0/1	0/1	0/13	
126	0/0	1/0	0/0	0/0	0/16	Group I
183	0/2	3/1	0/1	0/4	0/25	
220	0/0	0/0	2/1	0/1	0/3	
224	2/0	0/0	0/0	0/0	0/10	
Total	5/2	5/9	2/7	1/14	0/82	
Percent -*ed*	71	35	22	7	0	
41	1/0	0/0	0/1	1/0	0/7	
103	0/0	4/0	0/3	0/1	0/15	
108	0/0	1/1	0/3	0/4	0/17	
117	0/0	3/0	0/0	0/3	0/48	
125	0/0	1/1	2/0	5/1	0/10	
160	0/0	0/1	0/0	1/0	0/3	Group II
169	5/0	1/5	2/1	2/0	1/10	
186	0/0	1/0	1/0	0/5	0/34	
214	1/0	0/3	0/3	0/1	0/10	
223	1/0	0/0	2/0	0/0	0/6	
225	1/0	0/0	1/2	1/2	0/10	
Total	9/0	11/11	8/13	10/17	1/160	
Percent -*ed*	100	50	38	37	0.6	
Total I & II	14/2	16/20	10/20	11/31	1/242	
Percent -*ed*	87	44	33	26	0.4	

NOTES: Numbers before diagonal slashes indicate number of -*ed* morphemes realised; numbers after slashes indicate number of -*ed* morphemes unrealised. Group I = speakers who have no evidence of 'strong' past forms; Group II = speakers who have evidence of 'strong' past forms. V = verb, PP = past participle, + syll = stem ending in /t/ or /d/, − syll = all other weak (-*ed*) verbs.

TABLE 3.11 Implications of *-ed* environments

Speaker	Environment			
	V − syll	PP − syll	V + syll	PP + syll
121	0	0	0	+
214	0	0	0	+
224	0	−	−	+
100	0	0	x	−
101	0	0	x	−
108	0	0	x	−
183	0	0	x	⓪
160	0	−	x	−
41	0	0	+	+
126	0	−	+	−
103	0	0	+	−
117	0	−	+	−
220	0	x	⓪	−
225	0	x	ⓧ	+
223	0	+	−	+
186	0	+	+	−
125	0	+	ⓧ	−
169	x	ⓧ	ⓧ	+

NOTES: 0 = no cases of *-ed*; x = variable presence of *-ed*; + = invariant presence of *-ed*; − = no evidence; V + syll includes *start(ed)*. Deviations are ringed: scalability = 89.29%.

prior possession of *have* or *be* (Table 4.1 indicates that *had* is usually acquired before *have*). The acquisition of the *-ed* form proper is shown in Table 3.10. (The implicational relationships which hold for these data are illustrated in Table 3.11.) This table shows the *-ed* output of eighteen mesolectal speakers, chosen by the following criteria: first, all speakers who produced no *-ed* (whether because they lacked the form or failed to produce contexts for it) were excluded; then, all speakers who produced either more than 50% *-ed* or more than twelve *-ed* occurrences were excluded; then, all speakers who had recorded less than five hundred words were excluded, in order that unduly small samples should not distort the results. The residue of eighteen speakers was assumed to be representative of those speakers who are in a fairly early stage of *-ed* acquisition.

As Table 3.10 shows, a factor second only in importance to deverbalisation is the phonological structure of the affixated stem. English verb stems which have C[+ coronal, − continuant] as their final segment invariably add a syllable when *-ed* is affixed; those which have any other type of segment do not. It would seem that this feature gives the former class of verbs (which we shall in future refer to as V + syll) an unusual degree of phonological salience for Guyanese speakers, and to understand the reasons for this salience we must glance briefly at certain aspects of Guyanese phonology.

Guyanese, in common with pidgins and creoles generally, permits far fewer consonant clusters in syllable-final position than does English. Except near the acrolect, clusters of more than two consonants seldom if ever occur even in the slowest and most formal speech, while rapid and careless speech virtually reduces Guyanese syllable structure to a CVCV pattern. In semi-casual speech, dual clusters can be dealt with by apocope, metathesis or nasalisation. Metathesis affects only non-homorganic voiceless-fricative plus voiceless-stop clusters, so that one gets *huks* 'husk', *krips* 'crisp' etc. Loss of nasal consonant plus nasalisation of the preceding vowel is an option for all nasal plus voiceless-consonant clusters, though apocope can affect these and indeed all types of dual cluster except liquid plus voiceless-obstruent, which seems never to be reduced (unlike Black English, where *hep* 'help' is reportedly common). Thus all final C + /d/ and most final C + /t/ clusters are simplified by loss of the coronal stop.

However, the majority of English verb stems have final consonants. Affixation of -*ed* therefore has the effect (except with V + syll) of automatically creating clusters where there is only a single final consonant, and complicating clusters where these already exist. Moreover, all these resultant clusters have coronal stops as their final members. This means that the production of most English 'weak-past' forms is impossible within the limits of Guyanese Creole phonology, and indeed the study of reading and dictation exercises given to Guyanese children indicates that, for basilectal and perhaps many mesolectal speakers, there may be a complete lack even of aural discrimination between affixated and unaffixated forms.

It would be as well, however, to emphasise here that the Guyanese use of the stem form in past contexts cannot possibly have arisen through phonological deletion processes. If this were the case, the vast majority of English 'strong' verbs, which form their past tense without any kind of phonological complication (e.g. *take:took, write:wrote, come:came* etc.) would have remained unaffected. In fact, forms such as *took, wrote, came* are never used by basilectal and seldom if ever by many mesolectal speakers. For example, the speakers of Table 3.10 are divided into two groups on the basis of whether or not their recordings contained any examples of 'strong' pasts. Those of Group I members did not, even though their speech contained more tokens of strong than of weak verbs: even among Group II members, 'strong' pasts were sporadic and rare. There can therefore be no doubt that the complete absence of *-ed* over the basilectal end of the continuum is a grammatical and not a phonological fact. However, from the moment that the first *-ed* forms are acquired, grammatical and phonological constraints begin to interact in a complex and interesting way.

The earliest forms to be acquired are the past participles of + syll verbs. A majority of these forms are clearly, for their speakers, 'learnèd words' – *populated, accommodated, admitted, inoculated, excited* etc. – and since the unaffixated forms of these verbs (*populate, accommodate* etc.) are seldom if ever used by Guyanese speakers at this level, we may conclude that they are acquired as formal vocabulary items with no question of any productive process being involved. Indeed, the contexts in which they are used are almost always suggestive of some degree of formality:

> 3.99 Well, when I get this 'immediately X-ray', they prove that I have to stay until – it was a Saturday I *admitted*, and I have to stay until the next Tuesday. (121/8/155)
>
> 3.100 Well, with religion, ahm, long ago people I find was more *religiously minded* than nowadays. (223/17/279)
>
> 3.101 Even when fevers was reigning there was no present kind of [medicine?] just to be given or *to be inoculated*. (225/11–12/286)

Only two syllabic past participles are left unaffixated, and this involves only a single speaker and two tokens of the same form. In fact, these probably are not 'psychologically' syllabic at all:

> 3.102 You know, to get *suspend* for a month now to get the light. (183/12/235)
>
> 3.103 Two year them summons we – we *suspend* in court now. (183/22/235)

For 183, a slightly bemused but respectable old Indian artisan, *suspend* obviously carries a vague general meaning of 'delay, adjourn, remand on bail' etc. More importantly, from our viewpoint, it is phonetically [sɔspen]. Now if, for this speaker, its underlying as well as its surface form has been reduced by the regular rule of final-voiced-stop deletion, it would no longer, for him, fall into the V + syll class; its participial form would be *sospen + ed → sospend →* (by stop-deletion) *sospen*, which is the observed surface form.[13] Some evidence which tends to confirm this analysis will be given when we examine 'verbal' V + syll forms.

Introduction of these participial forms raises the question of a passive transformation. In Chapter 2, we noted that the basilect had two resources

---

[13] Note that this analysis removes 183's deviance from Table 3.11.

for dealing with expressions which require a *be* + PP passive in standard English: an unmarked intransitive stem form (described as an 'inchoative construction' in DeCamp's discussion of the Jamaican equivalent [1971a:362–3]) and a form consisting of *get* + stem. Lacking both *be* and past participles, an English passive is impossible at this stage. In the mesolect, it seems likely that passives are learnt, not as the product of a freshly acquired rule, but by a gradual and piecemeal process. Evidence on this point is not easy to come by, but one small piece is worth mentioning. One of the few cases of a 'learnèd word' being used verbally as well as participially is 121's

> 3.104 Well, the doctor *admit* me – he say I have to *admitted* to the hospital.
> (121/29–30/154)

The second construction can hardly be regarded as a transform of the first, at least not by any rules in the grammar of general English.

In all probability, the order of passive acquisition is represented by Examples 3.102, 3.103; 3.99, 3.104; 3.100; 3.101, in that order. Examples 3.102 and 3.103 represent the two basilectal passive equivalents; 3.99 and 3.104 represent the use of the newly acquired participial form in place of the stem, but without *be*-insertion; 3.100 represents the acquisition of *be* with participial adjectives (a natural development, since *be* before predicate adjectives begins to be acquired at this stage; cf. Bickerton 1973b); 3.101 represents full-fledged passive constructions. Note that, although at least *iz* is generally acquired before even syllabic participles, no examples of *be* + stem occur in our recordings; the order of changes given must therefore be general if not universal. Indeed, even the possession of both *be* and participles does not mean that passives will automatically be produced. Both 121 and 183 (speakers separated by eighty miles of space and over fifty years of age, incidentally) use *be* and *-ed* forms, and 183 even has the beginnings of number concord, but this is apparently not enough for them to put the two together in an English-type passive construction. Again it would seem that the production by the speaker himself of isolated passives (probably borrowed as lexical items from other speakers) must precede the formation of any generally productive rule.

The second environment for the acquisition of *-ed* is V + syll, or rather one particular member of V + syll. Table 3.10 is quite instructive in this respect. Speakers who have not yet acquired strong pasts affixate *start* five times as often as other V + syll verbs; speakers who have already acquired them have reduced the advantage of *start* to a mere 25%. Of all the V + syll verbs, *start* is by far the commonest in Guyanese speech, therefore intrinsically the likeliest to be first affected by any change.[14] However, for all speakers, and for all V + syll verbs, affixation is still highly variable, and it is worth asking whether other than phonological features may be involved.

For at least one speaker there is a clearly grammatical constraint. Speaker 101 has nine occurrences of V + syll including one *start*, but only one *-ed*. We already noted (Example 3.25 above) that this speaker is a *did*-user and that she used *did* in a past-before-past context. In the course of the same recording she used her solitary *-ed* in an identical manner:

> 3.105 After she *feel* better she *go* back – you taking me? – when she *go* back she *go* to the direct spot where she *planted* this seed. (101/5–6/120)

Note, however, that this only occurs in accordance with the basilectal [+ anterior] rule, that is to say when a speaker inverts normal narrative order (i.e. refers to an *earlier* event *after* a later one). In normal narrative order, or where reported speech brings the narrative 'baseline' into non-past time, the same verb remains unaffixated:

> 3.106 She only *plant* it that afternoon and she *go* home. (101/1/120)
> 3.107 The pumpkin seed that she *plant grow* and after it *grow* it *run*. (101/3/120)
> 3.108 She say, 'Pumpkin, since you missy *plant* you, me child, a now [sc. it is only now] you missy able for come back come see you.' (101/8–9/120)

However, there is no clear evidence that any of the other speakers in Table 3.10 follow this rule. The majority of *-ed* occurrences in that table could not possibly be regarded as falling within the scope of the [+ anterior] rule, and must be interpreted as bearers of a category new to the Guyanese system, that of English simple past:

> 3.109 When she finish bathe and sing this song, climb this tree, she *started* to sing, 'Benra Brama, two two tiger want to eat you.' (126/12–13/176)
> 3.110 When tractor come in we *started* now with big quantity plant. (183/24/231)

Where *-ed* is not affixed to V + syll, the reasons are most probably phonological; for instance, the distribution of *-ed* tokens for four speakers in Table 3.10 (100, 108, 169 and 183) can be accounted for fully by assuming a rule which permits *-ed* everywhere except before a following (perhaps hom-

---

[14] It is also worth noting that *start* is, almost by definition, [+ punctual]. However, in its patterns of behaviour it is very like a modal, and all modals are [− punctual]. It may be for this reason, rather than for any phonological cause, that some speakers systematically omit *-ed* when *start* is followed by *to*.

organic only) stop. Those who believe in sociological explanations for linguistic facts should note that there is very little in common regionally or socially between these speakers, who are, respectively, a fifty-year-old skilled African labourer from Georgetown, a lower-middle-class, middle-aged African housewife from the interior town of Bartica, a prosperous forty-year-old Indian shopkeeper from Bushlot, and a poor semi-retired seventy-year-old Indian artisan from Bushlot. However, 117 and probably also 103, near neighbours of 108, affixate all *start* and no other V + syll, irrespective of following environment.

The existence of the following-stop rule goes some way towards explaining why V + syll members other than *start* are able to catch up with *start* in their percentages of *-ed* affixations. *Start* is followed with high frequency by the complementiser *to*, and while this feature follows some other V + syll verbs with some frequency (e.g. *want*, *decide*), it does not do so with all of them.

Another factor to be taken into consideration is the possibility of apparent exceptions to the V + syll rule arising through differences between English and creole underlying forms. This point arose in our discussion of participles, and the following examples provide further evidence – evidence that is all the clearer in that the speaker (as the extracts indicate) is a highly self-conscious one:

> 3.111 We [atɛn] the Albion Canadian Presbyterian Church at Christianburg. (225/13/284) (Clearly past from context.)
> 3.112 Later on we [plantɪd] the rice and after ten weeks or a period of from twelve to fourteen weeks you [haavɪs] you rice. (225/25–6/284)

The clusters in *attend* (nasal plus voiced stop) and *harvest* (voiceless fricative plus voiceless stop, but homorganic) are ones which are obligatorily reduced in Guyanese phonology, while *plant* has a final cluster which is only optionally reduced. It seems reasonable to suppose that the underlying forms are *aten*, *haaves* and *plant* respectively, and that the first two verbs are therefore not members of V + syll. While this factor does not apply in all cases of non-insertion, it means that the percentage of marked V + syll is rather higher than Table 3.10 indicates.[15]

It is only with PP-syll that following environments become a relevant factor. If we divide the data into two classes based on following segment – on the one hand, vowel, semivowel and juncture; on the other, all conso-

---

[15] This also means that a further deviance, that of 225, can be removed from Table 3.11, raising the level of scalability to 92.86%.

nants – we find that while the twenty unaffixated participles are divided evenly ten/ten between these classes, seven out of the ten affixated ones are in the 'vowel etc.' class and only three in the 'consonantal' one. Again, the difference is slight, but it marks the emergence of a factor which has been found to be highly significant in studies of Black English (Labov et al. 1968, Fasold 1972 etc.) and to which we shall return in the following chapter.

However, there is no question of any phonological factor other than verb-stem constitution affecting V-syll, the final class in Table 3.10. With only a single affixation in 242 cases (and that from the most 'evolved' of the eighteen speakers in the table), it is clear not only that following environments are altogether without effect, but that there cannot even be any discrimination, by these speakers, between verbs in which affixation produces final clusters and vowel-final verbs in which it produces only single consonants. The latter, one might have thought, present no greater phonological obstacle than do V + syll verbs. However, the sole criterion at this level is not 'phonological ease' per se, but simply whether the underlying stem form terminates in a coronal stop. Moreover, the difference in the treatment of − syll participles and − syll verbs is clear indication that these constitute two conceptually distinct classes for the mid-mesolectal speaker, and are handled by separate rules.

A good deal of controversy over Black English (see especially Loflin 1967, 1970 in addition to sources previously cited) has turned on whether it possesses certain standard English forms, e.g. copula, perfect, past tense etc., and subsequently deletes them (sometimes in a majority of cases), or whether it lacks them altogether (in which case one invokes 'dialect mixture' to account for instances actually found in empirical data). The foregoing analysis indicates that this is a false dilemma, arising partly from the attempt to view Black English as a homogeneous object, partly from a confusion of past tense, a semantic category, with past tense marking, a morphophonemic feature. Of course, a category can hardly be said to exist if no observable feature represents it. However, one can acquire an English category without necessarily giving it an English representation, just as one can acquire an English category without giving it the same extension that it has in English. Both these developments seem to be present in the mid-mesolect. As regards the first, most verbs previously analysed as [− anterior, + punctual] but now analysed as [+ past, + punctual] retain their previous surface representation, at least in affirmative sentences; it is not entirely clear whether this surface representation is identical with underlying representation, but there seems no *a priori* reason why this should not be so. As regards the second, we have already seen evidence (and in Chapter 4 we shall see more) that non-punctual past-reference verbs are handled quite differently from punctual ones, and that what, in English, are formal markers of non-pastness (e.g. *don't*, stem form, and – at a later stage – even third-person-singular *-s*) are frequently attached to them.

However, it may not be quite correct to suppose that the mid-mesolect actually adopts a version of (semantic) English past which excludes non-punctuals. What may really happen can be better conceptualised if we briefly review the changes already discussed. To avoid irrelevant complications, *don* and irrealis forms are excluded from this summary.

The basilectal rules may be given as:

(1) + stat + ant → *bin*
(2) + stat − ant → ∅
(3) − stat + ant + punct → *bin*
(4) − stat + ant − punct → *bina*
(5) − stat − ant + punct → ∅
(6) − stat − ant − punct → *a*

To these rules, the following changes take place, in approximately the order given:

(7) − stat − ant − punct → − stat − ant − punct ± cont
(8) − stat − ant − punct + cont → *a*
(9) − stat − ant − punct − cont → *doz*
(10) *a* → *-ing*
(11) *bin* → *did*
(12) − ant → ± past/ − punct + cont
(13) + past − punct + cont → (*waz*) *-ing* [16]
(14) − past − punct + cont → (*iz*) *-ing*
(15) − ant → ± past/ − punct
(16) + past − punct − cont → ∅
(17) − past − punct − cont → (*doz*)
(18) + stat → − punct − cont
(19) − ant → ± past
(20) + past + punct → (*-ed*)

When *doz* finally disappears (as will be described in Chapter 4), rules (16) and (17) will have an identical output, and at least some speakers may simplify their grammars by substituting (21):

[16] Bracketed items are variables which alternate with ∅

(21) α past − punct − cont→$\emptyset$ (-s)

Thus, states and iterated actions could be conceptualised as past while still being treated in the same way as non-pasts.

We may note in passing that the most radical changes, and those that bring mesolectal Guyanese Creole closer to the system of English, affect the [−anterior] section of the paradigm before they affect the [+anterior] section. This is precisely what any diffusion theory would lead one to expect, since utterances with [−anterior] reference are much more frequent than those with [+anterior] reference.

Our survey of the Guyanese continuum has now brought us to a point somewhere near the centre of the mesolect. This level is characteristic of many working-class speakers in Georgetown, in neighbouring coastal villages, and in interior mining towns, while it is shared, in intimate and informal usage, by many members of the urban lower-middle class, and in formal and monitored usage by many members of the rural poor. For one of the most striking features of the continuum is its linearity: one man's hypercorrection is another man's vernacular, all the way up the line until the acrolect is reached.

4 From mesolect to acrolect

The processes that we observed in the developmental phase between basilect and mid-mesolect consisted to a large extent of introducing formatives modelled on English ones, using them (at least initially) in a quite un-English way, and only slowly and gradually shifting the underlying semantic system in the general direction of English. But at the level our description has now reached, a change in the nature of these processes occurs which makes the present chapter-division more than a mere matter of convenience. Increasingly, from this point, English forms are added to the grammar in pretty much their English functions, while non-English forms either drop out altogether or are crushed and distorted into patterns that become steadily closer to English ones.

Table 4.1 gives us a very general overview of this process. It shows the relative order of acquisition for eleven standard-English features, together with number of occurrences in each case. It does not indicate the stage at which a speaker loses competing (non-English) features. This fact explains why several speakers we have classed as mesolectal (e.g. 236, 196) are found near the foot of the scale, in a position that would indicate they are not far removed from the acrolect. In fact, these are 'broad-spectrum' speakers who, in addition to a sprinkling of standard items, use a great many non-standard ones, and who style-shift with frequency for expressive purposes. On the other hand, speakers such as 105 or even 100, who have few types of standard feature, also have fewer non-standard features, at least in those samples of their output we have on record. In Chapter 5, we will discuss some of the implications of such differences in range.

Table 4.1 shows a striking consistency in the order in which features are acquired. Only nine of the thirty speakers in the table show any standard features 'before time', so to speak, and none of these shows more than two features in this way; moreover, the very low figures in almost every case indicate that such 'premature acquisition' is always marginal. 'Delayed acquisition' is at least equally rare, since a number of the gaps on the right-hand side of the table are 'accidental' ones, i.e. arise simply because suitable environments for the feature were lacking in the outputs actually recorded.

If standard forms are acquired in a regular order, one must ask whether

TABLE 4.1 Acquisition of standard-English features

Speaker	Doesn't	Am	3rd pers. sing. non-past -s	Were	Are	Will	'Strong' past	Have	'Weak' past	Had	Was
98											2
99					1	1				1	
216	1						1			5	13
177						1				3	3
101									1	2	
100			2	1					3	13	1
121								1	3		
220					1			5	2	1	2
224					1			7	2	6	3
183	1				3			2	3		1
160							2		1	6	3
214						2	1	1	1	5	2
192							1	1	2	2	4
186							1	2	5	1	3
41					1	1		2	2	4	2
223			1		2	3	1	18	2		9
238		6			7	3	3	6	2		6
209					1			7	8	17	20
105				9	1	1	36	3	18	11	26
108			3		1		3	6	1	28	28
225			2		4		4	5	3		10
169			1	1		4	7	2	12	6	11
226			3	4	11	1	11	6	18	5	15
103			3	1	1		10	4	4	2	8
125		1	1		1	2	8	5	11	2	17
117		2	4	3			7	2	3	14	32
227		2	3	2	11	3	1	12	2	1	2
236		3	1	2	3	7	6	9	4	10	25
196		5	2	4	5	4	12	7	12	13	37
241	3	8	5		18	9	10	16	13	1	2
Total	5	27	26	32	73	44	133	134	124	161	284

this order is a purely accidental one, or whether there exist inter-rule constraints which effectively determine it. Perhaps the only way to answer this question unambiguously would be to demonstrate that an identical or almost identical ordering held good for all situations in which an anglo-creole was being decreolised. To date, however, there exists no study of decreolisation detailed enough for us to make the necessary comparisons. However, what is so far known of the process in Jamaica, in Hawaii, in the Gullah area and elsewhere seems to indicate that there are no immediately obvious counter-examples, and that a constrained and quasi-universal English-feature acquisition order would constitute a strong and interesting hypothesis for the comparative studies that will eventually emerge. In this chapter, as we examine both the loss of non-standard features and the acquisition of standard ones, we will try to see what support for such a hypothesis is offered by Guyanese data.

The principal developments which we shall examine in this chapter are: the loss of *doz, did* and *don*; the appearance of *have* and the emergence of a perfective category; the appearance of *will* as a pure future; the emergence of number-concord with *have* and third-person forms; the gradual acquisition of 'strong' past and participial forms and the spread of *-ed* to the V-syll category; the standardisation of negative forms.

doz

In the upper mesolect, *doz* becomes restricted to non-past environments. The heaviest user in this phase of the continuum [1] is 43, with thirty-three occurrences. Of these, twenty-nine are unambiguously non-past and one is doubtful. Only two have unambiguous past reference:

> 4.1 She *was* the only black girl and they start to say that she *does smell* stink and she *does smell* this and she perspiration high and all, and they make like a deputation in writing, sign their name. (43/26–9/37)

[1] The reader may well question the consistency of including 43 among mid-to-upper-mesolectal speakers in this chapter, when in the preceding chapter she was cited as a low-to-mid-mesolectal speaker. As the same criticism can be levelled at the treatment of other speakers such as 125 and 196, it must be dealt with fully. In fact, the inconsistency is more apparent than real. In the first place, positions on the continuum are really abstract levels, not the fixed locations of actual speakers. Although implicational relations hold over the continuum generally, strict implicational relations do not necessarily apply to all speakers in all areas of the grammar. The output rules a particular speaker has for negation, for example, may represent a level of the continuum different from that which is represented by the same speaker's rules for the handling of past-reference verbs; or vice versa. This is to some extent the case of 43, who uses *en* much more frequently than the typical mid-to-upper mesolectal speaker, but has numerous strong and even a few V-syll past forms, which the typical low-to-mid-mesolectal speaker lacks. In the second place, speakers differ widely in range – not just in overall range, but in the extent to which they style-shift within the context of the same situation. How one rates such speakers depends entirely on one's criteria. If they are rated on the kind and number of non-standard forms they use, they will be found to be closer to the basilect than the acrolect. If they are rated on the kind and number of standard forms they use, they will be found to be closer to the acrolect than the basilect. Speaker 43 is also just such a broad-spectrum speaker. In Chapter 5 we shall see whether it is possible to determine the position of such speakers more unambiguously by ignoring surface forms and concentrating on their underlying rules.

Here, however, it could be argued that the reporting of speech involves a shift of focus; moreover, Guyanese speakers in general, even when they introduce reported speech with a complementiser such as *se* or *that*, usually adhere to the conventions of *oratio recta*. Leaving aside for a moment 43's thirty-third *doz*-token, we note that the two speakers interacting with her in the quoted conversation, 41 and 44, use *doz* only in non-past contexts (four and five times respectively) while other upper-mesolectal speakers, if they retain *doz* at all, keep it exclusively for non-past reference.

Restriction of *doz* to non-past environments runs parallel with *doz*-deletion. In addition to being excluded from the stativised environments mentioned in Chapter 3, *doz* now begins to disappear from hypothetical or generic utterances (in particular those with generic 'you' as subject). This process starts fairly early on in the mesolect; 125, for example, is variable on 'you' sentences:

4.2 You *does price* them, put on them extra, half-cent extra. (125/27/173)
4.3 You *lick* it [sc. the cane-stalk] down and you can cut two by the time that fall down – by the time the man lash one. He *take* the time, you just *scramble* and *knock* and *gone*. (125/6–7/173)

In the upper mesolect, deletion is categorical in generics and hypotheticals, and *doz* is inserted only where actual behaviour by named persons is being described. Finally, it becomes variable even here:

4.4 They *rent* a plane and *pass* overhead so nothing *pass* through Bartica now, the only pork-knocker that *does pass* here is what we *call* the bad pork-knocker. (111/4/142)

From this point, it is only a step to the complete elimination of *doz*.

Since the disappearance of *doz* occurs at a stage of development when past marking is very far from complete, one finds a number of speakers who simultaneously have many unmarked forms in both past and non-past environments. Of course, as we saw in Chapter 2, the varied uses of unmarked forms in the basilect present no problem there, since basilectal grammar is based on a [± anterior] not a [± past] opposition. However, since *doz*-disappearance largely coincides with a shift from the former to the latter opposition, one may well ask how it is that problems of communication do not arise through the difficulty of assigning unambiguous time-reference to a given unmarked verb.

The answer seems to be that, as marked non-pasts decrease, so marked pasts increase, in such a way that (cf. Bickerton 1974) the percentage of non-past verbs marked with *doz* will not fall below 30 until the percentage of past verbs with standard-English marking has risen above that figure. Whether this is necessarily or only accidentally so is far from clear, but the effective result is that, even leaving aside contextual clues, it is possible to determine the time-reference of almost every utterance, given rules (16) and (18) in Chapter 3 plus the *doz*-deletion environments mentioned here.[2]

Before leaving *doz*, however, we must return to 43's odd *doz*-token mentioned above:

4.5 If the husband know that the mother does ill . . . (43/7/35)

At first sight, this may look like a case of English obsolescent and hyperformal 'to do ill', and indeed the immediate context is so confused, interrupted and based on knowledge privy to the participants that one cannot rule this reading out altogether. However, it is possible that *ill* is here substituted for the commoner Guyanese *sick*. *Doz* can of course occur with adjectives –

4.6 *son doz hat he bad* 'The sun gets very hot here.' (160/15/198)
4.7 People does jealous him. (99/4/117)

– given, of course, that we interpret *hot* and *jealous* as adjectives and not merely the Guyanese forms of the verbs 'to heat' and 'to envy'.[3] If the latter analysis is correct, then 'is frequently sick' is the meaning of *doz ill* here.

At this level, however, all speakers have variable copula insertion, and this affects all environments including pre-adjectival ones: *John sick* alternates with *John is sick*. But what happens when the speaker wishes to say 'John is frequently/usually sick' and lacks the necessary adverbs of frequency? He must use *doz*, just as in other contexts, but if (unlike the speakers of 4.6 and 4.7) he simultaneously inserts the copula, the resultant form is not *doz iz*, but *doz be*. Since *be* is not acquired until the later mesolect, the heaviest *doz*-users do not produce it, and indeed there is evidence that speakers who have just acquired it do not regard it in any sense as a non-standard form, but rather as an item more formal than their vernacu-

---

[2] For more specific discussion of this point, see Bickerton 1974.
[3] The latter would undoubtedly be the case if we were dealing with the basilect. However, at some stage in the development of the system, 'adjectival' stative verbs must be reinterpreted as 'true' adjectives. Though it is difficult to determine the precise stage at which this development takes place, one can only assume that it must precede acquisition of *iz* before adjectival predicates, since (even hypercorrectively) there are no cases of *iz*-insertion before other types of stative, e.g. **iz want*, **iz no* etc. On the other hand, it can be argued that, since 'to heat' and 'to envy' are not contained in the lexicon at this level, these two particular cases are true verbs, regardless of the status of adjectives generally. Many items shift word-classes in Guyana, e.g. *wachman* 'to keep watch on', *kobweb* 'to clean thoroughly' etc.

lar; for instance, in conversation with my wife, 160 immediately and spontaneously rephrased 4.6 as

4.8 The sun does be hot some days you know. (160/15/198)

Doz be occurs only half-a-dozen times in our recordings, but it is far from
being as rare as this might indicate; the recordings are biassed rather heavily
in favour of the previously unstudied rural areas and outlying townships,
and *doz be* users are commonest in the capital. A number of occurrences are
noted by Allsopp (1962, II:117), who attributes them to Irish influence. Of
our six recorded occurrences, three are with predicate adjectives, two with
locative expressions, and one is in 'exposed position' with a pre-posed
WH-nominal:

4.9 . . . for what he say he account does be. (99/4–5/117)

There are no occurrences of *doz be* + *-ing* either in our recordings or Allsopp's, but Allsopp has at least two cases in his field notes (1962, I:241).

The importance of *doz be* is that it constitutes a possible source for Black
English 'consuetudinal' *be* (cf. Labov et al. 1968, Fasold 1970 and 1972, as
well as numerous other writers on Black English). This suggestion, first
made by Rickford (MS.), is an extremely plausible one, for a variety of
reasons. The only other possible source would appear to be Irish English,
but none of the innumerable writers who have invoked Irish English to account for Caribbean or Black English expressions has ever established the
necessary chain of reasoning: (a) that there were sufficient speakers of Irish
origin in any particular region to have plausibly influenced Black speakers,
(b) that those speakers of Irish English actually used characteristically Irish
constructions, i.e. remained immune to those processes of levelling which
affected all speakers of regional varieties of English in the New World, and
(c) that there was sufficient contact between such speakers and Black
speakers for forms to have been transmitted. In addition, the development
can be explained in terms of regular decreolisation processes, without invoking any external influence. Let us merely suppose (for which there is abun-
dant evidence) that the progenitor of Black English was a creole substantially
similar to basilectal Guyanese Creole, that it acquired *doz* in the same way
that Guyanese Creole did, and that it underwent similar, if not identical,
decreolisation processes. In the course of the latter it would, like Guyanese
Creole, lose *doz*, and for this stage we have some direct evidence in that
Gullah still has *doz* while most if not all mainland varieties do not have it.
Now in Guyana, *doz*-loss seems to be accompanied by loss of *be* in finite

non-passives. This is hardly surprising, since *doz be* does not become established until shortly before *doz*-loss. However, one of the things that distinguish Black English from Guyanese Creole and other creoles is the comparative slowness of the processes involved (after a much more rapid start),
which in turn stems from obvious social causes: the continuing social depri-
vation and caste-like status of Black people in North America as opposed to
their much higher mobility in Caribbean society.[4] This slowness means that
each phase of decreolisation is longer drawn out, giving time for *doz be* to
become much more firmly implanted in the vernacular than it is in
Guyana. Thus, at the stage of *doz*-loss, there would have been correspondingly less chance of *be* following *doz* into oblivion.

Alongside rate of change we must consider motivation. The Guyanese
non-user of *doz* must be aware, from an early age, of the existence of a large
class of *doz*-users; therefore the fact that he is different from them represents a conscious and deliberate choice. The speaker who rejects *doz* because of its non-standard nature is hardly likely to retain non-standard *be*.
The U.S. non-user of *doz*, however, probably does not even know that *doz*
exists. We do not now know what motivated Black English *doz*-loss, but to
judge from the current condition of most speakers, it can hardly have been
that actual or imminent elevation to the middle class which most frequently
prompts *doz*-loss in Guyana. Retention of *be* after *doz*-loss would therefore not have exposed him to the ridicule of his peers.

If this analysis is correct, we would expect residual *be* to preserve the
meaning of *doz be*, and *doz be*, like all other *doz* + V forms, carries the
sense of either a frequently recurring action or state, or of an action or state
which, though possibly rare, has the same characteristics whenever it *does*
recur. Such a definition is virtually identical to that of 'distributive *be*' as
given in Fasold 1972 or in Wolfram 1969:188 ('an activity or state which
takes place at various non-continuous intervals'). But this topic, although a
fascinating one, really lies beyond the scope of the present work.[5]

---

[4] I do not wish to suggest that anything like full equality of opportunity exists in Guyana
or in other areas of the Caribbean. On the contrary, there are large masses of poor dark-
skinned people existing at a level that would shock the most deprived inhabitants of
U.S. ghettoes. But it is still true that the bright child of poor parents in the Caribbean
has more and better chances of going further than his U.S. equivalent, and is therefore
more strongly motivated in the direction of linguistic change. Moreover, since those
who rule him are of his own colour and yet speak standard English, there is no 'negative
motivation' that he will be replacing his own speech with the language of 'The Man'.

[5] I shall, however, continue to refer, albeit briefly, to Black English/Guyanese resemblances where these occur. A much fuller study is obviously required to do justice to
this subject. At least the correspondences shown in this chapter should be strong enough
to indicate the desirability of such a study.

did

Since *did* is of less frequent occurrence than *doz*, the stages of its disappearance are less easy to chronicle. However, there is evidence that the further one moves from the mid-mesolect, the more likely it is that a *did*-occurrence will represent, not a [+ anterior], but a simple English-type [+ past] referent.

Of the speakers discussed so far, 209 is one of the most decreolised; the solitary examples he and 242 give of *did* are both quite clearly [− anterior]:

> 4.10 He break all two [sc. both] at the same time and then he did set it up. (209/28/265)
>
> 4.11 Somebody else's house he did going to repair, and maybe the person is some benefit to him, but nothing to me, therefore I did not go. (243/6–7/326)

In a speaker still closer to the acrolect, it is even questionable whether creole *did* or 'counternegative' English *did* is represented:

> 4.12 Transportation was a problem and when we did get it, well, you're packed in each car. (226/29–30/287)

This example is even odder in that, while Guyanese *did* is unstressed with stressed verb, and while English *did* is stressed with unstressed or lightly stressed verb, both *did* and *get* here receive equal (and heavy) stress; it seems some odd halfway-house between the two.

However, the clearest evidence is provided by 43, who, although upper-mesolectal on some counts, is an extremely heavy *did*-user. Of her thirteen tokens, five (including the one already quoted as Example 3.26) are fairly clearly [+ anterior] as well as [+ past], three are doubtful because of obscure reference or interruption, and five are pretty unambiguously [+ past] but [− anterior]:

> 4.13 43: This time we had a colonial secretary name Waddington –
> 44: Yes, I know Waddington.
> 43: Afterwards he did ask Burton . . . (43, 44/29–30/37)
>
> 4.14 He used to give the grandmother, the mother, everybody. When the child *did born* – the child *did born* a serious little child but somebody else child. (43/26–7/51)

It would seem, therefore, that prior to its disappearance *did* ceases to be a specifically [+ anterior] marker and is reduced to simply another alternative for expressing [+ past]. The precise mechanism would probably be as follows. First, forms tied specifically to [− anterior, + past] – i.e. *neva*, *had*, *waz* – are introduced into the lexicon; second, *didn* (as opposed to *did*) spreads from [+anterior] to [−anterior, +past] environments; third, the first *-ed* forms appear, and, as these spread to finite verbs, the grammar is restructured to replace [±anterior] by [±past]; fourth, *did* is reinterpreted to conform with this underlying shift (i.e. as a pure [+past] marker); fifth, *did*, now the disfavoured competitor of other forms of past marking, is abandoned.

don

Our recordings contain no evidence concerning the disappearance of this form. Its meaning seems to be constant across the continuum until, shortly after the mid-mesolect, it vanishes altogether. It may be that its absence merely reflects less frequent use. Certainly one would suspect the veracity of any Guyanese informant who claimed he hadn't heard it or didn't know what it meant. On the other hand, *don* would be hard put to it to exist in a grammar that contained an established perfective aspect with *have*; the two forms, though by no means synonymous, would be in competition for the same semantic niche. If we now examine *have*, we will see that *have + -en* begins to establish itself at around the time of *don*-disappearance.

have

In the basilect, possession is expressed verbally by *gat*, and obligation by *ga(t) fi/fu*, which subsequently alternates with *ga(t) tu* (see Bickerton 1971a: 479–80 for the somewhat eccentric behaviour of this construction). Since, as we have seen, the basilect has no true equivalent of perfective aspect, the third major context for *have*-occurrence is also missing, and in consequence fully basilectal speakers such as 137, 9/188 or 28/178 never use it at all.

For many speakers, it would appear that *had* is acquired before *have*. As this is at first sight a rather unusual development, and as there is some counter-evidence, we had better examine the data rather carefully.

Of Guyanese upper-mesolectal speakers, the majority use both *have* and *had*. However, in the lower and mid-mesolect there are a number who are recorded as using only one form or the other. Ten, producing a total of thirty-five *had*-occurrences, use *had* only; nine, producing a total of forty-six *have*-occurrences, use only *have*. This evidence looks inconclusive until we examine it in more detail. We then find that, of the nine *have*-only speakers, five come from the same area – the Port Mourant–Albion district of the Corentyne – and were recorded by the same student interviewer who recorded another grammatical anomaly, *bina* + 'adjectival verb'. Again there exists the possibility that something in the interviewer's approach may have affected the data. However, it is worth noting that the three large villages of Port Mourant, Albion and Rose Hall (the latter of which contains a substantial Black population) have virtually merged and would, if incorporated, constitute a township of some 40,000 people, easily the second largest in the country; here, a form of urbanisation rather different from that of Georgetown may be producing somewhat different linguistic results. Of the remaining four speakers, one (227) is clearly upper-mesolectal (he is a foreman in charge of rail transport in a bauxite mine), and the subject of our conversation, his daily work routine, contained no opportunities for past forms.

In contrast, the *had*-only speakers are drawn from a wide range of areas (two from Essequibo, two from West Demerara, one from Georgetown, one from Bushlot and four from different parts of the Corentyne), and in only two cases (101, 216) was their speech limited to past narrative; at least four, on the other hand (99, 100, 160, 197) spoke extensively of present states and events.

However, if we distinguish between modal *have* (*to*) and main-verb *have*, there emerges the curious and interesting pattern of Table 4.2. It should be

TABLE 4.2 Distribution of modal and main-verb *have* for early acquirers

	had-only users	*have*-only users
Modal only	171	121, 183, 221, 222, 224
Modal/MV	100, 197, 216	225, 227
MV only	99, 101, 160, 172, 174, 177	164, 223

clear from this table that we have to do with two quite distinct processes. As shown in Table 4.3, the majority pattern is to acquire main-verb *have* first and modal *have* later. However, a minority reverses this order. It would appear that those who acquire the modal first acquire it in its non-past form, while those who acquire the main verb first acquire it in its past form.

Against this position, it could be argued that the distribution of *have* and *had* is merely a performance feature; that all speakers acquire *have* and *had*, modal and main verb simultaneously, but that by some accident of discourse which is no concern of the linguist, some happened to use one set of forms, some another, on the occasions on which they were recorded. However, there is a good deal of evidence that such arguments will not hold.

In order to understand *have/had*, we must understand its relationship with *gat*. The data we have suggest that *had* is acquired as the past of *gat*, i.e. is a replacement for basilectal *bin gat*. Six out of the ten *had*-only users have cases of present-tense *gat* as opposed to only three of the nine *have*-only speakers, and they produced more than twice as many tokens (27:11). The tense distinction is a perfectly unambiguous one:

> 4.15 We had the Snake in the Grass, we had Fedi Bandula boys, we had Farm Cutter boys – in them days a poor policeman dead in he boots, as soon as they say, 'Your beat is Albuoystown,' he say, 'Sergeant, I left the work!' (100/15–17/117).
>
> 4.16 Today we got pave [sc. pavements] and we got tar road – but come and see the condition of where we living. (100/28/117)
>
> 4.17 That is long years back, you know? I had a field here – pine [sc. pineapple] field – had corn, pumpkin and so at this very spot here. (160/1–2/197)
>
> 4.18 When they fishing we does buy, you know – when we got money we buy. (160/20–1/198)

None of the *had*-only speakers uses *had* in any non-past context. None uses *gat* in any past context, unless that context is also [− anterior]. Here, however, *gat* may be used:

> 4.19 But this place, mussy 'bout twelve, twelve to thirteen years since I got this place. (160/27–8/199) [6]

This would indicate that *had*, at the time it is acquired, is a [+ anterior] rather than [+ past] marker, and that it is only subsequent to acquisition that it becomes associated with the [± past] opposition. However, we have little direct evidence on this point.

Among *have*-only speakers, there is a curious scarcity of possessive verbs, whether *gat* or *have*. While *had*-only speakers produce fifty-eight possessive verbs in just over 7,000 words of text, *have*-only speakers produce only forty in about 12,500 – if we remove 223, an almost obsessive possessive-*have* user, they produce only twenty-four in 11,000 words. This almost looks like deliberate avoidance of a verb, *gat*, which is socially stigmatised (Bickerton 1971a:480) – rather than choose between two forms, one despised, one

---

[6] Advocates of the Thompson–Whinnom 'monogenetic' theory of creole origins (Thompson 1961, Whinnom 1965) which would derive all Caribbean and most other creoles and pidgins from the Mediterranean lingua franca might be interested to note that Romance languages treat sentences of this kind with a tense sequence identical to that shown here, e.g. Sp. *hace doce anos que yo obtengo esta finca* (literally 'it makes ten years that I obtain this farm', i.e. 'I have had this farm for ten years') – a virtually word-for-word, tense-for-tense translation of 160's sentence. It could, of course, be sheer coincidence.

marginal to them, they structure their sentences so as to eliminate possessive verbs altogether.[7] *Have to*, however – which alternates with *gat to* in the speech of most of them – is apparently influenced by the loss of the stative–non-stative distinction dealt with in Chapter 3, which results in all [– punctual] verbs appearing in stem-only form irrespective of time-reference:

> 4.20 Well the doctor admit me, he say I have to admitted to the hospital. (121/29–30/154)
> 4.21 Water used to flood around the houses and [we?] used to tie stop-off [sc. fasten the sluice-gates of the drainage–irrigation system] and bale the water out, and at times we have to go to the factory. (224/7–9/283)
> 4.22 The man who cut the cane now have to load the cane. (221/11/275)

For *have*-only speakers who also use main-verbal *have*, past–non-past neutralisation applies, as one would expect, to that form also:

> 4.23 Well today you have combine and tractor and thing like that working ricefield. But long ago you have people with them hoe and cutlass and shovel and whats-not going to the ricefield from early morning, and you have cow was mashing [sc. threshing] rice – today you have combines cutting rice. (223/8–11/278)
> 4.24 The long [sc. *longtime*, i.e. 'olden'] days you have an equal and a living worth living – but today . . . (225/1/286)

In these cases, however, one must note a possible alternative explanation. Speaker 223's *you have cow was mashing rice* is a morph-for-morph translation of basilectal *dem gat kau bina mash rais* 'There were oxen threshing the rice.' Compare

> 4.25 *i ga wan granson bina main* (118/7/149) 'She had one grandchild she was looking after.' [8]
> 4.26 *?i bin ga wan granson bina main.*
> 4.27 *i bin ga wan granson a main.*
> 4.28 *wan a dem a di man bin gat di bam* (98/21/119) 'One of them was the man who had the bomb.'

---

[7] The quantitative description of stylistic choice is something currently regarded as lying outside the domain of linguistics proper; conversely, those linguists who do practice it do not see it as feeding into linguistic theory in any significant way. However, once one accepts that speakers within the same system don't all have the same output rules, it becomes relevant to ask whether what seem, on the face of things, purely performance features might not yield interesting clues as to how one such set of rules may differ from another.

[8] Literally, '. . . one grandchild who was being looked after [by her]'. Passivisation, embedding within a higher NP and equi-NP deletion must all be involved in the derivation of this sentence, which is a highly complex one by creole standards.

4.29 *wan a dem bina di man bin ga di bam.
4.30 ** *wan a dem bina di man ga di bam.

There is apparently a basilectal rule which deletes tense-marking in higher (possessive or existential) sentences.[9] It may be that in sentences such as 4.24 and 4.25, past–non-past neutralisation of *have* should be attributed to retention of this rule rather than to the general unmarking of anterior statives. But whatever the cause, all *have*-only users (except 164 and 227, for whom, on overall performance, *had*-absence can be assumed to result from absence of appropriate environments) use both modal and main-verbal *have* without tense-distinction.

But whether *have* or *had* is first acquired, there can be little doubt that the majority of speakers acquire the main verb form first, and the modal form subsequently. Of the forty-two speakers summarised in Table 4.3, nine have main verb and no other form and twelve have main verb and modal and no other form as opposed to only six who have modal and no main verb and four who have main verb and perfect but no modal, while of the remaining eleven speakers there is only one who (possibly accidentally) has no main verb form, i.e. at most only seven out of the forty-two can have acquired modal before main verb rather than vice versa (or perhaps, in some cases, simultaneously).

From the viewpoint of the present study, however, our main interest must rest with acquisition of a perfective aspect marker, for which the acquisition of verbal/modal *have*, though interesting in itself, is only a necessary but not

---

[9] I am assuming that, at the basilectal level, the underlying structure of sentences of this type is something like:

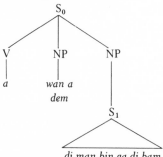

Relativisation seems to play no part in the derivation of such sentences (cf. Peet 1972 for some comparable sentences in Hawaiian Pidgin), nor is there a second occurrence of *di man* to be removed by Equi. Indeed, the whole relationship between embedding processes in pidgin–creole languages and those in 'standard' languages could do with much closer inquiry; cf. the discussion of Example 3.38 in Chapter 3.

TABLE 4.3 Stages of *have/had* acquisition

Speaker	has	Perf.	have to	MV have
99, 108, 160, 164, 172, 174, 177, 223, 229	–	–	–	63
121, 171, 183, 221, 222, 224	–	–	13	–
41, 100, 103, 162, 169, 186, 197, 209, 214, 216, 225, 236	–	–	26	96
101, 157, 226, 228	–	8	–	29
105, 122, 124, 125, 192, 196, 226	–	21	22	51
107, 111, 117, 242	7	7	8	51

NOTE: Figures for Perf., *have to* and MV *have* all include *had*. All figures show totals of recorded occurrences for each sub-group.

sufficient condition. Table 4.3 shows us that there are thirty-six perfect *have* forms, plus three perfectives with *has*, out of a total of 402 *have/had/has* tokens produced by the forty-two speakers. That only fourteen of these speakers produce perfectives indicates that non-perfective *have* must have to be established pretty firmly in the grammar before perfectives can be acquired.

When we examine these thirty-eight perfectives, we discover facts which would be quite inexplicable if the upper mesolect had no antecedent basilect to relate it to. First of all, five out of the six perfectives with *had* are quite unambiguously [+ anterior], and three out of these five are also [– realis]. Of the two [+ realis, + anterior] cases, one has already been noted –

4.31 . . . she go back to see what had happen to this seed. (101/30/119)

– while the other, though more complex, is conceptually identical:

4.32 So when they started to work they had already had been provided with means so that they can run they business. (122/20–1/163)

(Note the repetition of *had* indicating that the form is only marginal.) The other three examples of *had + -en* can best be understood if we reverse the procedure of Chapter 2 and translate 'back' into the basilect rather than 'forward' into standard English:

4.33 'And if it had land there it would have killed a lot of children' *if i bin lan de i bin go kil nofnof pikni*. (105/9/126)

4.34 'Had I gone trying to go ashore I would not a catch shore' *if mi bin trai fi miit sho mi na bin go kech am.* (242/27/318)

4.35 'Had he known he would have never tell me that' *if i bin no i na bin go tel mi so.* (242/28–9/325)

At first glance, the *had* X *Ven* looks like a highly formal, indeed literary and stilted, expression, and in all probability such usage forms the model for these sentences.[10] However, the question one should ask is, how is it possible for a speaker such as 242, who lacks an established perfective, number concord, question inversion and many other rules and features of even nonstandard English, to borrow, let alone use correctly, a rare form eschewed by many metropolitan speakers? The answer is that, if we are correct in assuming that *had* is originally a [+anterior] marker, a substitute for *bin* slightly more sophisticated than *did*, then the *had* X *Ven* construction merely adds subject–verb inversion to a morph-for-morph translation of the basilect.

Such a suggestion might seem to contradict what we have said about replacement of [±anterior] by [±past]. However, we indicated at the end of Chapter 3 that this replacement affected the [−anterior] part of the paradigm before the [+anterior] part; since, as we have observed in Chapter 2, [−realis, +anterior] represents a fairly rare feature combination, basilectal elements in this area would be likely to persist much later than elsewhere, and in particular where, as here, there is little conflict between the polar grammars at a non-superficial level.

Where the so-called 'present perfect' is involved, however, the polar grammars are quite distinct. In consequence, we should not be surprised to find that of twelve speakers who use *have* + *en* forms, only five use correctly the ordinary present perfect form. One, 117, knows the form but is not sure how to use it:

4.36 Well I work all this time doing this pulling at this boat until I have become a bowman [sc. man who stands in the bows to ward off obstacles – NB he was not a bowman at time of speaking]. (117/14/145)

Six others use only what look superficially like much more complex forms: *would have killed* (4.33), *would have never tell* (4.35), *would have put, might have been, could not have worked* etc. But again, successful use of these forms depends on their relationship with basilectal antecedents. At a

---

[10] The flowery rhetoric of a certain type of diamond prospector is legendary in Guyana; numerous examples are given in Abrams 1970.

very early stage, basilectal [− realis, + anterior] *bin go,* itself a replacement of earlier *bin sa,* gives way to single markers: *wuda, kuda, konta* ('couldn't have'), etc:

4.37 *yu get big peepa, man, yu kuda get jab* (197/7/159) 'You've got good qualifications, man, you could have found work.'

4.38 *dem konta jain an mek di rood yet* (137/8/184) 'They couldn't have got together to make the road yet.'

As we have seen, 197 is a *had*-only user, while 137 has no *have* in any shape or form. Clearly *kuda* etc. are acquired not as sandhi versions of *could have* etc., but as frozen forms, analysed by the speaker as monomorphemic. However, once *have* has become established in the grammars of such speakers, they are free to re-analyse the items as bimorphemic, and as sandhi of the standard-English modal + perfective series. They thus present far less difficulty to the Guyanese speaker than the present perfect, for which there is no true antecedent.

Of the five speakers who correctly use present perfect forms, one is a half-Portuguese in the timber trade in Bartica, one is an Indian shopowner who goes round without shoes but saved up enough to fly to India, one is the African owner of a small house-painting business, and one is an African policeman of virulent pomposity. The only one with neither money nor pretensions is a self-styled 'old African midwife', a charming old lady who, after admitting that she had no paper qualifications for her trade, explained that

4.39 Long years gone by they didn't have no certify midwife − all is the old-time African midwife. But they had the experience. They have done it and I can do it. (192/16–18/250)

Two contextual facts are relevant here; her need to justify herself to the interviewer and the fact that she 'grew in town with Mr Nightingale − the Commissioner Mr Nightingale' whose servant she was. Moreover, this is a solitary occurrence. Even 122, the heaviest passive user, seems hardly at home with the form: of his eight present perfects, six occur with the same verb − *I have seen* − which he uses as a set formula to introduce his experiences in India (note the persistence of subjectless impersonals, copula deletion and non-standard definite-article assignment in his speech):

4.40 In the northern India is the worst, in Behar state − is bad in the northern India. That is what I have seen and observe, and − ahm − you see the people in India is only two classes of people I observe there in India, the upper and the lower class, but in our country here all classes of people, middle class, lower class, third class, upper class and all you see. And the system that we living in this country, British Guiana,[11] is paradise what I have seen. (122/1–6/162)

The full distribution of perfect forms by type for all perfect users is given in Table 4.4.

Number-concord is the last feature of *have* to be acquired. Even the handful of speakers who produce *has* do not maintain concordial rules. Sometimes *has* looks like a hypercorrection:

4.41 When you has two paddles you able to brace it back [sc. hold the boat against the current]. (117/8/146)

Sometimes, *have* and *has* alternate for third-person-singular in the same sentence:

TABLE 4.4   Distribution of perfectives

Speaker	−Realis, +anterior	+Realis, +anterior	Present perfect	Total
101		1		1
105	3		1[a]	4
111	2		3	5
117			1[b]	1
122		1	8	9
124			1	1
125	1			1
157			4	4
192			1	1
196	3			3
220		1[c]		1
226	2			2
228	1			1
242	4			4
Total	16	3	19	38

NOTES: [a] 105's solitary present perfect is a quotation, and not necessarily evidence that she has free use of the form; [b] 117's use of the form is incorrect, as noted above; [c] 220's *had* form cannot unambiguously be assigned.

[− realis, + anterior] markers include *would have, could have, might have, could not have,* and *had;* [+ realis, + anterior] marker, *had* only; Present perfect markers, *have* or *has.*

[11] Older speakers for whom it is a matter of habit still from time to time refer to Guyana by its former name, despite overt correction from their younger and more nationalistic compatriots.

4.42 He have a house to repair in West Coast and, ahm, when he gone I
   says, 'Well, this old fellow he has a house to repair in West Coast – that
   is not my house.' (242/4–5/326)

Acquisition of *has* is, of course, linked with acquisition of general third-person -*s*, which we will shortly discuss; for the moment, one may simply note that the acquisition of concordial forms characteristically has two stages, (a) acquisition of the form itself, with no concord rule, and (b) acquisition of a concord rule.

Before leaving *have*, it is worth pointing out that (if we exclude the *kuda*, *wuda* forms referred to above) none of the characteristic English sandhi forms ('*ve*, '*d*, *hadn't*, *haven't* etc.) occur in Guyanese speech except among the most educated, and even here, usually only when the speaker has had a period of residence in North America or England. This is all the more remarkable when we consider the extent of the similarities between Guyanese mid-to-upper-mesolectal Creole and Black English, and the fact that phonological reduction and deletion rules have been invoked to account for so many of the characteristics of the latter (Labov et al. 1968, Labov 1969, Wolfram 1969, Fasold 1972 etc.). The natural reaction of the creolist is to assume that phonological explanations have been used much too freely. But though this may be true in some particular cases, one could also argue the

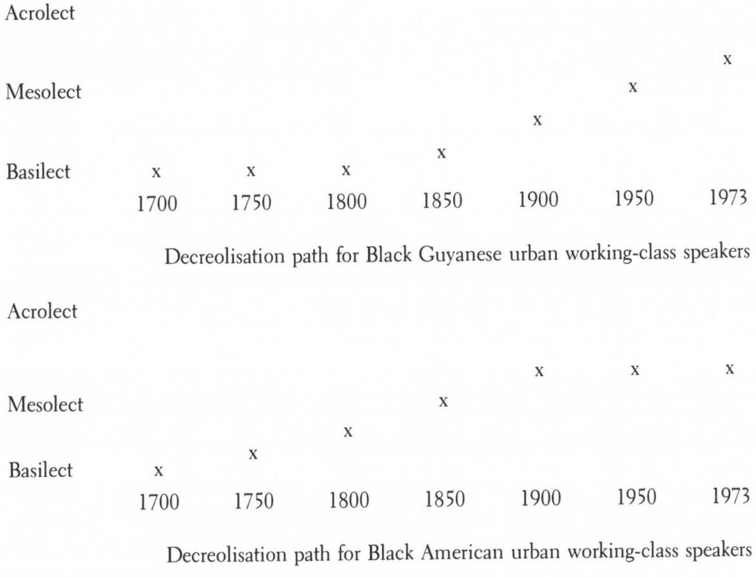

Acrolect

							x
Mesolect						x	
					x		
				x			
Basilect	x	x	x				
	1700	1750	1800	1850	1900	1950	1973

Decreolisation path for Black Guyanese urban working-class speakers

Acrolect

					x	x	x
Mesolect				x			
				x			
Basilect	x	x					
	1700	1750	1800	1850	1900	1950	1973

Decreolisation path for Black American urban working-class speakers

Fig. 4.1. Comparative decreolisation (Guyana/U.S.)

following: that the decreolisation of Black English reached a mid-to-upper-mesolectal stage much earlier than did that of Guyanese Creole (owing to the far higher percentage of white models available), that it then stagnated at that level because of the social and political stagnation the Black community underwent after the Civil War, and that this long period of stagnation, unknown in Guyana, maintained the late-mesolectal grammar largely unchanged in general outlines but gave time for complex morphophonemic reduction rules to be acquired. The decreolisation paths for the two communities would then be approximately as shown in Fig. 4.1.

will

This form begins to appear sporadically in the early mesolect, or rather in pre-mesolectal speakers who have had slight contacts with higher lects, and who are forced 'upwards' by nature of topic or by self-consciousness. Speaker 186, for example, produces her solitary *will* in over 3,000 words (and alongside eighteen occurrences of *go*) while talking about a Catholic priest she deeply admires:

> 4.43 That man will walk house house and give people. (186/4–5/242)

(That this is no accident of distribution is shown by the fact that her only two strong-verb pasts and seven of her twelve *iz*-tokens occur within the same 250-word section.) In the case of 177, linguistic insecurity in the author's presence occasioned a solitary (and inappropriate) *will*:

> 4.44 So they keeping watch a them place that, they, ah, ahm, the Negro people them will come and, ahm, burn down their property. (177/12–13/227)

Other 'premature *will*' users in fact employ a negative form, *won(t)*, which no more implies the existence of *will* than *doon(t)* implies that of *do*:

> 4.45 When he sober he want lick you down – he won' talk to you. (99/12/116)

One, and apparently only one, mid-mesolectal speaker has a rule which permits *will* to co-occur with *-ing* forms:

> 4.46 They have some old fellows will coming round and say, 'Mother-in-law, you can't live alone so I gon' take you and married you.' (236/9–10/300)
> 4.47 Over there I mean they will having people them to hire servants [sc. there are people who will hire servants]. (236/18/304)

In fact, for all speakers until the upper-mesolectal levels, *will* is a marginal and precarious feature, if indeed they have it at all.

Subsequently, however, it becomes established as either a formal or an emphatic variant of *gon*. Speaker 227, for instance, uses *will* in formally describing his work-schedule but *gon* in quotation and in casual conversation with his interviewer:

4.48 He wait for one of those lights. If is the green then the green will bring him in. (227/16/291)

4.49 One of these cars derail, we can say, 'Look, boy, we gon' give you fifteen minute, try and eat fast and let we push.' (227/30–1/295)

4.50 You gon' come up later? . . . So I gon' check back by three o'clock. (227/6–8/298)

Speaker 43, on the other hand, uses *will* five times (as against *gon* twenty times) either to underline the seriousness of a situation:

4.51 43: I say, 'And, H——, you must cool you temper. Everybody know woman strength is they mouth. And if you gon' get in always in that passion, one of these days –'
41: He gon' murder her.
43. 'You will kill her!' (41, 43/13–15/45)

or to express hypothetical as opposed to probable conditions:

4.52 43: Well she think it best to write home to say them – [41: Yes] – to T——thinking that – [41:He is there.] – she'll write and she'll feel that he will get it. (43/17–18/34)

4.53 You talk nicely to me, and when I will talk nicely to – [interrupted]. (43/1/41)

Speaker 43's use of *will*, which in 4.52 includes even morphophonemic reduction, differs from acrolectal usage only in the case of insertion in hypotheticals introduced by *when* or *if*. Speakers of lects 'higher' than 43's avoid even this feature:

4.54 If you remember you will see, if you consider. (122/16–17/163)

4.55 If I happen to live your age I will have – at seventy-five I'll have no fears, at seventy-five you closer to you coffin but you braver than anybody. (241/26–8/312)

The last example is striking in that, as the content indicates, it was addressed to an acquaintance, not the interviewer, and in fact took place in the course of an animated bar-room conversation. Though control of the acrolectal future is complete, the speaker still retains many non-standard forms, e.g. zero copula before adjectives and non-standard second-person possessive adjective before consonants.[12] It would appear that the relatively unstructured nature of the irrealis aspect permits acrolectal rules to be acquired more quickly and easily here than in the heavily structured realis aspect. [− Realis, + anterior] shades almost indistinguishably into [− realis, + past, + perfect], as we saw in our discussion of *had* and *wuda* forms; [− realis, − anterior] simply divides between *will* and *gon* (which may now acquire the shape [goːɪntʌ] in careful speech) on the same fuzzy, mainly probabilistic basis that the [− realis, − past] divides between *will* and *going to* for metropolitan speakers (McIntosh 1966). Where rules can simply be added, a grammar can change quickly and fairly smoothly, but where rules must be replaced or restructured, change is correspondingly more tortuous and slow.

Number concord

Lack of subject–verb number-concord, especially between third-person singular subjects and non-past verbs, has been noted by all quantitative and many non-quantitative analysts of Black English as one of its commonest phenomena: Labov goes so far as to claim that 'there is no underlying third singular -*s* in [non-standard Negro English]' (Labov et al. 1968 I:164). However, as has again been noted by many observers, -*s* frequently appears after non-past verbs when the subject is other than third-person-singular.

Both phenomena can be observed in the Guyanese data, and here, too, both are sporadic and unevenly distributed. However, the distribution is different in several ways. Few speakers in the Guyanese system have faulty number-concord, because few have any trace of number-concord at all. Fewer still have correct number-concord. Leaving aside the four purely acrolectal speakers 92–5, there are only ten speakers who each produce more than two occurrences of third-person -*s* (see Table 4.5). Of these, only five have cases of what Fasold (1972:133) calls 'hyper-*s*': affixation of -*s* to verbs without third-person-singular subjects.

As the term suggests, the most obvious explanation of 'hyper-*s*' is that it represents hypercorrection, the attempt of a socially insecure non-standard speaker to 'improve' his speech by tacking on a morpheme which he knows is characteristic of the standard language but which he has not yet learnt to use correctly. It is certainly true that all five of the hyper-*s* users in Table

---

[12] Since Guyanese speech in general is 'r-less', rC clusters are usually avoided even at word boundaries. The same speaker has *your* before vowels. However, this still represents a late stage of decreolisation, since most lects have obligatory *you* irrespective of phonological environment.

TABLE 4.5 Distribution of verbal affix -*s*

Speaker	+3ps+*s*	+3ps−*s*	−3ps+*s*	−3ps−*s*
117	1		3	3
240	3		4	
103	2	2	1	8
242	5	5	7	18
227	12	53	2	79
241	11	8		25
107	7	8		30
43	5	25		26
44	5	7		11
226	3			8
Total	54	108	17	208

4.5 were recorded by myself, and that some of them gave other signs, both linguistic and behavioural, that they had a dependency relationship on European culture, of which I was perceived as the representative. Speaker 103 was a church-warden and closely attached to his (English) High Anglican vicar; 240, a watchman by profession, was a ferocious autodidact and a poet in the vein of the notorious Scot McGonagal,[13] who was shocked and upset when asked if he knew any 'old-time story', and who subsequently had to be publicly reproved by the rest of the company (all Guyanese) when he tried to cadge cigarettes from me, the European, rather than from them ('I am a sport, why cou'nt you ask me, man? I am a Guyanese like you, why cou'nt you ask me?' [241/2–3/315]). In the face of such clear extra-linguistic evidence, it must seem unnecessary to examine hyper-*s* further, and yet there are a couple of odd facts about it which seem worth mentioning.

By no means all hyper-*s* (and, for that matter, not all 'correct'-*s*) is affixed to non-past verbs. Of the eleven users shown in Table 4.1, five affix -*s* to verbs of past reference only, while others behave variably:

4.56 Oh, my dear friend, those days was really terrible, greedin' – working greed in the interior. All they looks at, selfishness. (242/26–28/325)

4.57 My mother was poor – lives in trash house. (117/22/144)

4.58 No steamer takes you from this [sc. there] straight over to town – there were no trains in those days. (196/23–4/257)

4.59 We have two steamer, one goes in the morning and one come in the afternoon – one was 'Sproston Wood' and one was 'Lady London'. (236/9–11/303)

[13] A Victorian writer of excruciatingly bad verse, who enjoyed something of a vogue in post-war England. At its height, 240's muse produced the following memorable couplet: 'Bewitched, bewildered, like a frog in a pitcher/ I think of life, I think of death, I think of nature.'

If these are dismissed as the hypercorrections of mid-mesolectal speakers, we still have to explain, first, why, for instance, *-ed never* occurs with non-past reference (though it may occur hypercorrectively on non-finites with past reference), and second, why *-s* occurs in past contexts in situations where hypercorrection is intrinsically unlikely, such as a 'danger of death' story by a man whose boat-engine stalled just as he was about to pull out of a dangerous rapid:

> 4.6 226: Just on the brink of going over she stop. For about half a minute.
> Int: How did you feel?
> 226: I can't – I can't describe the feeling.
> Int.: I can realise it.
> 226: You glance behind and is sure death dey behind there – sure death if you – as the boat turns in the falls. Eventually we went over . . .
> (226/5–9/289)

All of these cases bar the last, plus virtually all other cases of past *-s* in the data, affect verbs which have clear [– punctual] reference. If, therefore, we take them in conjunction with past–non-past neutralisation of *have*, loss of marking of past statives, and the appearance of both *en* and *doon* in past, non-punctual contexts, we have yet further evidence for the hypothesis that stative is lost as a distinct category and that [α past, – punctual] becomes, for some speakers, a category in opposition to [+ punctual, + past]. It could even be argued that, as this development occurs around the time of *doz*-loss, and as *doz* reduces to *-s* or *-z* in rapid speech, this *s/z* marker of [– punctual] remains in category but is simply transferred from pre- to post-verbal position, i.e. represents a hypercorrected version of *doz*.

Whether or not the latter suggestion is correct, a [– punctual] category would account for some otherwise puzzling facts about Black English. While only six of Fasold's forty-seven Washington speakers had hyper-*s*, and while these used the form on only 13.4% of possible occasions (1972:133), Labov found that 'some individuals [use hyper-*s*] a great deal . . . one speaker from South Carolina . . . used an extraordinary amount . . . it was almost the norm with her' (Labov et al. 1968 1:165). Yet Fasold drew his data from interviews which 'were conducted in a variety of circumstances, all of them rather formal' (1972:27), while most of Labov's data came from sessions of spontaneous peer-group interaction. If hyper-*s* resulted *only* from hypercorrection, one would expect Fasold's data to show more hyper-*s* than Labov's. There is also the testimony of many more anecdotal and literary descriptions of Black speech. It is easy enough to dismiss these (as Labov does) as literary creations which have made variables invariant; that this tendency does undoubtedly exist in fictional versions of dialect does not of itself prove that such versions are invariably inaccurate, nor can it disprove the possibility that they may have faithfully recorded forms which were once frequent but are nowadays on the decline. If there were really *two* hyper-s's – a [– punctual] one as well as a purely hyper-corrective one – and these occurred at different stages of development, the first earlier, the second later, then the situation would indeed be difficult to unravel. However, we have shown how the same phonological shape (e.g. *did, doz*) can have quite different meanings and functions at different developmental stages within the same system, and if Black English is indeed a system passing through the final stages of decreolisation, we might well expect to find similar, if less salient, phenomena.

As with Black English, there is little evidence for supposing that -*s* affixation is phonologically conditioned in any way. However, it should be pointed out that what appear to the standard-English speaker to be omissions of concordial -*s* may not always be construed in this way by the upper-mesolectal speaker. Although frequently dismissed as a 'simplified' form of English, there is at least one respect in which Guyanese Creole is richer than English, that is, in the surface forms of its determiners.

English lacks a surface non-definite, as a result of which 'a badger', 'the badger' and 'badgers' may stand equally as representatives of the species, and a sentence such as 'everyone's mad at a guy who's seducing his wife' is at the least three ways ambiguous. Guyanese Creole, however, can distinguish readily between *di dag* (a definite dog), *wan dog* (a not-as-yet identified but in reality equally definite dog, to become, in due course, *di dag*, as in English), *di dag-dem* (definite dogs) and *dag* (one or more truly non-definite dog or dogs – if non-definite really means what it says, it can have no number). The latter form never carries any marker of plurality (e.g. *dem*) or singularity (any article), and the rule of grammar that prevents such co-occurrence is strong enough to persist up to acrolectal levels (an official notice in the Georgetown Zoo informs the visitor that a certain species of bird 'frequents tall *tree*'). Naturally, speakers are slow to extend third-person-singular -*s* to verbs that have non-definite subjects:

> 4.61 Foodstuff come from roadside. (107/25/129)
> 4.62 Something mean that – (241/29/310)
> 4.63 Nobody ride across or drive across. (227/23/289)

Acquisition of -*s* in such environments probably represents the final step to the acrolect in this area.

Negation

With regard to negation, the upper-mesolectal phase essentially consists in eliminating remaining non-standard forms and shifting the reference of quasi-standard forms where acrolectal rules require this, e.g. dropping the use of *never* as an equivalent of *did not*.

In the fifteen outputs of upper-mesolectal speakers summarised in Table 4.6, there are only six occurrences of *na* and ten of *en. Na* occurs only in direct quotations; we may conclude that speakers at this level know it passively and only activate their knowledge for the mimicry of lower lects. *En* is a rather different case; it occurs only once in quotation, indicating that at this level it is still a regular variant in certain environments, albeit an informal one. However, if we compare Table 4.6 with Tables 3.8 and 3.9, we will

TABLE 4.6   Upper-mesolectal negation

Speaker	+Past	+Perf	−Past	Have	(Be)	−Realis	Imp
103			*don't* 1	*hadn't* 1 *never* 1		*wouldn't* 1	
105	*didn't* 1 *never* 3 *don't* 1		*don't* 3		*weren't* 1		
107	*didn't* 1 *never* 1		*doesn't* 4 *don't* 6	*don't* 1	*not* 2	*wouldn't* 4	
108	*didn't* 5 *never* 1		*don't* 9	*haven't* 1 *hadn't* 3 *don't* 2	*wasn't* 2 *isn't* 1	*wouldn't* 1	
114			*doesn't* 1 *don't* 1	*en* 2	*'m not* 1	*wouldn't* 2	
122	*didn't* 4 *never* 3	*never* 1	*doesn't* 1 *don't* 1	*en* 5 *haven't* 1	*not* 1 *en* 1 *is not* 1		
124			*don't* 9		*wasn't* 1 *am not* 1 *are not* 1	*wouldn't* 2	
157			*do not* 2	*hadn't* 1	*am not* 1		
169	*didn't* 1 *don't* 1		*don't* 1				*no* 1
226	*never* 1		*en* 1 *don't* 1		*'re not* 1 *wasn't* 1		
227	*didn't* 2		*don't* 5	*don't* 3		*wouldn't* 1 *won't* 1	*don't* 1

TABLE 4.6   Upper-mesolectal negation

Speaker	+ Past	+ Perf	− Past	*Have*	(Be)	− Realis	Imp
228			don't 1		weren't 1 wasn't 1 not 1 's not 1 en 1	won't 1	
240	don't 1		don't 1	haven't 1			don't 1
241		never 2	doesn't 4 don't 4	hadn't 1	en 1 'm not 3 're not 1	should never 1 shouldn't 4 wouldn't 2 will never 1	don't 1
242	didn't 1 never 1 na 2 did not 3	never 1	don't 6 doesn't 2 en 1 na 1	na 2	is not 3 am not 1 wasn't 1	wouldn't 1	don't 1
Sub-total	didn't 15 never 10 don't 3 did not 3 na 2	never 4	don't 49 doesn't 12 en 2 na 1 do not 2	en 7 na 2 have/ hadn't 9 don't 6 never 1	(be)n't 24 en 3 not 4	wouldn't 13 won't 2 shouldn't 4 never 2	na 1 don't 4
Total	33	4	66	25	31	21	5

NOTE: '*Have*' category includes possessive *got*.

see that *en* has already been eliminated from past environments, and in other environments is greatly reduced in frequency.

The continued appearance of *never* in past environments, and its rarity in perfect environments, may be a trifle misleading. It is still occasionally used as a preterit negator:

> 4.64 When I get to Bartica I was sick. I never went in hospital, I went home because I was living there. (242/21–3/318)

However, it generally occurs with a reference unmistakably equivalent to the English perfective 'not-at-all-from-then-until-now' sense:

> 4.65 He never come back to Guyana – he remain there until he die. (107/18/132)
> 4.66 He never was found until this day. (105/19/127)

From examples such as these, from the rarity of 'true' perfectives, and from the existence of 'imperfect perfectives' such as 4.67 –

> 4.67 He would have never tell me. (242/29/325)

– it would appear that the perfective *category* may be acquired before the perfective *form*; or, to be more precise, that the category forms (as we have seen other categories form) about a specific negator, *never*, as this is displaced from the past category, before *have* + *-en* has been acquired or at least before it is fully established in the speaker's grammar.

The retention of *don't* in past environments, though now rare, provides further evidence for the rule-changes affecting past statives and other non-punctuals already discussed in this and the preceding chapter:

> 4.68 The doctor we had in those days was Dr Pollard, he worked for years at the Mental Hospital. You know he could speak very loudly and he don't like people making a fuss, you know. (105/26–7/127)
> 4.69 Everybody got excited, some running in the streets, some running out and – you know, they don't know what to do then. (169/27–8/217)
> 4.70 Some don't wore a shoe before coming here. (240/6/308)

Like the mid-mesolectal cases of *en* and *doon* in past contexts (see Chapter 3), these examples are all clearly [– punctual].

Non-past reference is by now almost exclusively covered by *don't* or *doesn't*, although, as we might expect, number-concord is still erratic:

> 4.71 Those who doesn't make any money. (107/27/128)
> 4.72 Those who don't make money. (107/28/128)
> 4.73 When he doesn't make money. (107/33/128)
> 4.74 He don't eat all. (107/26/131)

En has virtually disappeared from this category, even before statives; it is found most frequently in those environments, i.e. with *have* and *be*, where, it was suggested in Chapter 3, the form first originated. In fact, the bulk of its occurrences in the *have* category occur with *got*, although it is sometimes retained even when *got* is replaced by *had*:

> 4.75 They en got no time like for this. (122/16/162)
> 4.76 You en got to put on fifty pounds of clothing on you skin to walk on the street. (122/22/162)
> 4.77 We en had nothing to do. (122/31/162)

Once main-verb *have* has been acquired, *don't have* seems to be preferred to *haven't* as its negative form.

Negation of *be* continues to be affected by the rarity of copula insertion before *-ing* forms. Of the twenty-four occurrences of negated *be*-forms (*'s not, wasn't, are not* etc.), no less than twenty-one occur before nouns, predicate adjectives or adverbials, and only three (two of which, significantly, are *wasn't*) before *-ing* forms. Of the remaining seven negations in this category (three *en*, four *not*), there is only one which fails to occur before an *-ing* form. The use of *not* in this environment is interesting, since it seems to occur when *en* is perceived as too non-standard a form but before the speaker has a rule for regular *be*-insertion before *-ing*: thus 228 has both

4.78 He en giving no particular report. (228/23/293)

and

4.79 We not travelling so fast, we are travelling around fifteen miles an hour. (228/20/292)

One might plausibly state that the sequence *be* + *not* + V*ing* will occur only under heavy emphasis:

4.80 Int.: You know Sultan?
242: Sultan, I heard of him.
Int.: You never met him?
242: No, never, I heard of him, he had a joke [sc. there was a story about him]. Eh, Sultan – *I am not telling* you nothing that I – I have knowledge of. When I say knowledge, experience. Doesn't know the man personally but I hearing jokes about him, he was just terrible – a man? – he was a beast! (242/7–12/323)

It was stated in Chapter 3 that forms such as *don't* and *didn't* were originally acquired as single unanalysable morphemes, rather than as *do/did* + *not*. However, at least two of the speakers in Table 4.6 (157, 242) give practical proof of their ability to analyse these forms into their constituents, and it may be that for other speakers too they have acquired their English underlying representations.

The final development in upper-mesolectal negation is one which, unfortunately, falls outside the scope of the present study: the acquisition of English negative-concord rules. That these have yet to be acquired even by some of the more decreolised speakers is shown by examples such as:

4.81 No, no potato never sell in British Guiana for cent a pound, never yet at no time. (122/22/160)
4.82 Nobody died nor they weren't badly injured. (105/19/126)

In discussing similar rules for Black English, Labov comments: 'But so far as the rules of negative attraction and negative concord are concerned, we are looking at the further development of traditional, well-established English rules with no reflection in Creole structures' (1972:774, note 4). Labov gives no justification for this remark, and it is hard, in view of examples such as 4.81 and 4.82, even to imagine the form that such justification could take. Speakers 105 and 122 are certainly not 'developing English rules', but merely retaining rules that originated with basilectal creole speakers. If, indeed, creole negative-concord and attraction rules are the last to be lost, and if, as Labov admits in the sentence before that cited, many Black English rules may derive from creole origins, I can see no valid reason for rejecting the possibility that, in negation just as much as in any other area, differences between White standard and Black English derive from the creole ancestry of the latter.

Strong and 'weak non-syllabic' past-tense forms

In the preceding chapter, we saw how past-tense forms were originally acquired through a combination of two factors: addition to the lexicon of past-participial adjectives, and affixation of -*ed* to verbs whose underlying forms terminated in coronal stops. We now have to examine two processes which might, on the surface, seem to be one, but which, as we shall try to show, can and must be distinguished if the true nature of past-tense acquisition is to be appreciated: first, the acquisition of 'strong' past-tense forms (*go:went, teach:taught* etc.) and 'weak non-syllabic' past-tense forms (*watch:watched, remember:remembered* etc.), and second, the distribution of these forms in conformity with English rules for past-tense insertion.

In order to do so, we shall analyse the outputs of all speakers who satisfy the following criteria: (a) speakers should produce not less than five standard past-tense forms in at least one of the two categories strong and weak – non-syllabic, and (b) speakers should produce not less than thirty occurrences of past-reference verbs (marked or unmarked) including examples of strong pasts or V – syll pasts or both. These criteria leave us with the fourteen speakers whose outputs are shown in Table 4.7 and Fig. 4.2 and who between them yield no less than 1,400 past-reference verbs.

The first three speakers in Table 4.7, unlike the remainder of the speakers in that table, and also unlike the eighteen speakers of Table 3.10, have either strong past forms without having marked V + syll forms, or (in the case of 196) strong forms with more than double the frequency of V + syll forms. All the remaining eleven speakers in Table 4.7, except for one trivial

TABLE 4.7   Acquisition of strong and V − syll past

Speaker	V + syll			Strong			V − syll		
	+	−	% +	+	−	% +	+	−	% +
236	0	1	0	8	82	9	0	45	0
209	0	4	0	8	37	18	0	13	0
196	1	11	8	15	57	21	9	43	17
108	1	7	13	6	43	12	0	20	0
43	8	6	57	24	155	14	2	50	4
117	3	2	60	10	34	23	0	41	0
125	7	1	87	13	27	32	2	15	12
242	5	6	45	49	80	38	8	48	14
169	8	0	100	9	40	18	4	17	19
122	9	2	82	33	19	63	8	15	35
107	11	0	100	18	13	58	12	15	44
105	4	0	100	41	11	79	15	17	47
226	3	1	75	13	3	81	16	14	53
241	1	0	100	22	2	92	7	3	70
Total	61	41	60%	269	603	31%	83	356	19%

NOTE: + = morphologically marked; − = morphologically unmarked; % + = percentage of morphologically marked verbs in category.

exception (226, whose marginally lower V + syll percentage probably results from sample size), have a higher percentage of marked V + syll than of marked strong past forms. Taking in conjunction the evidence of Tables 4.7 and 3.10, we can state with some confidence that for all but a small minority of speakers (three out of a possible twenty-five) V + syll pasts are acquired before strong pasts. Indeed, the proportion may be even higher than these figures indicate. Speaker 236 used only a single verb in this subclass; in the case of 196, *start* accounted for eight of the eleven zero V + syll forms, and we have seen how some speakers may treat this verb as a [− punctual] modal (Chapter 3, note 14). As for 209, it is questionable whether he can be regarded as a native speaker of Guyanese Creole, since he was born in Barbados and came to Guyana at the age of seventeen.

Similarly, in every case but one, the percentage of marked strong pasts is greater than that of marked V − syll pasts; in the case of the solitary exception, 169, the reverse difference amounts to only 1%. Moreover, there is nowhere any case of a speaker who has V − syll past marking and who lacks it in either the strong or the V + syll category. We may therefore conclude that past forms are acquired almost without exception in the following order: V + syll, strong, V − syll. The strength of this relationship is shown by the

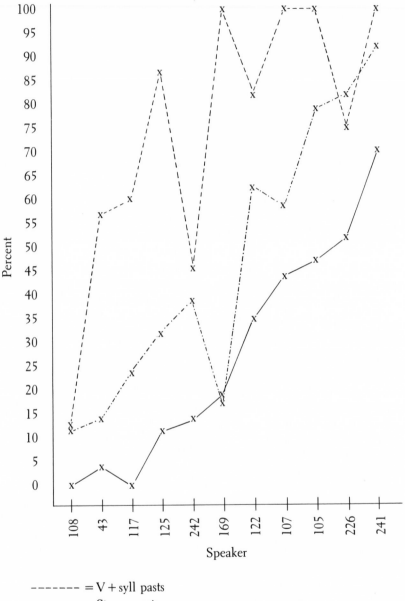

Fig. 4.2. Percentages of past forms in three environments

fact that, even in written composition, Guyanese schoolchildren regularly produce correctly more V + syll pasts than strong pasts, and more strong pasts than V − syll pasts (Bickerton 1971b).

Regularities of this type are frequently expressed in terms of variable rules (e.g. Labov 1969, Sankoff MS., Cedergren and Sankoff MS. etc.) which, whatever their precise formalism, indicate that a given rule will consistently operate with greater frequency in one environment than in another. Certainly such a rule could be formulated on the basis of the data shown here, but it is questionable whether it would convey all the information which those data yield. Though such a rule would account for the inter-environmental relationships shown by speakers as diverse as 108 and 241, for example, there is no way in which it could express the surprising evenness with which percentages ascend (as shown in Fig. 4.2) or the fact, implicit in that figure and our preceding analysis, that the variability involved is not some quasi-permanent condition, but represents simply a transition stage between a state of having no overt marking for any simple-past-reference verb and a state of having overt marking for every such verb. We should be able to say, not merely that 108, an elderly rural housewife, and 241, an up-and-coming young technician, exhibit identical proportions in their outputs, but also that 108 is only just past the beginning of this transition stage and that 241 has almost reached the end of it. It is hard to see how any variable-rule format thus far suggested could handle such facts.

Although on a gross count the acquisition of strong pasts and that of V − syll pasts seem to follow a similar pattern, we find on closer examination that two quite distinct processes are involved. Broadly speaking, phonological features play only a small part in the first process, but a very large one in the second.

Clearly, in the case of strong verbs, the following phonological environment could hardly be expected to have any effect on the form of the past. In a majority of cases, past formation has no effect on the constitution of the final segment of the verb, and thus cannot cause that complication of consonant-clustering at word-boundaries which is so frequently a cause of -*ed* absence in Black English and, as we shall see, in the Guyanese upper mesolect also (e.g. *come back* and *came back* represent an equal degree of phonological complexity, while *slipped back* is more complex than *slip back*; and, while *came up* and *slipped up* are both less complex than *came down* and *slipped down*, there is no obvious way of simplifying *came* before the consonant, as there is in the case of *slipped*). Similarly, even in those strong verbs which do increase their own complexity by past formation (e.g. *hear*, *heard; go, went*), it would stretch the imagination to suppose that any speaker would consistently select his alternant on the basis of following environments alone (e.g. *I went out and go downstairs, When he hear the concert he heard a false note* etc.).

However, one might reasonably suppose that the phonological constitution of the past form itself might influence order of acquisition; that is to say, one might expect that among the earliest past forms to be acquired would be those with vowel change only (*see, saw; throw, threw,* etc.); that past forms ending in a single consonant might next be acquired (*buy, bought; make, made,* etc.); and that forms ending in consonant clusters (*go, went; sleep, slept,* etc.) would be the last to be acquired. Plausible though such a hypothesis might seem, it is certainly not borne out by the facts. Table 4.8 shows us how the speakers of Table 4.7 deal with the three phonological categories discussed. In order to remove certain factors that might have worked against the hypothesis, several verbs were omitted from the data. For example, if the verb *say* had been retained, it would have severely skewed the results, since of all strong verbs it is the one whose past form is least frequently produced (as is true of Black English [Labov et al. 1968 I:138]) even though it is by far the commonest of its class in our data.

TABLE 4.8 Phonological categories for strong-past formation

Speaker	− V			− C			− CC		
	+	−	%	+	−	%	+	−	%
43	7	6	54	17	41	29	3	53	5
105	2	4	33	27	5	84	6	2	75
107	1	0	100	7	8	46	10	3	77
108	0	5	0	5	12	29	1	8	11
117	0	3	0	5	10	33	3	9	25
122	7	3	70	8	7	53	17	1	94
125	1	4	20	5	11	31	5	5	50
169	0	2	0	6	20	23	3	10	23
196	0	1	0	11	19	37	3	19	14
209	1	2	33	4	13	23	3	6	33
226	2	0	100	6	2	75	5	0	100
236	1	7	12	5	41	11	2	5	28
241	−	−	−	6	1	86	8	0	100
242	4	8	33	15	28	35	21	11	65
Total	26	45	37%	127	218	37%	90	132	40%

NOTES: −V = verbs whose past form ends in a vowel (e.g. *see, throw, grow, lie* etc.). −C = verbs whose past form ends in a single consonant (e.g. *buy, take, bring, catch* etc.). −CC = verbs whose past form ends in a consonant cluster (e.g. *go, tell, feel, send* etc.). + = + *-ed*; − = *-ed*; % = % + of + and − total.

Other verbs excluded are *get, leave, lose* and *break. Get* has a rate of past-form appearance only marginally higher than that of *say*, probably because of the need to keep it distinct from the possessive verb *got*; while since *leave, lose, break* have the basilectal stem forms *lef, los, brok*, respectively, the upper-mesolectal speaker is generally careful to avoid forms (*left, lost, broke*) which are so close to the stigmatised ones which he may himself have only just abandoned. Inclusion of these verbs would have given the 'middle' category, − C, an unfair disadvantage as against other categories, since the criteria in these cases are clearly non-phonological; however, once these verbs are excluded, the percentages of realised past forms are virtually identical for all three categories, as shown by Table 4.8.

TABLE 4.9 Past frequencies of commonest strong verbs

	No.	% past		No.	% past
1. say	178	8	7. take	34	41
2. come	116	40	8. hear	26	35
3. go	113	48	9. bring	23	13
4. get	56	9	10. run	20	20
5. tell	55	35	11. make	17	53
6. see	48	44	12. give	17	23

If we examine in detail the individual speakers in this table, we see that only one speaker, 43, follows the predicted relationship 'more past in − V than in − C, more pasts in − C than in − CC'. Indeed, more than half the speakers have their highest percentage of past forms in the least-favoured − CC category. We may conclude that the phonological constitution of the past form of strong verbs has no influence whatsoever on the choice between past and stem forms.

Another plausible suggestion might be that those verbs which are used most frequently acquire their past form first, while the most rarely used would be the slowest to acquire distinctive pasts. Again, however, the data render any such hypothesis implausible. If we take the twelve commonest strong verbs in our data, we see (Table 4.9) there is no connection whatsoever between frequency and past form. Moreover, of sixteen once-only-occurring verbs in the data, six occurred in their past form, giving a past percentage of 37 – better than slightly more than half of the most frequently occurring verbs.

Further, it can be shown that acquisition of strong pasts is not constant as between individuals. Table 4.10 shows that no implicational relationships hold between ten of the most common strong verbs; that one speaker will

TABLE 4.10   Acquisition of past-tense forms in ten of the commonest strong verbs

Speaker	Take	Say	Get	Tell	Hear	See	Go	Bring	Come	Make
108	−	−	−		−	−	−	−	x	+
236	−	−	−			x	x	x	x	⊖
209	−	−	−	−	x	x	x		⊖	
43	−	−	−	−	x	+	⊖	x	x	ⓧ
117	−	−	x			⊖	x	⊖	x	+
122	−	−	+	+		⊖	+		x	⊖
196	−	x	⊖	⊖	⊖		⊖	x	x	
169	+	⊖	⊖	⊖	⊖	⊖	ⓧ		x	ⓧ
125	⊖	x	⊖	+	+	ⓧ	⊖		⊖	
241		x		+						+
242	ⓧ	x	x	ⓧ	ⓧ	ⓧ	ⓧ	⊖	x	⊖
107	+		⊖		ⓧ	+	+	⊖	x	
226		⊖				+	+		x	
105	+	+		+	ⓧ	ⓧ	+		+	

NOTES: − = stem form only; x = variation between stem and past form; + = past form only.

Scalability: if ringed deviations are scaled, 64.5%; if strict implications are observed (i.e. everything under the line which is not + counted as a deviation), 51.4%.

consistently use the stem form of verb A and the past tense of verb B, while another speaker with equal consistency will simply reverse this relationship.[14]

Is the acquisition of past forms purely a random process? For certain verbs, particular explanations can be suggested. One has already been put forward for the persistence of past-reference *get*. *Say* is a rather more puzzling case, unless a report of what someone else has said can be considered in some sense stative; and in fact, many standard-English speakers use non-past forms for speech-reporting, e.g. 'John says he saw Bill', which is easily as common as 'John said he saw Bill', and certainly commoner, in speech at least, than the prescriptive back-shifting of pedagogic *oratio obliqua* 'John said that he had seen Bill'. If this explanation is valid for *say*, it may also cover a verb of similar meaning, *tell*. But it is less easy to detect any such principle underlying the variation which affects verbs of motion such as *go*, *come*, *run* etc.

In fact, several influences are at work here. One is stylistic. *Go* and *went*

---

[14] The scalability figure of 51.4% in Table 4.10 should be of interest to those who have expressed doubts about scalability figures, and suggested that, given freedom to interchange rows and columns, scalability percentages of 90 or better are always obtainable. The difference between the data in this table and those in other implicational scales should be readily apparent.

may be related diachronically as successive forms indicative of past actions, but synchronically they are style markers: *went* is formal, respectable; *go* is casual and intimate. For example, a speaker such as 242, who shifts style sharply and consistently when he reports dialogue, uses *go* exclusively in the latter but *went* fairly consistently in narrative passages.

However, division between styles is seldom as clear-cut as most writers on 'language in context' seem to imply. For example, in 242's story of Sultan, Tengar and their boy assistant, each of the three pork-knockers in turn goes to sell diamonds, keeps the money for himself and claims that he lost the diamonds. The first incident is recounted by 242 as follows:

> 4.83 Sultan went and sol' diamonds, he came back and he say, 'Diamond lost.' (242/16–17/323)

But by the time 242 reaches the third incident, the background atmosphere of the story has overcome his formal narrative style:

> 4.84 When the boy go to sell, the boy come back, he say, 'Diamond lost.' (242/28/323)

Factors such as these can account for much of 242's variability. However, they cannot account for all of it, still less for that of speakers who maintain a more consistent style.

Where non-stylistic variation is involved, probably the most important factor is verbal aspect. We saw in this and in the preceding chapter how past statives came to be treated as non-punctuals and how non-punctuals after *doz*-loss retained stem form even when their reference was clearly past. The effect of these developments is to delay if not completely inhibit the acquisition of past forms in non-punctual environments. For example, 236 uses the verbs *go* and *come* with past reference thirty-one times. Only five of those occurrences are in the English past form, and all five of these are both [+ punctual] and in non-temporal clauses:

> 4.85 And another time again they going in the bush, you know, they *went* through tramping, they see a little one [sc. jaguar] lie down. (236/19–20/303)
>
> 4.86 I can't tell you the year that I *came* here. (236/10/304)

Of the twenty-six unmarked forms, seventeen are non-punctual: e.g. *come from* in the sense of 'be a native of' –

> 4.87 Int.: But your grandmother came from Dutch country? Where?
> 236: She come from – where they call the place? – Surinam. (236/1–3/301)

– *come in contact* in the sense of 'maintain a lasting relationship with' –

> 4.88 Well is from there I come in contact with Mr S——[sc. her future husband]. (236/26/301)

– *come* in the sense of 'become' –

> 4.89 They [sc. her grandchildren] grow up in my eye sight, they come big and they say, 'I know this same old lady been living there for years . . .' (236/13–14/300)

– or simply *come* or *go* with iterative or habitual reference –

> 4.90 When my husband was living here everything is boat, boat, boat, boat, boat – who have their own boat, well, they can cross over, but who en have, you have to pay these boatmen to cross you then to go over there, and then we go over there. (236/5–8/302)

Of the remaining nine punctual occurrences, four occur in temporal clauses. We saw in Chapters 2 and 3 that such clauses are favourable environments for the deletion of aspectual markers, and it would seem that for at least some speakers this deletion-rule may generalise to include tense marking also:

> 4.91 When the dog come he raise right up. (236/28/303)
> 4.92 When I come here to live there was no bauxite nor nothing. (236/29/301)

Thus 236 has a 50% past-insertion rate in [+ punctual, − temporal] environments (five pasts, five zeros); a zero past-insertion rate in [+ punctual, + temporal] environments (no pasts, four zeros); and a zero past-insertion rate in [− punctual] environments (no pasts, seventeen zeros).

These factors of temporality and non-punctuality cross-cut with the stylistic factors mentioned above, and are in turn affected by the stage of general strong-past acquisition that the speaker may have reached. Thus a speaker at the beginning of the process, such as 236, will insert strong pasts rarely, and then only in the most favourable environment ([+ punctual, − temporal]), and even there insertion will only be variable. On the other hand, a speaker such as 226 who is near the end of the process will insert categorically in that environment and in temporal clauses and will use the stem form only in [− punctual] environments – even there, only variably:

> 4.93 His name was Bell, we *call* him Bell. Holding the bell he *rings* his bell, *say*, 'Well, you have dance tonight, dance tomorrow night and dance

the other nights,' and he *give* you the place where they have the dance. (226/14–16/287)

4.94 A dollar *meant* quite a lot for a man. (226/21/288)

To write a variable rule of the type

$$V[+strong] \rightarrow V[+past] \ / \ \underline{\hspace{3cm}}$$
$$\left\langle \begin{array}{c} +past \\ +punctual \\ +temporal \end{array} \right\rangle$$

would account for virtually all the data that are not stylistically determined. It would, however, completely obscure the steady change-process that underlies the data, and would oblige us to treat both 226 and 236 in the same terms, ignoring the differences that exist not only in their outputs but in the internalised grammars that generate those outputs.

A similar change-process affects 'weak' past forms – similar, but far from identical, since here, phonological factors are of some importance. If we take just three following environments – C –, where the segment following the verb is [+consonantal], V –, where the following segment is [– consonantal], and #, where a clause- or sentence-boundary immediately follows the verb – we find that the nine speakers in Table 4.7 who produce past forms in weak (– syll) verbs can be divided into four groups: one which produces past forms only in V – environments, one which produces past forms in C – and V – environments, one which produces past forms in C – and V – and variably in # – environments, and one which produces past forms in C – and V – and categorically in # – environments. It is not clear whether the changes in the # – environment indicate a 'rule-acceleration' (C.-J. Bailey 1973) or result from small sample size: the outputs for all speakers are shown in Table 4.11. However, as is made clear in Fig. 4.3, the relationship between C – and V – environments is a constant one.

Our findings with respect to the influence of following environments differ little from those of Labov (Labov et al. 1968), Wolfram (1969) and Fasold (1972) for Black English. However, the effect of the segment immediately preceding the *-ed* affix, i.e. the final segment of the verb-stem, seems to differ between the two communities. Fasold's treatment of this topic (1972:67–72) is the most detailed; he finds (as did Wolfram, though not Labov) that what he regards as the 'deletion' of *-ed* occurs more frequently after sonorants than after spirants, and more frequently after spirants than

TABLE 4.11   Environments for past marking of weak verbs

Speaker	V− +	V− −	# +	# −	C− +	C− −
43	2	23	0	3	0	34
169	4	6	0	1	0	10
Group I	6	29 (17%)	0	4 (0%)	0	44 (0%)
242	6	23	0	4	2	21
Group II	6	23 (20%)	0	4 (0%)	2	21 (9%)
107	9	6	1	2	2	7
196	5	22	2	1	2	20
226	9	6	2	2	5	6
Group III	23	34 (40%)	5	5 (50%)	9	33 (21%)
122	3	3	3	0	2	12
105	7	8	4	0	4	9
241	5	2	−	−	2	1
Group IV	15	13 (54%)	7	0 (100%)	8	22 (27%)
Total	50	99 (33%)	12	13 (48%)	19	120 (13%)

NOTES: V− = verbs with following [−consonantal] segment; # = verbs with following clause/sentence boundary; C − = verbs with following [+ consonantal] segment. + = with -ed; − = without -ed.

after stops. For Guyanese speakers, however, these constraints do not appear to operate. Figures are given in Table 4.12. Nor does the voicing or non-voicing of preceding consonants appear to have any effect. The only influence of preceding environment that has any significance can be shown if we include the class of verbs whose stems end with vocalic segments, and ab-

TABLE 4.12   Effect of preceding environment on -ed

	Sonorant__	Spirant__	Stop__
-ed produced	19	21	24
-ed not produced	61	60	78
% -ed	23.8	25.9	23.9

stract from consonant-ending stems all those which, prior to affixation, already terminate in a consonant cluster, i.e. which on affixation yield triple clusters (e.g. *watch*, *jump* etc.), since it was observed in Bickerton 1971b that in reading aloud, Guyanese schoolchildren produced triple clusters significantly less often than double ones. The results of this further analysis are given in Table 4.13. The triple-cluster constraint does not seem to have been mentioned in the literature on Black English.

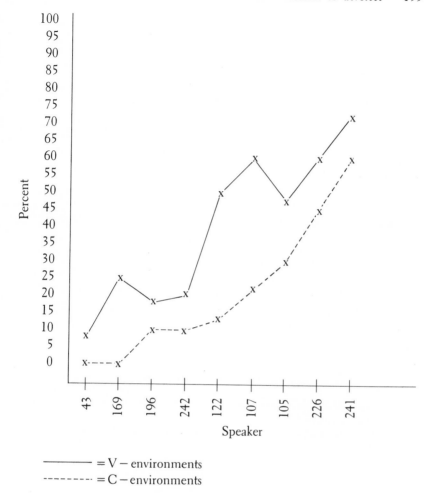

Fig. 4.3. Affixation of -*ed* in V− and C− environments

As Table 4.13 indicates, insertion of -*ed* is rare even in the most favoured environment, where it occurs in only just over a third of cases (as opposed, for example, to 83% insertion in the same environment for Washington speakers [Fasold 1972:46]). When we consider the closeness of the Guyanese speakers concerned to other Guyanese speakers who have no past morpheme at all, and the fact that not one of them has 100% strong-past forms, we must naturally be sceptical of any suggestion that phonological processes of

TABLE 4.13   Further preceding environments for *-ed*

	-ed produced	*-ed* not produced	%*-ed*
Triple __	3	19	14
Double(+voi) __	30	84	26
Double(−voi) __	31	96	24
Single __	17	29	36

'*-ed* deletion' are responsible for the absence of English past tense forms. Indeed, in view of the features noted in our analysis of 236's output, we must now consider, despite the evidence of Figs. 4.2 and 4.3, whether phonological factors are really the primary ones in past-tense acquisition.

Let us propose the hypothesis that the most important factors in the process are those of punctuality and non-punctuality, as described above, plus the past-participle constraint that was noted in Chapter 3. For the moment I shall group as one category [− punctual] verbs and verbs in temporal clauses. I shall also exclude those verbs which, it was suggested above, follow minor rules of their own, since the inclusion of these could only serve to obscure tendencies that were otherwise general (particularly in view of the very high frequency of two of the verbs concerned). These verbs are *get*, *say*, *tell*, *leave*, *lose* and *break*. The outputs of all our fourteen past-using speakers are analysed into the above categories in Table 4.14 and Fig. 4.4.

The evidence as here presented shows quite clearly that grammatical con-

TABLE 4.14   Rates of past insertion for strong, weak and V + syll verbs in three grammatical environments

	[+Participial]			[+Punctual]			[−Punctual]		
Speaker	+	−	%	+	−	%	+	−	%
43	7	2	78	24	78	24	3	40	7
105	10	2	83	36	17	68	8	9	47
107	14	2	87	20	10	66	7	15	32
108	2	3	40	5	35	12	0	27	0
117	1	1	50	9	23	28	0	55	0
122	8	1	88	25	13	66	9	19	32
125	5	2	71	10	20	33	3	7	30
169	7	0	100	7	24	23	2	8	20
196	4	1	80	15	33	31	5	65	7
209	1	2	33	7	28	20	0	17	0
226	10	0	100	12	3	80	10	16	38
236	2	2	50	8	37	18	0	50	0
241	10	2	83	9	2	82	1	1	50
242	7	0	100	43	44	49	4	47	8
Total	88	20	81	230	367	38	52	376	12

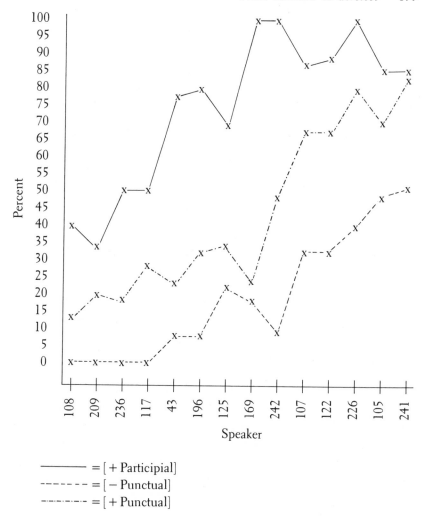

Fig. 4.4. Graphic representation of data in Table 4.14

straits outweigh phonological ones in past acquisition. Identical relationships between grammatical categories (in terms of mores and lesses) are
maintained by all fourteen speakers; indeed categories are more sharply and
consistently differentiated than the phonological ones in Fig. 4.2. Further,
the data in Fig. 4.4 conform more closely to the S-curve pattern already
shown to be characteristic of linguistic change. In Fig. 4.2, percentages are
evenly distributed between the upper, middle and lower thirds of the scale;

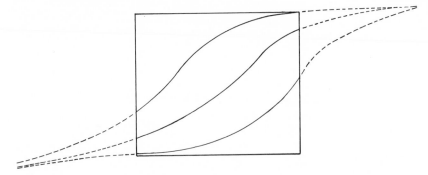

Fig. 4.5. Idealised S-curves for Fig. 4.4

in Fig. 4.4, only six of the forty-two percentage figures fall between 33 and 66, and of these, no less than four result from cells in Table 4.14 which have five or less occurrences. A very slight idealisation of Fig. 4.4 would give us the pattern of three consecutive S-curves (indicating three consecutive changes) shown in Fig. 4.5. Even if we now sub-divide the [− punctual] category of Table 4.14 into [− punctual] and [+ temporal] (i.e. verbs in temporal clauses), grammatical relationships still hold with only two exceptions (see Table 4.15 and Fig. 4.6). Except for 122 and 242, who simply reverse priorities for [− punctual] and [+ temporal], all speakers have more past marking in participles than in finite verbs, more past marking in verbs with punctual than in verbs with non-punctual reference, and more past marking in verbs with non-punctual reference than in verbs in temporal clauses.

This patterning is only what one would expect from the grammatical analysis of the last two chapters. We saw in Chapter 3 that past marking appears with participles before it appears in any other environment; on the basis of the general principle that 'earlier means more', we would expect to find, at a later stage of mesolectal development, that participial past marking outnumbered all other kinds. Both in Chapter 3 and earlier in this chapter we had occasion to note the wide generality and numerous effects of the

TABLE 4.15   [− Punctual] and [+ Temporal] environments for past tense

[−Punctual] +	3	4	2	2	3	7	5	9	7	1
[−Punctual] −	26	48	41	8	7	11	18	12	6	1
% +	10	8	5	20	30	39	22	43	53	50
[+Temporal] +	0	1	2	1	0	0	4	1	1	−
[+Temporal] −	14	17	6	7	7	4	1	4	3	−
% +	0	5	25	12	0	0	80	20	25	−
Speaker	43	196	242	169	125	107	122	226	105	241

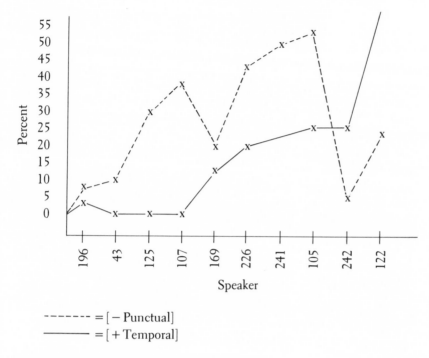

Percent

Speaker

- - - - - - = [− Punctual]
—————— = [+ Temporal]

Fig. 4.6. Graphic representation of Table 4.15

collapse of the stative–non-stative distinction and the loss of *doz*, which together served to create a tense-neutral non-punctual category in opposition to the (increasingly marked) punctual (and incidentally, past) category. We would therefore expect that, after participials, punctuals would be most frequently marked, to distinguish them from the morphologically unmarked non-punctuals. The final distinction, between non-punctuals and temporals, is, as the data indicate, both the least important and the one least consistently held. Sample size may be critical here. Many of the speakers who have zero insertion in temporal clauses are ones whose overall insertion rate is so low that, statistically, one would not expect even a single insertion among their handful of temporals; for speakers in this category, no special rule need be posited. For others, it might well prove significant to distinguish between punctual and non-punctual temporals, i.e. between 'when the boat sank, someone was drowned' and 'when a boat sank, someone was always drowned'. The latter is semantically very close to the 'pure' hypothetical, 'whenever a boat sinks, someone is likely to get drowned', and we saw in Chapters 2 and 3 how hypotheticals are favourable environments for non-insertion of pre-verbal markers. But to obtain significant answers we would need larger samples of speech from more speakers at this particular stage of development.

In any case, such issues are minor beside the demonstration that, even so late in the decreolisation process, grammatical constraints can exercise such powerful effects. Given the rules demonstrated above, it is not necessary to posit any special phonological rules for the process of past acquisition. Though a full analysis lies outside the scope of the present study, one can state that the process which enables Guyanese to acquire terminal clusters generally (perhaps with the addition of some kind of feature-weighting for 'morpheme boundary') would largely account for the steady increase in the more phonologically complex types of past marking. The process would seem to be as follows: at any time, a speaker has n grammatical categories open to past marking, each of which will be filled by V + syll, strong, and V − syll pasts in the proportions shown in Fig. 4.2. In a category not yet open to marking, even the most favoured phonological category will not appear. In the opposite extreme − a category in which marking is obligatory or almost so − most phonological categories will be obligatorily represented, and only the most disfavoured one(s) may have variable representation. For intermediate cases, let us assume a speaker X who has 70% past insertion for [+ punctual] and 30% insertion for [− punctual], and who at the same time affixates 60% of V − syll verbs before [− cons] and 40% before [+ cons]. Let us further assume that [− cons] and [+ cons] following environments are equal in frequency. Then out of every 100 [+ punctual] verbs in [− cons] environments, we might expect 84 to be marked for past tense; out of every 100 [+ punctual] verbs in [+ cons] environments, 56 to be marked; out of every 100 [− punctual] verbs in [− cons] environments, 36; and out of every 100 [− punctual] verbs in [+ cons] environments, 24.

Of course, in practice, things never are equal. There are additional constraints, such as the triple-consonant one, which have to be taken into consideration, and even if there were not, unpredictable performance fluctuations in token-occurrences for all the categories involved would make it impossible for such consistency of patterning to show up except over texts far longer than those analysed here. One may, however, predict with some degree of confidence that such texts, when obtained, will support the present hypothesis about the relationship between phonological and grammatical constraints. For the present, it is surely remarkable enough that speakers should preserve phonological consistencies so strictly that they could be taken as the primary rules, while simply following the grammatical rules and rule-changes that are in fact the primary determinant of past-tense acquisition.

The possible significance of these findings may be indicated by a brief glance at what may prove to be a parallel case. In Black English, the linguists who claim grammatical differences between standard and Black past tenses are ones who have not carried out quantitative studies; Labov, Wolfram, Fasold and (to the best of my knowledge) all other linguists who have made studies of this kind are unanimous in supposing that Black English has an underlying past indistinguishable from the standard one, which is then subject to fairly extensive deletion. They have produced massive statistical evidence in favour of this interpretation.

Despite the evidence they have presented, could the quantitativists be wrong? The data we have just analysed show that they could. It could well be that the phonological patterns they have revealed, so similar to those in our own data, merely serve the same purpose of masking the factors which in reality take precedence over phonological ones. However, 'could be' is a long way from 'must be'. Is there any independent evidence that would support such an assertion?

Here, the linguist who does not have access to a very large quantity of raw data is at an obvious disadvantage. However, at least one source of recorded Black English conversations is generally available (Loman 1967), and a number of passages in it are extremely suggestive. There is the speaker who distinguishes between 'causative' and 'non-causative' *scare:*

> 4.95 And the ghost *scared* him out [twice repeated] . . . So the coloured man went in there, and he say – and he *scare.*' (Loman 1967:21) [15]

'Causative' *scare* is of course [+ punctual], 'non-causative' *scare* is [− punctual]. Elsewhere, another speaker answers a past-tense question with a stem form, for reasons which should be sufficiently obvious to any reader of the present study:

> 4.96 PJ: Did you do that last year?
> JD: Yeah, we do it sometimes. (ibid., p. 77)

Finally, a much longer but even less ambiguous passage:

> 4.97 Anita, you remember when we – it was a long time ago. We used to – when somebody used to be crying in our house we used to do just like this. We used to do our fingers – all like that – do like this to 'em – we

---

[15] Loman's orthography, designed to illustrate certain phonological features of Black English which are not relevant to our concerns, has been conventionalised in this and succeeding extracts.

used to say, ching ching ching ching ching ching ching ching. We doing all that old stuff [AP: oo cha li boo, oo cha li boo], and sometimes we *make* them laughy. They – we *make* somebody laugh when we be doing that you know. Who ever it be crying, we *make* them laugh so hard – that they – they – that – that they be steadily – they be steadily crying and laughing back. And then we *say* – and then we used to say – when they *do* that – we used to say: 'Crying when you laughing!' [LAUGHS]. (ibid., pp. 24–5)

It must be perfectly clear from the use of *remember, was a long time ago* and *used to* that the period the speaker is discussing lies in the past – note the reformulation that even replaces tense-neutral *say* with *used to say* so as to avoid any possible confusion on the part of the hearer. The only plausible reason that can be advanced for the other four italicised verbs lacking morphological change is that their referents are not single-point actions, but series of actions which were repeated on frequent occasions in the past – in other words, are marked [− punctual]. This particular case is all the more impressive in that the verbs are strong ones, and the alleged near-universality of strong-past forms has been claimed (by e.g. Fasold 1972:38–40, Labov et al. 1968 1:138) as the strongest evidence for supposing that the category 'past tense' in Black English (if not its morphophonemic representation) is identical to its standard-English equivalent. On the basis of such evidence, plus the analysis of Guyanese past-formation which preceded it, there would seem to be a strong case for the re-examination of Black English (both northern–urban, which is well documented, and southern–rural, which is not) to see whether factors similar to, if not identical with, those discussed above are not generally present.

Before we leave Guyanese past-information, two connected points must be made. We have already noted the dubious status of statements to the effect that 'creoles indicate time adverbially'. It is interesting to observe that where time-adverbs occur in a sentence, mid- to upper-mesolectal speakers characteristically use the past form, even when they have a very low overall rate of past insertion; conversely, where there is no adverbial, the past form is less frequently realised. Thus, from 43, we have

4.98 He brought her to this place nineteen twenty-eight. (43/34/46)
4.99 I saw him couple months ago. (43/12/48)
4.100 A [sc. one] night this woman came to me. (43/8/50)

even though in the vast majority of sentences where she has no adverbial, there is no past form either. The presence of the adverbial seems to have the effect of reinforcing the [+ punctual] marking of the verb.

The second point concerns a reflex of the basilectal anterior rule with statives. As noted in the previous chapter, the collapse of the main stative rule means that statives thereafter are generally treated in the same way as non-punctual non-statives. However, where it is clear that an anterior state of affairs has definitively been replaced by a *contrary* state, the former may be marked. Two examples from the same speaker may illustrate this point:

> 4.101 123: He's at Bartica
> 125: Bartica – I *thought* he was some East Bank side [sc. somewhere on the east bank of the Demerara River]. (125/1/171)
> 4.102 Last crop [sc. at the time of the last sugar harvest] people *know* about it, they found out this. (125/18–19/172)

In 4.101, 125 had thought something, but after 123's information he no longer thinks it; in 4.102, people found out something, and as a result knew it, but of course continue to know it until the present moment. With reference to the preceding comment on adverbials, it is also worth noting that, while the time marker *last crop* has no effect at all on the stative, it does impose past marking on the non-stative verb in the sentence.

Remaining forms

Even if we limit ourselves to realis forms, we will realise that there are at least three standard-English forms about which nothing has yet been said – *had + en*, *have been + -ing* and *had been + -ing*. These forms simply do not occur in the recordings of Guyanese speakers we have so far discussed. It is true that this does not in itself constitute proof that these speakers have no knowledge of these forms. Their occurrence in the conversation of native standard-English-speakers is relatively rare. However, it would be quite reasonable to suppose that they depend on the prior establishment of a perfective category, and we have seen how marginal any such category is even among the more evolved of the upper-mesolectal speakers we have discussed.

That the management of past tenses presents problems even for highly educated Guyanese speakers can be shown by the following extract from a speech delivered at a teachers' conference:

> 4.103 And this is what I discovered. I didn't get all right all the time, but I was able at least to help the children to correct their own work and see *where they have gone wrong*. Of course, it's a tedious drill, as Mr—— told you, it is something that will have to go on and on and sometimes *I have to use* the whole of the second term doing something like that

> and then leave the third term – now the third term, and when *I am sa-*
> *tisfy – and when I was satisfied* that *they had got* this in, the third term
> now, they would write their continuous essays. (94/22–8/110)

At the time of the conference, the speaker was no longer a practising teacher
and there is therefore no contextual explanation of his slips into non-past
tenses. In any case, standard-English tense-sequence rules indicate that the
first italicised verb should have been pluperfect. The second italicised verb
probably takes its form from a conjunction of two factors – the reference to a
teaching method in the abstract coupled with the speaker's memory of having used it repeatedly (non-punctually) in the past. However, having maintained the non-past sequence in the third italicised verb, the speaker 'catches
himself' (to use a vivid Guyanese idiom), and reformulates according to
standard-English rules. Having done this, he correctly produces the italicised pluperfect that follows. We may conclude that, at the acrolectal level,
Guyanese speakers have all the English tense rules within their competence,
but that they do not always realise these rules because of the upper-mesolectal rules which equally lie within their competence, and which conflict with
the English ones.

Conclusion

We have now, in our analysis of the Guyanese continuum, reached a point
at which the only major differences between Guyanese and English outputs
are distributional (English tense-aspect forms are not always realised, or, if
realised, not always in appropriate environments). With the relatively trivial
exceptions mentioned in the previous section, the underlying representation
of the verbal system in the minds of acrolectal Guyanese speakers may be
regarded as substantively identical with that of metropolitan speakers of English.

In Chapter 3 we detailed the underlying and superficial changes necessary
for the basilectal system to evolve into the mid-mesolectal one. At that stage,
the rules that generate realis forms can be summarised as

$$(1) \quad + \text{past} - \text{punct} + \text{cont} \rightarrow (waz) \text{ -}ing$$
$$(2) \quad - \text{past} - \text{punct} + \text{cont} \rightarrow (iz) \text{ -}ing$$
$$(3) \quad + \text{past} - \text{punct} - \text{cont} \rightarrow \emptyset$$
$$(4) \quad - \text{past} - \text{punct} - \text{cont} \rightarrow (doz)$$
$$(5) \quad + \text{past} + \text{punct} \rightarrow (\text{-}ed)$$

(6)   + ant   punct − cont → *did*

(7)   + ant − punct + cont → *did/been -ing*

To these rules, the following changes now take place:

(8)   (*doz*) → ∅

(9)   α past − punct − cont → ∅

(10)   + ant → + past

(11)   *did* → ∅

(12)   *been -ing* → ∅

(13)   + perf → *have(-en)*

(14)   + past + punct − temp → (*-ed*)

(15)   + past + punct → (*-ed*)

(16)   + past − cont → (*-ed*)

(17)   − past − cont → ∅ (*-s*)

This series of rule-changes, together with those given at the end of Chapter 3, serve to establish an unbroken chain from a basilectal level whose underlying (semantic) structure is quite different from that of English to an acrolectal level whose underlying structure is virtually indistinguishable from that of English. At every stage of this unbroken chain, the rule-changes postulated yield the outputs observed at that stage, and nowhere is there a point at which one could draw any valid boundary that would separate the two extremes. The Guyanese continuum, however unlike traditionally conceived language systems it may appear, may legitimately be described as a system by virtue of the fact that all of its superficial confusion can be shown to represent the operation of consistent and interrelated factors which can be described in a principled and systematic way.

In the final chapter, we shall look at some of the questions which the existence of such a system poses for general linguistic theory.

5 Implications for linguistic theory

The findings described in the preceding chapters are at variance with many assumptions which are widely accepted in current linguistic theory, although they should not cause surprise to anyone versed in the Labovian paradigm, and indeed issue logically from insights into language and approaches to linguistic description developed in recent years by C.-J. Bailey, DeCamp and others, as well as by the present writer. In this final chapter I shall try to indicate the precise ways in which these findings challenge those assumptions, and to formulate possible alternatives. In so doing, I shall be obliged to suggest a model of human language which, while it has been considerably influenced by the above-mentioned writers, will probably differ in a number of respects from any which they might propose, and for which, therefore, I must take full responsibility. For, heterodox as this model may appear, it can be justified point by point, as I shall try to show, by detailed and specific reference to the empirical studies described in preceding chapters. At the same time it will, I hope, be general enough to cast light on theoretical problems already known to exist in linguistic theory and in descriptive practice, and thus justify at least consideration as a possible competitor to models at present more generally approved.

To elaborate on all the possible issues involved would entail, in effect, writing another book, so I shall confine myself to only two. However, these two seem to me to be central to, and critical in, any general theory of language, and, once they are settled, decisions on lesser issues are largely constrained by them. They are, first, the meaning of the concept 'system' in language and its relationship to change, and second, the nature of the internalised ('psychologically real') grammars of individual speakers.

First of all, it might be as well to dispose of the objection that our findings are not such as would necessarily occasion any drastic re-evaluation of existing theory. Such an objection might take either of two forms: it might argue that the facts described here pertain to an aberrant and possibly unique dialect system, or that they are specific to a limited and again, perhaps, unique area of the grammar, the tense-aspect system. In either case, the argument might go, they lack the necessary generality and therefore the burden of proof must continue to lie with the advocates of re-evaluation. One does not abandon a good theory for every mite of counter-evidence.

In fact, the objection will hold in neither form. As regards the first; even if we could rule out the possibility that processes of pidginisation, creolisation and decreolisation may have affected many nowadays 'standard' languages,[1] the claims made here would not be in any way affected. To unseat a putative universal requires no more than a single counter-example, and it is putative universals that we are dealing with here. Claims such as 'dialects of the same language differ only in low-level rules' become meaningless if they have to be rephrased as 'dialects of most languages differ only in low-level rules' – we both lose any principled distinction between 'language' and 'dialect' and are left with only ad hoc methods of determining membership for the two kinds of language we are now forced to assume.

A similar argument could be used against the second form of the objection: a single deep-structural difference is all that is needed to refute the 'low-level only' position. However, anyone who rested his case on such a claim would invite scepticism as to the accuracy of his analysis. One would expect either that varieties within a language would differ only in low-level rules, or that underlying differences, if they proved to exist, would be plural rather than merely singular or dual. We have shown, within the Guyanese continuum, the co-existence of polar varieties, one of which has [± anterior] tense, [± punctual] aspect, and grammatical distinction between statives and non-statives, while the other has [± past] tense, [± continuous] and [± perfective] aspect, and no consistent grammatical distinction between statives and non-statives, i.e. there are not less than three clear and non-low-level differences in the tense-aspect system alone. But outside this system, underlying differences are equally widespread; the underlying representations of lexical items differ between poles of the continuum,[2] and the stocks of transformations also differ, as we can soon find out by trying to provide identical

---

[1] More than one linguist would nowadays claim that they have; Alleyne (1971) mentions this point with specific reference to English. That English is a creole by origin, and that Germanic is a creolised form of Indo-European, is certainly maintained by C.-J. Bailey (personal communication). But while there can be little doubt that pidginisation etc. have often occurred in the past, and may be responsible for many hitherto puzzling historic phenomena, there is an obvious danger that their definitions may be widened to include all forms of linguistic change, rendering them vacuous. Claims of prior pidginisation etc. are hypotheses that require empirical testing, rather than corollaries that follow from studies of synchronic variation.

[2] On this issue, see two interesting papers by Barbara Robson (1972, 1973). Further evidence is provided by the analysis of -*ed* acquisition for weak-syllabic verbs in Chapter 4 above.

derivations for such basilectal sentences as *na ponish di govmen a ponish awi?* (186/22/238) and their acrolectal equivalents, e.g. 'Making us suffer, isn't that what the government's doing?' (For a version of one non-English transformation involved in this particular case, see B. L. Bailey 1966:86, Rule 51.)

We are therefore fully justified in concluding that differences between varieties in the Guyanese continuum are such that, where they run counter to prior assumptions about the nature of linguistic systems, it is the assumptions rather than the varietal differences that should be called into question.

Hitherto, it has been generally supposed that language, in its most general sense, could be divided into a number of entities called languages, which could be further sub-divided into entities called dialects. Doubts about the validity of the latter term were quoted in Chapter 1; these can now be extended to the former as well. For Guyanese Creole clearly does not constitute a language, in so far as one end of it is indistinguishable from English. Yet it cannot be a dialect, since dialects are supposedly more homogeneous than the language that contains them, while Guyanese Creole is less homogeneous than English. So what is it? In a passsage quoted in Chapter 1, Labov (1971b:57) suggested a third term, 'system', and though in that place he defined it as less, rather than more than a language, this does not seem a necessary part of the definition. Is there any sense in which we can call Guyanese Creole a system? I believe so, even though it may involve interpreting the term 'system' in a way rather different to that of common linguistic usage. When a linguist speaks of languages as constituting systems, he is usually thinking of static systems, systems with a fixed number of parts which hold invariant relations with one another. But there is no *a priori* reason why a system should be static, and indeed we know perfectly well that languages are not static. Guyanese Creole can claim to be a system by virtue of the fact that relationships within it, though not invariant, are systematic. There is, as I have shown, no trace of anything that could be called random mixing of elements; on the contrary, the rule-changes that give rise to different outputs are tightly interrelated and capable of principled description. The only difference between it and what have traditionally been called systems is that it is dynamic, not static.

But what precisely do we mean by a dynamic system? It was suggested in Chapter 1 that there was a relationship between 'dynamic' and 'diachronic', in that changes which could be observed synchronically in the Guyanese continuum resembled the changes that may be observed diachronically in standard languages. However, this cannot be the whole story. Historical syntax within the generative framework, e.g. Kiparsky 1968 and Robin Lakoff

1968, suggests that syntactic changes – even those which span many centuries, or what are popularly conceived of as 'different' languages, e.g. Latin and Spanish – involve shallower levels than had previously been assumed, and affect conditions on transformations rather than transformations themselves, much less phrase-structure rules or underlying semantic categories. If such analyses are indeed correct (and the evidence for them is persuasive), then the deep-level changes that have taken place within Indo-European languages throughout their recorded history may be less than those which we may observe today within a population of little over half a million people.

This conclusion is so startling that one must hesitate before accepting it. However, even if it should prove to be exaggerated, we have already shown it to be true to the extent that synchronic changes in Guyanese Creole are different both in kind and in degree from the diachronic changes that characteristically take place in more settled languages. Thus, while it remains true that a synchronic description of the continuum deals with what might, in other historical circumstances, have emerged as purely diachronic changes, these changes, even had they been diachronic in fact, would still have constituted unusual examples of their class.

These changes owe their nature to the distance between the polar grammars of the continuum. When we first noted this fact, in Chapter 2, it was suggested that the remoteness of the underlying basilectal grammar from standard English could derive from one of two origins: either the retention of at least part of a pan–West African or at least pan-Kwa underlying system, or the surfacing of some yet more abstract system from a level at which Kwa and English (or, perhaps, any pair of languages) would be indistinguishable. As was noted, the evidence for either hypothesis is extremely scant. However, the findings discussed in Chapters 3 and 4 may incline us slightly towards the former, if only because those findings indicate subsequent changes in kind rather than in complexity, instead of the progressive complication and diversification one might expect if the second hypothesis were correct.

There would be further corroboration if we could point to some other form of natural change in language which parallels in kind and scope the changes we have observed in the Guyanese continuum. In fact, there are persuasive similarities between the kinds of change predicated by our two hypotheses and two types of development which are not generally conceptualised in terms of linguistic change, but which consist, in fact, of series of linked and sequent changes, i.e. first- and second-language acquisition.

The 'deep-structure-recovery' hypothesis predicates changes of a type similar to those which take place in the course of first-language learning. At first sight, the analogies might seem persuasive. The child commences with an initial grammar which generates, not, it is true, deep structures such as these are currently understood by any school of linguistic theory, but one- and two-word structures which one feels intuitively are somehow 'simpler' or 'more basic' than later-child or adult language, and which are readily relatable to 'predicate-argument' type interpretations of underlying structure. From this base, the child evolves a series of hypothetical grammars (cf. Bloom 1970) each closer to the grammar of the adult language which constitutes its target, just as speakers in a creole continuum evolve a series of grammars each of which is closer than the previous one to the grammar of the superstrate.

However, when we come to examine the processes in more detail, the analogy breaks down. In the first place, there is negligible resemblance between the grammar the child starts with and the grammar the basilectal-creole- or pidgin-speaker starts with (the 'baby-talk' theory of pidgins–creoles being simply a reflex of the racist syndrome that called black males of all ages 'boy'). One is a fully articulated system in which any adult topic can be discussed and full understood,[3] the other is a partial and inadequate system in which very few topics can be discussed, and even these with a great deal of vagueness and ambiguity. Secondly, the development of a child grammar is intimately related to the overall mental and physical development of the speaker, while the development of a creole grammar is certainly not so related; contrary to some quasi-fashionable (and, of course, non-linguistic) theorising about the alleged conceptual deficit of non-standard-English-speaking people, basilectal-creole-speakers are in no way beneath acrolectal ones in their intellectual make-up, although they are naturally not adept at displaying their skills in the styles favoured by the educated middle class. As one would expect between two processes, one geared to maturational processes and one not, there are critical differences. For instance,

---

[3] It is not suggested that all topics may be discussed with equal ease. English is better equipped than basilectal creole to deal with abstractions, but that is simply because many more English than creole speakers have had time and leisure to think about such things. In fact, any statement, however abstract, can probably be translated into basilectal creole, sometimes at the cost of periphrasis, sometimes not. For instance, Descartes's *cogito ergo sum* translates smoothly as *a mi tingk mek mi de*, or, still more idiomatically, *a mi main gi mi se mi de mek mi de*. (Note that, unlike *think*, *mi main gi mi* is necessarily transitive, so an object must be supplied, and the one supplied here both seems the only one possible and underlines what has seemed to some philosophers (cf. Achemann 1965) the essential circularity of the Cartesian definition!)

Chomsky has observed that in first-language acquisition, 'advances are generally "across the board". A child who does not produce initial *s* + consonant clusters may begin to produce them all, at approximately the same time' (1964:39). As we have seen, creole changes operate along quite different lines: they generalise very slowly, and are characterised at every level by frequent variation. But even if Chomsky has exaggerated the absence of variation in child speech,[4] there are still other and more important differences.

These can best be understood if we take an actual process which in crude outline is similar in both child speech and the creole continuum: the acquisition of past-tense marking. The English-speaking child first acquires the past forms of a few of the commoner strong verbs. He then acquires a general *-ed*-affixation rule which overrides the minor morphophonemic rules he has just learnt, so that he produces forms such as *goed* or *wented* by affixing *-ed* either to the stem or an already learnt past form. Finally he learns, or, in the case of some verbs, relearns the irregular forms. The only real resemblance between this and creole past-acquisition is that some creolespeakers (e.g. 209) may begin by acquiring a handful of strong pasts – though such speakers are very much in a minority. However, no speaker acquires an 'across the board' *-ed* rule; on the contrary, the acquisition of *-ed* is a slow and complex process. Moreover, the affixation of *-ed* to strong-past verbs simply never occurs, even among the most self-conscious and hypercorrecting of speakers. On the contrary, strong pasts in general are acquired before weak ones, rather than vice versa. Finally, the creole process is subject to both grammatical and phonological constraints which seem to be largely if not entirely absent from the child process. All in all, the child process is what one would expect of a process which *added* a formal past–non-past distinction to a grammar where no comparable distinction had existed before, and the creole process is what one would expect of a process which *superimposed* a formal past–non-past distinction on a grammar which already had different distinctions and different formal means of expressing them.

Thus, while the process of first-language acquisition is probably what the decreolisation process *would* look like if it began from a quasi-universal, highly generalised base and proceeded gradually to add English category-dis-

---

[4] An extremely interesting paper by Hsin-I. Hsieh (MS.) indicates considerable intra-personal variation in the acquisition of tone sandhi by Taiwanese children. Hsieh's paper is supported by a richer array of quantitative data than were the studies on which Chomsky's opinion was based.

tinctions, it is not one which bears more than a superficial resemblance to the *actual* process of decreolisation. We may therefore conclude that any 'deep-structure-recovery' hypothesis for pidgin–creole origins is unlikely to prove correct unless heavily qualified in some way.

Our second hypothesis, the 'African-base' one, predicates changes which may well prove to be similar to those which take place in second-language learning.[5] The vagueness of the last sentence is wholly regrettable, but, in the present state of our knowledge, simply inevitable. For all the thousands of works which deal with second-language *teaching*, there are only a handful which deal with second-language *learning*,[6] and indeed, to the best of my knowledge, none at all which deal with the learning of second languages by untaught adults – the only arena in which the process can be studied free from possible contamination by the general maturational processes which govern first-language acquisition. In part, but only in part, this lack is traceable to some remarks by Halle (1964:344) (subsequently given a biological rationale in Lenneberg 1967): 'The ability to master a language like a native, which children possess to an extraordinary degree, is almost completely lacking in the adult. I propose to explain this as being due to deterioration or loss in the adult of the ability to construct optimal (simplest) grammars on the basis of a restricted corpus of examples.' This remark is sometimes interpreted as meaning simply that no adult can master a foreign sound-system. But even this version is questionable; moreover, if it were what Halle meant, one must question the propriety of his use of the term 'optimal grammar', since an optimal grammar contains vastly much more than the phonological component of a language. But most striking of all is the total lack of empirical evidence for Halle's claims – for even if we concede that

---

[5] Discussion of this second hypothesis is greatly indebted to four papers – Alleyne 1971, Richards MS., Traugott 1973 and Whinnom 1971 – as well as to the sources actually cited in the body of the text. I have, however, avoided specific references to them for two reasons; first, because their influence, though extensive, was sometimes indirect, and second, because I differ from each of them on some issues, but did not wish to bog down the exposition in controversies which are, I think, secondary to our points of general agreement. There is not space in this volume for a really thorough discussion of pidgin–creole origins, so I trust the writers concerned will pardon this blanket acknowledgement.

[6] By this I mean, of course, the processes by which innumerable speakers, often illiterates, acquire fluent knowledge of other languages without the aid of textbooks or any kind of formal instruction. David Reibel has drawn my attention to a paper by Dato (1971) on natural acquisition of Spanish, but the subjects discussed were children below the age of six and a half; moreover, the deep-level differences between English and Spanish are less than those between English and West African languages.

only the sound-system is involved, and that no adult has ever mastered a foreign sound-system, incorrect production of foreign sounds (the only evidence Halle could adduce) is simply a characteristic of production and no clue whatsoever, within the Chomsky–Halle paradigm, as to what the speaker's mental representation of (as distinct from his articulatory capacity to represent) the foreign sound-system might be.[7]

It remains a fact that adults do internalise second-language grammars of some kind, and since no such grammar has been even partially described, one wonders how Halle could with such confidence describe them as non-optimal. They may very well not be optimal, but they often function extremely well, and if there is indeed a difference between them and the optimal grammar the native speaker would construct, one would have thought such a difference would constitute a topic of far from trivial interest to 'anyone concerned with the study of human nature and human capacities' (Chomsky 1968:59). However, the Halle–Lenneberg formulation has deterred pure linguists from wasting their time in a supposedly non-existent field, while applied linguists have naturally refrained from too close examination of the ways in which people acquire second languages without the intervention of second-language teachers. Since it is obviously too late for the present work to fill this truly remarkable hiatus in our knowledge of language and the mind, the paragraphs that follow will have to depend heavily on anecdote, observation and personal experience.

We may agree with Reibel (1969:290) that the adult brings to second-language learning strategies which are qualitatively similar to those he employed on his first language as a child, but not necessarily with Reibel (1971:92) that he 'accepts the fluent native speaker as a suitable model'. On approaching a language for the first time, and indeed for some considerable time afterwards, the adult cannot understand a word the fluent native speaker is saying. All he can understand with any facility are non-native,

---

[7] By this I do not, of course, mean that there is any purely physical deficit in the articulatory capacity such as would prevent, literally, a speaker from producing 'foreign sounds'. On the contrary, foreign speakers of a language, in addition to being able to comprehend these strange sounds when directed at them, can very often produce such sounds when they are elicited separately or in isolated words. Such evidence indicates that they do indeed have an adequate mental representation of the foreign sound-system, but that their articulatory processes have become so routinised by consistently producing only the sounds of their native tongue for ten years or more that they are unable to actualise these representations at anything approaching the speed of normal speech, i.e. there is a purely performance restriction. The Hallean argument seems defensible only if one assumes that 'grammar' means merely 'grammar of production' – an assumption explicitly denied by Chomsky on numerous occasions.

non-fluent speakers of his own nationality, drunks (who, contrary to the 'whishky-pleashe' stereotype, often articulate with hypercorrect distinctness and repeat themselves oftener than a programmed-learning manual), people whose slowness of utterance amounts virtually to a speech impediment, and patronising, if well-meaning, individuals who address him in some kind of 'foreigner talk' (Ferguson 1971). Despite this handicap, he must talk back, if desired social benefits are to ensue. While accepting Reibel's dismissal of some mechanistic 'interference' which inexorably imposes L1 patterns on his L2 utterances, one cannot avoid the fact that the adult's success in learning his first language constitutes the solitary ray of hope to sustain him through the disheartening early days of his contact with his second. Inevitably, where direct and obvious evidence to the contrary is lacking, he will conclude that, hopefully, the target grammar does not differ from his own. Just as he clutches at lexical similarities, even should they turn out to be 'false friends', he also clutches at syntactic similarities, even though here as well, surface similarities may mask differences at a deeper level. He will begin by hypothesising a grammar that will generate simple sentences of a type similar to those of his own language: in other words, he will strip from his grammar all transformations that are 'marked' in the sense of some as-yet-unformulated theory of universal syntactic markedness. On this basis, he will begin to construct hypotheses about the target grammar. It is inevitable that many of these will be incorrect; many hypotheses children make about their native grammar are incorrect, even though they usually have fewer distractions and higher motivation than the adult learner. It is inevitable too that adult hypotheses will be coloured by knowledge the speaker has of his own language, which he cannot, at the language-teacher's bidding, entirely expunge from his memory, any more than, at the judge's bidding, the juryman can entirely expunge biassed reportage of the case he is considering, however conscientiously he may try to do so. However, the adult, like the child, will attempt to adjust his hypotheses, in the light of further and fuller evidence (i.e. utterances by speakers rated 'more native-like' which differ substantively from utterances generated by the existing hypothetical grammar).

It is at this stage that differences between child and adult perhaps more critical than differences in linguistic knowledge and experience begin to make themselves felt. It appears to be a well-established fact (cf. Smith and Miller 1966) that all children within a given language community acquire the language of that community in a series of identical steps which follow an invariant order. Although it has been suggested by Corder (1967) that a similar process may apply in second-language learning, there seems to be little empirical evidence either way. Indeed, since the corpus from which an adult induces the rules of a second language is generally very much smaller than that from which a child induces the rules of a first, and more especially since, in the adult, the process of acquisition is uncontrolled by any more general maturational process, it seems likelier that hypotheses are relatively unconstrained. One position would be that it matters not at all, in the long run, what hypotheses the adult makes, in so far as evidence such as we have already discussed would soon enable him to correct it. But this position is based on two assumptions, both of which are quite likely false. First, it assumes that a hypothesis H_n is neutral as between $H_{n+1(a)}$ and $H_{n+1(b)}$ – that is to say, no matter what one's choice of a hypothesis, one's choice of a successor for it will not thereby be constrained. This is an interesting question which cannot be settled here; some possible counter-evidence from a creole context is examined in Bickerton 1973a. Second, it assumes that sufficient evidence for correction will be presented. While we do not really know what would constitute 'sufficient evidence' (Reibel 1971:91, note 1), we may well suspect that the exposure to the target language of a majority of learners is simply not large enough for the corrective cycle to be completed. In consequence, while (excluding cases of gross physical or mental defect) children invariably proceed to full mastery of their native language, relatively few learners of second languages succeed in dominating them fully. Like runners in a long-distance race that is stopped the moment the leaders burst the tape, they are strung out over a considerable distance: some have reached the goal, others are almost there, some are much further off, while there are many who, despite their having run many laps, are as far from the finishing post as they were when the race began.

It seems to me that series of developments such as those described above are sufficient to account for the very varied levels of achievement reached by second-language learners, without the necessity of invoking any mysterious, otherwise unmotivated, and empirically unsubstantiable 'loss of language-learning ability'. Certainly they are not contradicted by any of the known facts about second-language learning. They are, however, strikingly similar to the developments which bring about a creole continuum, and which have been described in the foregoing chapters.

At the inception of a pidgin–creole cycle, the future pidgin-speaker is precisely in the position of the adult learner described above. He already has an established grammar of his own, and he is confronted with a grammar (that of the superstrate language) which is quite different from his own (considerably more different in Afro-European contacts than in inter-European ones). However, there is one interesting difference. The future speaker of a pidgin usually comes from an area where several different languages are already spoken; he is very often already a multilingual. Thanks to the total absence of study in this area, we cannot say what difference this fact might make to his acquisition of a language of totally different structure, but we might plausibly guess that he would bring to the task rather more generalised hypotheses than the monolingual would, i.e. they would be based, not on the grammar of his native language so much as on those grammatical features which he had found to be common to all the languages he knew.

This latter point, if correct, could explain an otherwise puzzling feature of pidgin–creole grammars in general. In Chapter 2 we noted that, while the tense-aspect system of Guyanese and other creoles differed sharply from European models, the languages seemed also to differ from specific African models in so far as the latter have been described. However, we also noted a small amount of evidence that the features most characteristic of creole verbal systems might be widely distributed among African languages. We can now suggest that, as described above, the future pidgin-speaker began by discarding from his hypothesised tense-aspect system all features pertaining to the individual languages he knew which were not shared by all of them, i.e. all features that would be treated as marked by a theory of universal markedness. If this were the case, the hypotheses formed by Africans would show a high degree of similarity irrespective of the individual's linguistic background. At the same time, they would be so generalised that, when the postulated rules were fleshed out with (somewhat reinterpreted) European morphemes, the resultant output would be just about comprehensible to European ears. However, this surface output would be interpreted by Europeans in the light of their own grammars, i.e. different underlying structures would be manipulated to yield similar surface structures, as proposed by Silverstein (1972) for the earlier stages of pidgin development. Thus, for instance, when an African speaker said '*bin*', the European would not say, 'Ah, he must be referring to one action which happened before another'; he would say, 'Ah, he must be referring to something in the past.' Similarly, when the African speaker referred to an obviously past event without the *bin*, the European would not say, 'Oh, I must have misinterpreted this man's grammar'; he would probably say something like, 'These ignorant natives can't tell the difference between past and present.'

Had Euro-African contact proceeded on non-exploitive terms, the situation would doubtless have developed along the usual foreign-language-learning lines, with some Africans speaking European languages fluently, others speaking them passably, others having only a smattering, but all retaining control of their native tongues. The slave trade disrupted this pattern, isolating many Africans at a very early or null stage of European-language acquisition and cutting them off from their own language communities, thereby virtually obliging them to use the imperfectly acquired European language as their only medium of communication. Thus those creoles which had minimal subsequent contact with European languages (e.g. Saramaccan and the other creoles of interior Surinam) would have underlying grammars which represented Africans' earliest and least-corrected hypotheses about European grammar; basilectal creoles in other areas (e.g. Guyana, Jamaica) would have slightly more corrected hypotheses. However, until after Emancipation, social divisions would insure that, for the vast majority of speakers, both evidence for correction and (perhaps even more important) motivation for correction would be extremely limited.

After Emancipation, the language-learning process so sharply interrupted by slavery was resumed, but it was resumed with a difference. The difference may be best illustrated by an analogy. The normal second-language learning situation may be compared to that of a man who already has a house building a second house. The second house will generally conform to universal ideas of what a house should be like, but it will be made of materials different to the first and may quite likely have a different design. While he is building his second house the man will not be comfortable in it but he can always go back and stay in his first house until he feels like doing some more work on the second. If and when the second house is completed he can commute freely between the two.

The pidgin-speaker is a man who has just begun to build his second house when some disaster destroys his first one. He has to abandon it and use what he can salvage from it to complete the second one. Naturally, the shape of the second house is constrained by the materials he has to use. It resembles neither the house he used to have nor the new one he envisaged. Still, his children grow up in it and to them it is home, a house in its own right like any other. But then, one day, generations later, an important someone comes along. This someone says that the house is only an inadequate copy of what it was meant to be. He produces what he claims were the authentic plans. He insists that the house must be remodelled to conform with them. Since there is nowhere else to go, this remodelling must take place while the family continues to live in it, regardless of the inconvenience and embarrassment that this may cause them. When he has gone, the family disagrees about what should be done. Some are for obedience, others for resistance, some are apathetic and will do what seems convenient. No agreement is reached, so finally everyone treats his own room as a separate entity. Some radically remodel theirs, others make superficial alterations. Others defiantly leave everything exactly as it is – and so the matter rests, to this day.

This constitutes a capsule history of the pidgin–creole–decreolization cycle, from which it should be clear that when I speak of 'correcting hypotheses', I do so in a technical, and indeed teleological, sense – certainly not in a prescriptive one. To conceptualise the overall cycle in linguistic terms, it is convenient in many ways to think of the Guyanese community as taking three hundred years to learn English, even though such a picture is (a) grossly unfair to the linguistic capacities of the speakers involved, (b) certainly not what they subjectively thought they were doing, and (c) in no sense what the author thinks they ought to have been doing. However, the analogy is particularly effective with respect to that part of the cycle with which we are most directly concerned, i.e. decreolisation. In the course of decreolisation, speakers are strung out across the continuum between 'native' creole and 'target' English in much the same way as second-language learners are strung out across the continuum between L1 and L2. In each case, the successive stages of the continuum constitute hypothetical grammars of the target language, each slightly closer to that target than its antecedent. But the relationships between stages are not forward-looking only, at least as far as creoles are concerned; each stage, as we have seen, represents a minimal adaptation of its predecessor, and can therefore be regarded as constrained by that predecessor more strongly than by the ultimate target. We do not yet know whether such constraints characterise successive stages of the second-language continuum, but there seems no reason to suppose the contrary.

There are, of course, some points of difference between continuums of the two types. These, however, seem to stem from extra-linguistic rather than linguistic factors. In the first place, second-language learners do not constitute a closed community, as speakers in the various stages of decreolisation effectively do. It follows that second-language learners very seldom speak to one another in their shared target language. The rare exceptions usually occur when two learners of the same second language with different mother tongues are obliged to communicate. Where a mother tongue is shared, however, one can observe a marked unwillingness to communicate in the language being learnt; although non-behaviourist teachers sometimes recommend this procedure for purposes of practice, speakers feel unnatural in it and quickly clam up or revert to their native language. Speakers in a creole continuum, on the other hand, have no-one but themselves to talk to, and nothing but their own variety of creole (or their neighbours') to talk in. In the second place, second-language learning is a conscious and consciously directed process, which the type of change characteristic of decreolisation very seldom is. It follows from the conjunction of these two facts that stages in the second-language continuum tend to be more transient (since the learner is striving to push on to the next stage) and that there will be a greater degree of apparently unpredictable variation (since stages do not become reinforced by positive feedback from other speakers at the same stage). Apart from such considerations, the analogy between decreolising speakers and second-language learners seems to be valid in most respects.

But if in fact the changes that occur within the Guyanese continuum resemble those which occur when a speaker acquires a quite dissimilar language, what are the implications for the concept of 'linguistic system'? In the first instance, let us get rid of the idea that a second-language-learning continuum is automatically debarred from constituting a system. In fact, the only real basis for that idea is that such a continuum is not *used* in the way a system is used, i.e. for communication *amongst* those who share it rather than *between* those who share it and those who control only the target language. If only linguistic factors were involved, there is every reason to suppose that it could be so used. For instance, most persons who speak a foreign language with any degree of fluency must have had the following experience: together with a compatriot who speaks the language less fluently you come into the company of a foreign monolingual; your compatriot addresses a remark to the monolingual; the monolingual fails to understand it; you, however, understand it immediately; you translate it into something that is at least closer to the foreign language than the original version; the foreign monolingual then understands it. You understand your compatriot's remark perfectly and immediately by virtue of the fact that you share with him the inter-system between your language and the foreigner's, whereas the foreigner does not; further, you share that inter-system precisely because you have travelled that path yourself – you have, yourself, begun from the same beginning and have, at some time in the past, stood at a position within that inter-system approximately if not exactly the same as that at which your compatriot stands today.[8] Of course, the inter-system does not work in the opposite direction. Though your less fluent compatriot will understand you better than he understands the foreign native speaker, it by no means follows that he will understand everything you say – precisely because he does not yet (and indeed may never) stand in the position where you now stand.

Similar, if not identical, phenomena may be observed in the creole continuum. Broadly speaking, it is easier for a person to understand 'down' than 'up'; the mesolectal speaker or the acrolectal speaker *born within the system* will generally understand pretty well everything the basilectal speaker says, whereas the basilectal speaker may often be confused by the acrolectal speaker if he is young or otherwise limited in experience (Reisman [1965:270] records a telling illustration of the general truth that even pedagogues who are bitter enemies of creole may be forced to use it to make children understand). The only difference between the two types of continuum is that in the creole one, knowledge need not be gained by going through the whole continuum in terms of one's own production, as the L2 learner does (though in fact the street speech of even upper-middle-class children is usually mid-mesolectal if not lower); it can be acquired through social contacts.

Thus, if the creole continuum constitutes a system (as we have given good reason to believe), the language-learning continuum between two distinct languages must equally constitute a system, and the 'Anglo-Chinese' and 'Anglo-Spanish' of native English-speaking learners of Chinese and Spanish must have as much right to the title 'system' as English, Spanish and Chinese (themselves all clearly 'multilectal' languages, it should be noted). But if the reader quite naturally revolts from innumerable new 'systems' of this kind, there is a preferable solution, first hinted at in Bickerton 1971a (p. 488). This is to regard neither Anglo-Chinese or Anglo-Spanish, on the one hand, nor English, Chinese or Spanish, on the other, as constituting systems – not because they are too pluralistic, as one would have to conclude from a static, monolectal definition of 'system', but because they are only partial and arbitrary interpretations of the unique repository of System – the human *faculté de langage* itself.

There is much to recommend such a decision. Sapir's notorious dictum 'all grammars leak' remains as true as when it was written, and indeed can

---

[8] It remains an open question to what extent such an inter-system would also be accessible to native speakers of a foreign language who had second-language English. An anecdote by Reibel (personal communication) indicates that English-speaking Russians could understand an English learner's Russian more readily than monolingual Russians could.

more clearly be seen to be true, in spite of (or perhaps one should say, because of) the existence of more efficient grammars. The boundaries of any language are therefore ill-defined. At the same time, increased concentration on underlying structure and putative universals has shown that languages overlap in terms of shared rules much more than Sapir's generation supposed. One can no longer claim with any degree of confidence that 'feature x is found in language A but not in language B'; feature x has an awkward way of suddenly turning up, either in some 'deviant' variety of B, or at some sub-surface level. The sharpest divisions that remain are merely lexical, and even these are disappearing as generative semantics disintegrates the autonomous word.

Yet, while 'languages' come to be perceived as increasingly overlapping and ill-defined, 'language' emerges as an ever more readily definable object. It is probably already true that we can say with more confidence 'x is or is not a feature of human language' than we can say 'x is or is not a feature of language A'. Fairly soon we may be able to specify with absolute precision what human language can and cannot contain. Indeed, it begins to seem as though there is a Second Saussurean Paradox.[9] Saussure regarded *la langue* as principled and describable, *la langage* as unprincipled and '*inconnaisible*'; a reverse relationship may well turn out to be closer to the truth.

Such a conclusion would fit well with a number of recent developments in linguistic theory. For instance, 'natural phonology' as proposed by Stampe (1969) suggests that what we actually do in first-language acquisition is not so much acquire rules as 'unlearn' natural rules, i.e. develop a set of constraints imposed on those rules. While such constraints may not be arbitrary in an absolute sense (they must be drawn from a stock of language-possible constraints, and presumably are interrelated in ways that would render impossible any kind of purely random selection by a given language), they must be relatively arbitrary as compared with the non-language-specific rules they constrain. Similarly, generative semantics suggests that there may be a finite stock of atomic predicates common to all languages, which different languages lexicalise in different ways. As such theories develop, both creole continuums and inter-systems will increasingly be seen as objects of study potentially more revealing than supposedly discrete natural languages, in so

---

[9] The First Saussurean Paradox is, of course, that stated by Labov (1970:32): 'The social aspect of language is studied by observing one individual, but the individual aspect only by observing language in its social context.' In terms of the present study, even the division of language into 'social' and 'individual' aspects is not a particularly meaningful one.

far as they pose more stringent tests of what language (as distinct from languages) can contain. At the same time, acceptance of the fact that there are no systems but only System, and that any arbitrary interpretation of that system (i.e. any so-called 'natural language') has the potential of merging into any other in a principled way, will enable us to reconcile the apparent paradoxes which arise from the four best-attested facts about human language: that all languages seem different, but that all are somehow alike, and that all languages are systematic, and yet that all are subject to continuous change.

Before we move on to consider the nature of internalised grammars, it is worth pointing out that the viewpoint of the last paragraph, heterodox though it may appear, is much more faithful even to the superficial facts about language than is the conventional one, if we exclude the artificial conditions of the last few centuries. Most of modern linguistics predicates large, stable, quasi-homogeneous language communities with predominantly monoglot speakers; but these did not exist prior to the emergence of the centralised state four or five millennia ago, and still do not exist, save sometimes on paper, over large areas of the inhabited globe. In those areas which the state has only begun to penetrate, the norm remains as it has been over the greater part of human existence: language communities too small to be fully viable social units, upon which patterns of exogamy and/or trade impose a high degree of bilingualism or even multilingualism. Indeed, in such areas, where illiteracy is widespread, the native quite often has fluent command of four, five or even more languages, while the average literate American or European can count himself lucky if he can make himself understood in any tongue other than his own; and although there have never been so many language-teachers as there are today, it is probable that the number of man-languages [10] is smaller now than at any previous time in man's sojourn on earth. It follows that the natural condition of an individual human speaker is to have a competence that embraces several possibly similar but certainly distinct varieties of language, plus all the inter-systems that relate them to his own.

Such a competence is considerably different from the monoglot competence envisaged by Chomsky and other early generativists. Unfortunately, there is little more we can say about it for the present, because the whole of linguistic inquiry has been geared to deliberately ignoring its existence. That fieldworkers were well aware of it can be shown by, e.g. Bloomfield's description of his Menomini informants (1927:437). That, forty years on, they

---

[10] This somewhat ugly, if useful, coinage is modelled upon, and similar in meaning to, 'man-hours', i.e. 'languages per man'.

were still determined to dodge its implications can be shown by solemn warnings against the use of bilingual informants (Samarin 1967b:35, Gudschinsky 1967:6), or desiderata for a 'good corpus' (Samarin 1967b:55 ff.), or anecdotes such as that of the linguist who dropped his Hausa informant like a hot coal when it was found that he was a native speaker of Ibo (Hodge 1958).[11] Methods were aimed at finding discrete languages, and sure enough, discrete languages were what they found.

In the absence of such knowledge, I am going to suggest that the polylingual competence of many speakers in such areas as the Amazon basin, Dahomey and the New Guinea highlands differs in degree, rather than in kind, from the polylectal competence of our Guyanese speakers, and that this, in turn, differs only in degree from the competence of speakers of a standardised language.

In Chapter 3, note 11, I referred to remarks of Chomsky such as 'competence (the speaker–hearer's knowledge of his language)' (1965:4) or 'a generative grammar attempts to specify what the speaker actually knows . . . the knowledge of the language that provides the basis for actual use of language by a speaker–hearer' (ibid:8–9). But as any dictionary will tell us, and as Ayer (1965:3–4) specifically points out, *know* is among the most ambiguous of verbs; to know a person or a place, Beethoven's Fifth or differential calculus, the date of Waterloo or how to play the piano, are all quite different things, some of which are themselves ambiguous. 'I know John,' for instance, may mean anything between 'I can recognise John when I see him' to 'I have a complete understanding of John's character, motives etc.' And while, as Austin (1946) showed, *know* is a performative verb, so that we do not have to have access to John's mind to say, 'I know that John is angry,' it is slightly less clear what is meant when *know* is predicated of persons other than oneself, e.g. 'I know that everyone knows his own language'; if, as in the Austin formulation, *know* is simply a claim to be sure of something, it is hard to know quite what is entailed when such a claim is made on another's behalf, and it is no clearer when one considers that 'another' in this case refers, not to a person, but an abstraction – the 'ideal speaker–hearer'.

This is not a mere game with words. Chomsky himself admits a 'system-

---

[11] In all fairness to Carleton Hodge, it must be emphasised that he subsequently realised the possible importance and interest of such speakers, and the paper cited discusses what he was able to salvage from his original data. One wonders how often similar experiences must have befallen other linguists, who have not told and, presumably, have not repented either.

atic ambiguity' between two senses of grammar, that already stated (the grammar that 'attempts to specify what the [ideal] speaker actually knows', i.e. the grammar the linguist writes) and that which 'the child has developed and internally represented . . . on the basis of observation of what we may call primary linguistic data' (1965:25). The knowledge that is envisaged in the first interpretation must be perfect and complete (and, presumably, without internal contradiction, though this is a point we will not press now). The knowledge that is envisaged in the second interpretation is obviously anything but these things; nobody knows 'all of English', and it is an open question to what extent the knowledge of English of any two native speakers is the same. Yet, by this device of 'systematic ambiguity', the ideal is smuggled into the real, and all the characteristics of the Chomskyan ideal are, by implication, fostered on the flesh-and-blood speaker and his individual representation of the grammar of his language.

Let us consider, then, what real speakers may really be supposed to know. One might begin by supposing that they would at least know 'their vernacular'. But in an evolving system like that of Guyana, what is their vernacular? If by 'vernacular' we imply some unitary, monolectal variety within the system that is somehow more natural to them than any other, there is no clear evidence that any such entity exists, since from an early age, speakers are exposed to a large part of, if not all, the range of variation that exists within the community. However, since the maturational cycle in creole society has not been studied in the present work, let us assume that such a relatively homogeneous vernacular is what is first acquired. But even if this is the case, then knowledge of other varieties must follow it rapidly. This knowledge is evidenced by the ability of speakers to adjust their output in a basilectal or mesolectal direction, to give imitations of the output of habitual speakers of other varieties, and to understand things that are said to them in those varieties. The question we have to answer is simply: how can such knowledge be stored in the mind?

Let us first dispose of two plausible suggestions. One would be that the different varieties are stored as sets of optional alternatives, e.g. *mi/a* for first-person-singular subject pronoun, *bin/did* for [+anterior], *na/not* for verbal negator, *a/-ing* for continuative marker, and so on. However, as we saw in Chapter 1, this hypothesis is a non-starter since, if it operated, strings which took random combinations from such options would all be equally grammatical; in fact, strings such as **mi did not a go* 'I was not/had not been going' are hopelessly ungrammatical. The second would be a more sophisticated version of this one, and would say, in effect, that the different options (or different combinations of the options) are socially, rather than linguistically marked, and that lectal mixtures like the one just cited are barred in a way and for reasons similar to those that operate in the case of sentences such as ' *procrastination drinks quadruplicity' – as the latter are judged semantically anomalous because semantically ill-formed, so the former would be judged socially meaningless because socially ill-formed. A very specific proposal to this effect, envisaging the fusing of several different options into units he calls 'dialemes', is made in Edwards 1968, but generally similar assumptions about relationships between linguistic rules proper and sociolinguistic rules underlie much recent work on 'language in context', e.g. Robin Lakoff 1972, Fillmore 1972, and indeed the whole Hymesian concept of 'communicative competence'.

This hypothesis, plausible enough at first sight, looks less certain the more one looks at primary speech data. While, with the help of a little hindsight, a plausible contextual explanation can be given for very many stylistic shifts, there are many more which operate in quite unpredictable ways. There is no conceivable reason why 242's speech to his friend's six-year-old son should be more formal, not merely than his speech to his friend, but than a good deal of his speech to me – and yet it is:

> 5.1 I want this piece of pencil for my birthday. C—— is going to give me [pretends to take child's pencil]. You will give me this pencil for my birthday, C——? True? Oh, well, you're a good boy. Come, let me hug you up, come, come, come, come [child determinedly holds on to pencil]. Well all right, put it up – don't let nobody use it. (242/25–8/317)

There is no conceivable reason why, among intimate friends, and with no contextual stimulus, 30 should oscillate between

> 5.2 *mi main tel mi a i – if na i, a hu mi mos se? a i sen am, mi main gi mi a i* (30/14–15/388) 'I think it was him – if it wasn't him, who could it have been? It was him sent it, I think it was him.'

and,

> 5.3 If I had a pen I woulda write C—— tonight because I don't know when again I'll – I'll write. (30/7–8/390)

in the course of the same conversation.

Similarly, any 'contextual' theorist would have predicted that when the same Bushlot speaker was recorded both by myself, an acrolectal stranger of a different race and complexion, and by Arnold Persaud, a native of the village who had known the speaker for many years (all other factors being kept, as far as possible, equal), my recording would invariably show a less basilectal speech level than Persaud's. In fact, while this happened in a number of cases (for instance, Examples 5.7 and 5.8 below), there were some where there was little or no perceptible difference in speech levels, and in at least three cases (2/186, 9/188 and 19/169) the speaker either followed basilectal rules more faithfully in my recording, or produced basilectal forms which did not appear in Persaud's, or both. For instance, 169, whose general level of production is indicated in tables in Chapter 4, actually produced a *sa* form (in quotation, admittedly) as well as a percentage of past-reference stem forms higher than that in his appearance as 19. Speaker 188 uses *yuus tu* and *das* with Persaud in contexts where she uses *a* with me:

> 5.4 *dem das plant dem faam an ting an dem das yuus tu stan de.* (9/27/10)
> 5.5 *dem a stan abak an dem a plant faam an ting an dem a stan rait de.*
> (188/21/247)

The examples discussed here form only a small part of the massive evidence that could be produced to demonstrate the independence of grammar from context. Choice of style is governed, not by any inter-subjective and objectively perceptible features in the situational context, but by the autonomous and fluctuating feelings of the speaker himself or herself. Obviously situations affect people's feelings, but they do so in puzzlingly different ways for different individuals, and in any case it is not the situation as objectively perceived by the observer, but the situation as subjectively perceived by the actor, which constitutes the operant factor – and only one among several, at that.

A further argument against the incorporation of social or contextual constraints in grammars is that any such procedure reverses the laws of cause and effect. The somewhat misleading title of Labov's seminal paper on sound change (Labov 1963) is worth noting in this respect. In fact, the phenomenon of diphthong-centralisation therein described does not represent a sound change *sensu stricto*. Centralised /ai/ antedated the social conditions responsible for its rapid contemporary spread; what happened was not that the influx of outsiders *caused* native Martha's Vineyarders to *introduce* a change, rather that they selected for intensification a feature that already existed as a variable in island speech and then generalised it to /au/ by dropping the original [-back] constraint.

This argument applies *a fortiori* in a creole setting. The complex layers of the grammar we have tried to unravel in the two preceding chapters represent an apparatus far more complex than could possibly be required to carry social or contextual information. However, it can be, and is, exploited by local speakers for purposes of this kind.

It could be argued that, for synchronic purposes, the purely linguistic origins of the continuum are irrelevant; if speakers now identify the different levels with different social and contextual parameters, even though, as has just been shown, such identification may not always be consistent or unanimous, surely we should identify them this way in our written grammar. But there are two important reasons why we cannot do this. One is that, as previous chapters have tried to show, the continuum consists of 'living linguistic history', as it were, and thus the synchronic–diachronic distinction is hardly tenable even if we are merely trying to account for what the synchronic speaker knows. This point is arguable, but the second is irrefutable. In the latter part of this chapter, I shall show that the kind of 'code-switching' or 'style-shifting' carried out within the Guyanese system involves not merely the alternation of socially codable forms within a fixed grammatical framework, but different grammatical analyses of the verbal system at different levels. Thus, even if outputs are socially coded, the grammar that generates them must be both polylectal and purely linguistic in nature, in so far as it must contain more than one set of distinct underlying rules in order to produce the correct surface tense and aspect forms. Such knowledge is linguistic knowledge, no matter what way you look at it, and it would not cease to be so even if the resultant outputs were 100% correlatable with extra-linguistic factors. For while socially oriented models may account for the distribution of surface forms (and may therefore have a limited validity where phonological features are concerned) they can have no function in accounting for inter-relationships between underlying rules. For instance, a speaker such as 242 has (as we shall show) probably got a 'communicative competence' rule which says something like, 'Merge continuative and iterative categories into a single non-punctual one when addressing or quoting a basilectal speaker'; but before he can have any such rule, he has to know, in some sense, exactly what continuative, iterative and non-punctual categories are, and to be able to handle them systematically. In other words, they must first be stored in his grammar in terms of purely linguistic information. Moreover, knowledge of this kind must be highly structured, more highly structured than sociolinguistic knowledge, since, as we have noted, sociolinguistic breaches are commoner than linguistic ones. The only question that remains is, how is such knowledge represented in internalised grammars?

The simplest model would be one which proposed that, in every case, a speaker had simply one set of underlying rules, plus a number of different spelling rules, so that the same bundle of underlying syntactico-semantic features may be represented by two or more surface realisations. A great deal of surface variation can be accounted for in this way. For example, a speaker whose output shows *a/-ing* variation, or *bin/did* variation, cannot therefore be said to have two grammars, or even one grammar with conflicting rules, except at a relatively superficial level. Even where much wider variations were involved, it would be possible to argue that a speaker was still adhering to what was (for him) a unitary set of rules. This argument is strengthened by the considerable degree of overlap between different levels of the continuum, which in some areas spans the entire system. Take an output such as *no* 'know'. This may as easily be produced by a basilectal as an acrolectal speaker, though, if the analysis of the foregoing chapters is correct, the identical output will be generated by two quite distinct underlying systems: one which first divides verbs into statives and non-statives, and then allots the zero form to non-anteriors, and one which first divides verbs into past and non-past, and then allots the zero form to non-pasts. On this feature taken in isolation there is no way of determining which underlying rule a speaker has.

Such cases, it is true, are rare, and it is usually possible to determine from other utterances whether a speaker has the main stative rule or not. However, there is still a possibility that when a speaker shifts styles, he maintains the same rules throughout, irrespective of the surface forms he may use. We have noted, in the last two chapters, a number of inter-personal differences in the handling of rules at what appears to be the same level – in the acquisition of *have*, of past tense forms, and so on. It could well be that such differences arise through precisely such shifting into (for the speaker) relatively little-known territory. To put it in prescriptive terms, a speaker handling a less familiar lect may well speak it incorrectly (if we take the outputs of habitual users of that lect as constituting the norm), although not so incorrectly as to provoke overt correction from a community which necessarily has an unusually high degree of tolerance for variation. Thus, even if the lects he appeared to control were widely distant, the underlying structure of his verbal (or other) sub-system would in fact remain the same.

Evidence on this issue is very hard to obtain, because of the impossibility of knowing what constitutes a speaker's total range, or even what part or quantity of that range he is utilising on any given occasion. A speaker may appear to be talking at his most acrolectal level, yet there is no guarantee that in, say, a job application or a court case he might not produce features yet more acrolectal. A speaker may appear to be talking at his most basilectal level, yet again, there is no guarantee that in, say, a fight with a neighbour or a meeting with a childhood acquaintance he might not produce something still closer to the absolute basilect. Similarly, for a person one records on only a single occasion, one cannot be sure what one has tapped; Labov's 'channel cues' (Labov 1964) are of limited use in a creole system, for I have had speakers breathe faster, laugh, open beer-bottles etc. while using what I could prove to be more acrolectal than their most spontaneous level of speech. As indicated by our discussion of 'contextual' variation above, it is quite impossible to forecast what effect an interviewer may have on different individuals.

It is true that one could always fall back on the argument, suggested in Chapter 1, that an assessment of competence within a creole continuum cannot be based on production alone, but must be related to the (putatively pan-lectal) range of the hearer. However, it would still obviously be preferable if we could produce evidence for polylectal competence in terms of hard speech data, and I shall now try to do this in addition to, subsequently, developing the argument from receptive capacity.

Until someone invents a reliable and replicable method of sampling a person's total productive range, anything said on this subject must be extremely tentative. However, a number of Guyanese speakers were recorded on at least two different occasions and either by different interviewers, or in different contexts, or both. On the basis of these recordings, one may make certain observations which, even if largely anecdotal, may be of some use and interest to future investigators in this field.

In the first place, speakers seem to fall, impressionistically at least, into two classes, which we may describe as 'single-range' speakers and 'split-range' speakers. A single-range speaker, wherever located within the system, appears to control contiguous lects. One unmistakable characteristic of such speakers is their tendency to shift lects without any apparent contextual or even topical motivation. For many such speakers, one gets the impression that conversation is an experimental art form, and that they take a positive delight in exploiting their wide linguistic resources to entertain and perhaps sometimes startle their listeners. Certainly, their formal speech is much less varied than their colloquial. We have seen, for instance, something of the range of variation which 30 covers in uninhibited conversation; however, in the company of acrolectal strangers, all her speech may be fairly represented by examples such as

5.6 Well J—— went away but B—— has a boy there who was working with
J—— for years, over twenty years and he left J—— and came across at
B——. B—— and J—— were partners and they came round, well, most

of B——'s girls came across with – ahm, J—— girls came over with
B——, so they have new girls there at Plaisance you know; all the old
girls there at Plaisance actually come across at B.V. [Beterverwagting,
another village], so they hadn't to start it from scratch because the girls
knew the work already. (30/6–11/397)

A split-range speaker, on the other hand, is one who appears to control
lects which are quite widely separated within the continuum, without con-
trolling intermediate ones. It could, of course, always be argued that a split-
range speaker is simply a broad single-range speaker who happens not to
have operated intervening lects in the presence of the observer. While this is
always a possibility, there is at least one good argument against it. This is
that a split-range speaker seems characteristically to have little room for
manoeuvre in either of his ranges; his outputs resemble those of a bilingual
rather than those of a person varying within a single system, in that while his
two discrete levels may interfere with one another, shifts from one to the
other are always sharply and unambiguously marked. Further, such speakers
are readily explicable on social grounds. They are rare, in comparison with
single-range speakers, and the only sure cases I know of are people from
rural Indian villages who have been exposed to the acrolect but who have
had very little exposure to lower-class urban speech. While it might seem
interesting to test the split-range hypothesis by engineering confrontations
between such speakers and urban mesolectal ones, the psychological and
ethnosocial obstacles involved (since the latter would inevitably be African)
would make any results hard to interpret.

Some idea of the variety in productive range in quite a small sample of
Guyanese speakers may be given by Fig. 5.1. It is admittedly impres-
sionistic, and inevitably based solely on the distribution of surface forms, but
although the precise limits of the spans may not be quite accurate, their extent and position relative to one another are reasonably so. As the figure indicates, there appears to be no constraint on the scope of ranges save that no
range can touch both ends of the continuum and perhaps no really broad
range can touch either end. This bears out Labov's observation that he has
'not encountered any non-standard speakers who gained good control of a
standard language, and still retained control of the non-standard vernacular'
(1970:52). It should, however, be noted that he is working in terms of a relatively simple model which postulates two discrete varieties with, apparently,
nothing in between. If, instead, one uses a model of many different but contiguous lects, as we have done, the sharpness of Labov's picture is blurred
somewhat; however, it appears to remain true that control of widely dis-
persed lects is indeed never absolute. Though all the empirical evidence

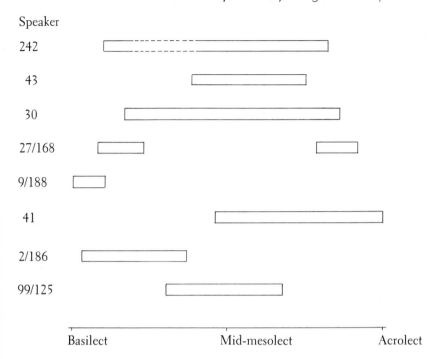

Fig. 5.1. Approximate ranges of Guyanese speakers

NOTE: Broken lines for 242 indicate a possible discontinuity in his range.

points in the same direction, it is still not clear to me whether this principle is necessarily maintained in all cases (one would like to meet a speaker whose life-style obliged him to generate approximately equal outputs of diverse varieties), and, if it is, what the precise cause might be. It hardly needs stating that the possibilities for research in this field, as in others discussed in the present chapter, are practically limitless.

However, some facts can be gleaned from a close study of those speakers whose outputs do vary substantially, whether within the same context or in different ones. Comparing two such outputs is never easy, since differences in content introduce uncontrollable variables, and even where content is substantially the same, it may not always be easy to tell whether the same or different rules are being applied. This may be illustrated by quoting two versions of the same story by a Bushlot informant:

> 5.7 *so wan nait wen dem soja bina patrool mi sidong in front mi shap pan*
> *wan bensh an mi si dem soja swing in pan mi an aks mi wa mi a du de, se*
> *if mi a wachman fi kil niigro, an de staat fi slap mi bihain mi hed an*

japaniiz slap mi an dem tek a beenet an dem spor mi an de se, kech op-steez, an mi – an mi ron laik hel! (12/25–9/13) 'So one night when the soldiers were patrolling I was sitting on a bench in front of my shop and I saw the soldiers swing in on me and they asked me what I was doing and whether I was watching out to kill Negroes, and they started to slap the back of my head and give me karate chops, and they took a bayonet and pricked me with it and said, "Get upstairs!" and I – and I ran like hell!'

5.8 About seven o'clock one – one night, four soldier was passing by the road and come in suddenly and ask us what we doing there. Well me tell the the the the the, ahm, the head soldier that, ahm, we just watching. Well he say, "Get moving!" and he start to, to take the gun with the bayonet and he start to spur me 'pon me ribs – to keep walking – oh, and to go up-stairs. (177/15–19/227)

If we compare the speed and vividness of the basilectal version with the relatively colourless and hesitant style of the mesolectal one, we can have little doubt which is more natural to the speaker; and yet, if one excises the hesitations and reformulations, the latter output differs little if at all from that which might be produced by a speaker to whom the mesolectal level does represent his own most natural speech. Let us look at some close verbal correspondences:

(a) *bina patrool* – was passing
(b) *swing in* – come in
(c) *aks mi* – ask us
(d) *mi a du* – we doing
(e) *mi a wachman* – we just watching
(f) *de staat* – he start

In (b), (c) and (f), both versions have punctual non-statives in the stem form, indicating no change in this category – though it is worth noting that the second version uses *start* + infinitive where the first uses a string of fi-nite verbs, *tek, spor, kech, ron* (behaviour typical of insecure speakers who choose structures which enjoy wide distribution over the continuum so as to avoid others, as e.g. here the English past, of whose existence they are pas-sively aware but which they are unable to process). However, (a), (d) and (e) are slightly more complex. The *was/ø* contrast between (a) and (d) – (e) might lead one to suppose that 177 must have acquired a ± past distinction, if only for continuatives, but this is not really the case. Although not strictly + anterior (unless the meaning is 'at the time when soldiers used to patrol', as it well could be) the use of *bina* in (a) is validated by the basilectal gram-mar just in case a durative past action happens to carry a definite time marker (see Example 2.58 and discussion thereof) such as *wan nait*. Thus *was*, far from indicating the introduction of an English-type past distinction, is for 12/177 simply a respelling of *bin*. That this analysis is fundamentally correct is indicated by the fact that the $\emptyset$ + -*ing* form, which at a slightly more advanced stage of the grammar would unambiguously indicate non-past, in fact does not do so here; the verb-phrases of both (d) and (e) require a past marker when translated into English. The speaker, then, is simply applying the ± anterior distinction to continuatives in a basilectal way; he has not yet acquired rule (12) of Chapter 3, unlike a 'born' mesolectal such as 99/125:

> 5.9 He say where he *was working* he *used* to look after workers. (125/6/174)
> 5.10 So he *pushing* them around ['now' clear from context]. (125/7/174)

If, however, we examine the outputs of speakers with a wider range than that of 12/177, we will find that more than the respelling of items in a unitary grammar is involved. Speaker 242 is a case in point. We noted in Chapter 1 that he controlled neither the basilectal nor the acrolectal extreme, and indeed he sometimes makes 'mistakes' more glaring than the ones noted there; for instance,

> 5.11 *mi no awi kudn a biin paas ya* (242/13/322) 'I knew we couldn't have got through here.'

should more properly have been

> 5.12 *mi no se awi na bin kyan paas ya.*[12]

if he was trying to represent the extreme basilect.

However, apart from such details, his analysis of the tense-aspect system substantially follows that of the present study. As noted in our discussion of context above, he uses, in his imitations of basilectal speakers, a single non-punctual category marked with *a*:

> 5.13 *dem a week mi. if mi a sliip somtaim dem a biit mi an week mi fu go mek ti* (242/16–17/324) 'They wake me up. If I'm asleep, sometimes they beat me and wake me up to go and make tea.'
> 5.14 *bai a wa yu a se?* (242/5/325) 'What are you saying, boy?'

[12] Not, note, *mi bin no . . .* – even though the English gloss must use *knew* – since the speaker *knew and still knows* what he states, i.e. the reference of the verb is not [+ anterior]. This example illustrates yet another of the ways in which the ± anterior distinction differs from the ± past one; for English *know*, on the other hand, could readily be interpreted as meaning 'I know now, though I didn't know then' in this and similar contexts, while *no* carries no such implication.

In free conversation with his friend, however, he uses *doz* in iterative contexts:

> 5.15 I does tell him that his eye bend [sc. I distinguish him by the fact that he squints]. (242/7/317)
> 5.16 Does be nice, man, you know. (242/19/317)

but *-ing* in continuative ones:

> 5.17 I say, 'Ruthie, what you doing?' (242/26/316)

where he now also makes a tense distinction, using *was* in contexts where no basilectal speaker would use *bin:*

> 5.18 She had that boy when she was nursing that puppy. (242/8/317)

In his speech to me, however, he uses stem-only for iteratives:

> 5.19 You generally go up with the small – the easiest side. (242/19/319)
> 5.20 Every mail boat that goes up the Kurupung River they sends money down. (242/9/324)

and *does* occurs in an English fashion:

> 5.21 Therefore a man just doesn't care what he say or what he does. (242/6/323)

This means that he must be operating at least three sets of rules. In one, there is a single non-punctual category opposed to the punctual one and marked with *a;* in another, what is covered by the non-punctual category in the first is divided into continuative and iterative categories, one marked with *-ing,* the other with *doz,* while an English-past-type distinction is imported into the former; in a third set, iteratives are now grouped with gnomic or stative non-pasts –

> 5.22 They calls him the general. (242/3/325)
> 5.23 Really, if you want to come home with money. (242/29/320)

– and all are left unmarked, while *do* appears regularly inflected as a support verb. Clearly, 242 cannot be working with a unitary grammar and a range of different surface forms. To generate the outputs he produces requires knowledge of conflicting rules at widely different levels of the continuum.

If space allowed, many more examples of rule alternation could be given. We shall limit ourselves to two equally striking ones. The first concerns 41. Earlier (Examples 3.17–19) we noted how 41 retains the basilectal rule that blocks aspect markers in non-specific temporals, and which therefore blocks *doz* in mid-mesolectal speakers:

5.24 (= 3.17) Then what you *does* talk, what you *does* talk when you and the girls get together? (41/23/180)

This and similar utterances occurred when she was talking to schoolchildren in Black Bush Polder, a predominantly basilectal area. However, when talking to schoolchildren in mesolectal Wismar, in school and in the presence of teachers, *does* appeared only in contexts such as the following:

5.25 Where *does* your father work? (41/20/59)

and in questions structurally similar to that of 5.24, no morphological distinction is made between iteratives and non-specific temporals, given that both are non-past:

5.26 Well when you *move* what *happen*, tell me when you *move* what *happen*. (41/9–10/55)

Whatever may have been the case in her childhood, the level of 5.25–6 now comes more naturally to 41 than that of 5.24. However, 5.24 and numerous examples like it show that when she does 'shift down', she does not simply relexify her current acrolectal grammar; if she did this, she would treat all iteratives alike, and 5.24 would have read, in part, 'when you and the girls *does get* together'. Whether she has retained the necessary rules or relearnt them, her output clearly shows that conflicting rules form part of her internalised grammar.

One might argue that 41 is a linguistically sophisticated speaker, whom one would expect to be a skilled manipulator of rules. This is true enough, though the rules involved here are not of a type likely to be known consciously, and to the best of my knowledge the non-specific temporal rule had never been formulated at the time she was recorded. But in any case, 242, an old pork-knocker and bush cook, could hardly be called sophisticated, any more than could 30, the supervisor of a small tailoring workshop, but with only primary education. Speaker 30, however, operates rule-systems fully as disparate as those of the previous two speakers. In Example 3.27, we noted her use of the anterior marker *did* with non-statives:

5.27 The one what he *did* get didn't enough? (30/1/390)

although, as 3.30 showed, she was not consistent in this:

5.28 If she only *know* was F—— had it she wunt a sent for it. (30/9/387)

At the same time, 3.23 showed that she preserved the ±anterior distinction with non-statives:

5.29 What she *come* for then? (30/25/386)
5.30 And the same the day when she *did come.* (30/2/387)

In other words, while she preserved basilectal rules affecting the anterior category, she was beginning to lose the basilectal main stative rule and treat all statives as (unmarked) non-punctuals, i.e. to acquire rules (18) and (21) as given in Chapter 3.

If we compare the rules she uses in familiar conversation with those she uses in more formal contexts, we find once more that much more than relexification is involved. As shown in Example 5.6, she uses English strong pasts in simple-past contexts with both punctual non-statives ('I——— went away', 'they came round') and statives ('the girls knew the work already'). At this level she completely discards the anterior rules, marks morphologically the past punctual non-statives she would otherwise have left unmarked, and, most striking of all, marks all past-reference statives *despite* the fact that this one would *not* have required marking under anterior rules – for clearly, the girls have not ceased to know what they knew already, and the reference is therefore not truly [+anterior]. We may therefore conclude that her grammar contains at least three different rules for dealing with past-reference statives: (a) a rule that marks [+anterior] statives with *did*, (b) a rule that lumps statives together with other non-punctuals, irrespective of time-reference, and leaves both unmarked, and (c) a rule that marks [+past] statives in the same way as [+past] non-statives.

The mere capacity to carry out morph-for-morph replacements on the surface forms of one's own otherwise invariant grammar, while it might account for outputs such as those of 12/177 and similar speakers (and see also Example 4.23 and discussion thereof), could not possibly account for the productive capacities of speakers such as 30, 41 and 242. Such speakers can only have internalised sets of quite distinct rules such as could not be reconciled within a rule-system as traditionally conceived, since they are in no way optional variants, but depend on several distinct analyses of the underlying tense-aspect system. Moreover, these distinct analyses are by no means idiosyncratic inventions of their users; as we saw in the two preceding chapters, each analysis is not only widely shared with other speakers, but also constitutes a distinct stage of development within the evolution of the creole system as a whole.

One could, perhaps, still argue that this type of speaker may simply have internalised two or three distinct grammars of the traditional type, much as speakers of one or more foreign languages may perhaps be supposed to do. An explanation of the data offered might then go something like this: there are really only two *underlying* grammars, the grammar of English and the grammar of (basilectal) Guyanese Creole; some speakers know only one and relexicalise it where necessary (e.g. 12/177); others know both, and, in addition to relexicalising, can switch from the rules of one to the rules of the other at will (e.g. 30).

However, many of the rules involved are neither rules of English nor rules of basilectal creole. For instance, the rule that unmarks statives and other non-punctuals, irrespective of time reference, differs both from the basilectal treatment (which deals with the two quite differently on the ± anterior axis) and the acrolectal one (which deals with them, again quite differently, but on the ± past axis. But 30 and 242 quite clearly have this rule, in addition to whatever other more basilectal or more acrolectal rules they may have. Indeed, it could be argued that this rule is more vernacular to them than any competing rule, and that, far from their being able to switch between English and creole grammars, their knowledge of both these extremes is equally defective.

The output of 41 provides further evidence against such an explanation. Speaker 41 quite obviously does have an acrolectal grammar. If, however, there are two underlying systems, then whenever she uses non-acrolectal rules she must have switched to the second, basilectal system. In fact, we know that she has internalised the basilectal rule for non-generation of aspect markers with non-specific temporals. However, as is shown by Example 5.24 above, her output differs in many ways from that of 'native' basilectals. In the course of her conversations in Black Bush Polder, non-punctual *a* was used to her on dozens of occasions, but never once did she return it. If what she had learnt was the basilectal grammar, how had she managed to avoid learning the basilectal lexicon? In fact, her knowledge extends only into the lower mesolect, where, as Example 3.16 showed, the basilectal rule in question is preserved. She can analyse acrolectal non-continuatives into mesolectal iteratives (marked with *doz*) and statives, hypotheticals etc. (unmarked), but she proved unable [13] to carry out the 'next step backwards' and generalise non-continuative iteratives and continuatives into the single basilectal category of non-punctuals (marked with *a*).

The only recourse would then be to postulate one or more discrete and

---

[13] Unable productively, that is to say. That she understood the basilectal system is obvious from the conversations, and she must have hypothesised the system underlying her interlocutors' utterances in order to process them. Her productive limitations can easily be accounted for by her relatively slight exposure to the basilectal level. She herself said to me that visiting Black Bush Polder was in many ways like visiting a foreign country; but it was a foreign country in which quite fluent communication could be maintained from the very beginning.

unitary grammars between the acrolectal and basilectal extremes. But such an attempt, even when based on underlying rather than surface structures, would still have to meet the objections levelled against a surface 'co-existent systems' explanation in Chapter 1; things that should be together would have to be separated, things which should be separated would be forced together. Moreover, it is difficult to see what would be the motivation for postulating any such additional underlying systems, other than the need to shore up traditional concepts of what a grammar of competence ought to look like. For there can be no empirical constraints on the postulation of such hypothetical inter-systems, nothing to prevent the investigator multiplying them, as new facts seemed to make this necessary, until his overall description came to differ from the present account of competence in name only. Once the 'underlying bilingual' hypothesis has been disposed of, there is no logical stopping-place short of a full acceptance of polycompetence.

Moreover, now that differentials in production have been documented, we can use the argument from receptive capacity in support of our case. For, as Chomsky has frequently pointed out (1964, 1965 etc.), a grammar should be neutral as between speaker and hearer, and we have already claimed that most native Guyanese speakers, whatever their productive capacity, can process receptively virtually any variety within the continuum. Indeed, one may often observe speakers in the same conversation producing at widely different levels and yet continuing to understand one another perfectly. Here, for instance, is 41 in a rural area:

5.31   41: Find it very hard in here then?
     137: Yes, bina haul, yes – till a Zambia me rice field dey over there.
     41: Zambia?
     137: Zambia.
     41: Oh.
     137: Every day me a walk –
     41: Zambia.
     137: Yes, where the black people a dey.
     41: Zambia, that's why they call it Zambia?
     137: Yes, them put he name so.
     41: [Laughs]. (41,137/21–4/183)

And here, a Bushlot conversation:

5.32   178: Well fix one-one time, nuh?
     166: Well you tell me when we can come, where you want us catch you there or you want us catch you –
     178: Oh me God no there!
     166: You na want?

178: No.
166: You want come do it here?
178: M-m, come a house, nuh?
166: Well you tell me when to come.
178: What o'clock a-we a come back?
180: Well a that me na know. When we go done there. (166,178, 180/10–14/229)

Evidence such as this is persuasive, but, taken by itself, it might not, perhaps, be completely convincing. It could always be argued that the participants were each using a unitary grammar of their own but understood one another by virtue of 'context', or some jury-rigged 'extension rules', extraneous to that grammar, which enabled them to convert the outputs of others directly into their own surface forms. While it is not easy to think of any empirical test of receptive competence which would decisively refute this possibility, the evidence we have so far surveyed works strongly even if indirectly against it. We have shown that the nature of productive competence implies the existence of complex internalised rule-systems which will generate widely dissimilar outputs. It seems reasonable to assume that receptive competence is based on such systems. The alternative would be to suppose that a speaker–hearer produces different varieties by operating internalised rules, but understands different varieties by means of some distinct interpretative device. Such an alternative would have to be stated in one of two ways. One, the more obnoxious, would suggest that when 41 *says* 'you does go?' she understands it by virtue of her internalised rule-system, but that when she *hears* 'you does go?' she understands it by virtue of her interpretive device. But if one rejects this violation of parsimony, one is left with a competence that is split into two halves: the speaker must understand things he can himself say correctly by virtue of the rule-system, but things he cannot say correctly, only by virtue of the interpretive device.

I can think of no evidence that would support such a position, apart from the fact, already documented, that no individual rule-system seems adequate to generate *all* possible outputs within the overall creole system. But this is not really evidence unless one happens to accept as axiomatic the isomorphism of speaker and hearer competence – a position against which Labov (1970:59–60) has presented hard evidence. It would seem more plausible to argue that a speaker in a creole system both produces and understands by virtue of the same set of internalised rules, and that the striking asymmetry which often exists between receptive and productive capacity arises through performance factors: in particular, limitations on opportunities for actual use of (and hence, full familiarisation with) particular varieties, imposed by particular life-styles, and overt social restrictions on what occupants of given roles may or may not say.[14]

Polycompetence, therefore, must exist, and must consist of diverse and conflicting internalised rules ordered in such a way that random mixing of their outputs does not occur, and selection of any rule entails a series of correlated choices. While the form in which rules are given in Chapters 3 and 4 may not represent the way in which such rules are stored in the mind, it is, at present, far from obvious what would constitute a simpler or a more efficient means of storage, consonant with the wide variety of outputs which, as we have seen, have to be generated.

Finally, it may be convenient briefly to summarise the findings of this study. We set out with the problem of accounting for a wide range of variant structures, all produced within the same quite small speech community, and all, apparently, understood by most if not all members of that community, even though the varieties that deviated most sharply from standard English were quite unintelligible to the uninitiated native English-speaker. We claim that this range of structures is produced through prolonged contact between on the one hand a creole language, probably already containing considerable variation, and deriving in the first instance from inhibition of normal second-language learning processes, plus first-language loss, in a non-European population, and on the other the European language that formed the target of that creole's antecedent pidgin, in this case English. As social divisions separating speakers of the two languages weakened, social contacts constrained speakers of the language adjudged 'lower' to borrow surface forms from that adjudged 'higher'. Even if we rule out the possibility of massive restructuring of a grammar within a speaker's own lifetime (a possibility discounted by orthodox generativists, but never empirically disproved), we can see how borrowed forms would constitute part of the input to subsequent grammars. The next generation of speakers would then be obliged to incorporate both borrowed and 'original' elements into their grammars, which they could only do at the expense of a certain degree of restructuring. However, social pressures, and the amount of creole data that would still have to be incorporated, would keep such restructuring to a minimum at each stage.

---

[14] For instance, a student of mine who addressed a shopkeeper in the basilect was sternly reproved by her: 'Schoolteachers shouldn't talk that way!' To admit the importance of such factors is not to concede the type of 'socially dominated' theory of language variation discussed above. 'Should do' is a very different bird from 'can do', and social speech rules, like other social rules, are made to be broken.

If all members of the Guyanese population had been equal and if that population had been ethnically as well as socially homogeneous, continuation of this process would have eventually brought the whole of that population close to standard English. However, the different positions of individuals in ethnosocial space gave them differential exposure to the superstrate. In consequence, while the more favoured groups were able to carry out sufficiently radical and/or numerous restructurings to approximate to their target, the least favoured groups proved unable or, perhaps in many cases, unwilling to make more than minimal, if indeed any, restructuring. Between these two extremes there came into being intermediate groups with grammars which had undergone reconstructions more drastic and/or more frequent than those of the disfavoured groups, but less drastic and/or less frequent than those of the favoured. Thus the end-product of the process was a continuum of lects between the two polar varieties, and this continuum is now the potential input to any internalised grammar. That this potential is not always fully realised is a necessary result of the fact that a given individual may not be exposed to all of it or at least may be exposed to some levels more and/or earlier than to others. Thus the ranges of different individuals may differ, especially as regards production; however, each will receive, and be at least potentially able to produce, every variety within the creole system. The competence of such individuals will therefore differ from traditional accounts of competence in just the same way as the internal structure of such a system will differ from traditional accounts of linguistic systems, be these languages, dialects or idiolects; that is to say, both competence and system will be capable of reconciling conflicting rules, in so far as such conflicts have arisen through some natural development in the dynamics of language, whether decreolisation, second-language acquisition or the more widely known and better-accepted processes of linguistic change.

For there is no reason to suppose that the models of competence and system we have discussed are in any way peculiar to Guyana, or to similar arenas of decreolisation.[15] It is true that such arenas impose stresses on the human language faculty which are different from, and probably considerably greater than, those that occur in more settled regions. However, it does not follow from this that that faculty itself should differ, and indeed it would

---

[15] They should, however, emerge more rapidly and obviously from the data in decreolisation situations and other cases of language contact. Such situations have been common at all times in human history (see Mitrovic 1972 for two interesting nineteenth-century cases in the Austrian Empire), but with the massive population movements and large-scale urbanisation characteristic of modern society, there is good reason to believe that they may be on the increase. In particular, the bulging cities of Asia and Africa should provide particularly rich fields for research.

be very remarkable were we to find that there were really two distinct types of competence and two different types of linguistic system, unevenly distributed at different times and different places upon the face of the globe. It might even seem preferable to try to account for the many problems that arise in the grammars of standard languages, or in the attempted reconstruction of proto-languages, by assuming that polycompetence and polysystematicity represent norms rather than perversions of natural language. But such a suggestion, plausible as it may seem in the light of what has gone before, carries us, at the present stage of knowledge, well into the realms of speculation; our task here is ended, and the extent to which the principles observed may be generally applicable must be left as a topic for future study and debate.

Appendix I Methodology

Since the choice of a methodology for any linguistic investigation is largely determined by the investigator's general theoretical orientation, and since that orientation in this instance is broadly generative, it might have been expected that the use of native speaker intuitions would have bulked large in the present study. This, however, is not the case.

Dissatisfaction with the evidence of intuitions has already been expressed within a generative framework by Labov 1970, and is for that matter implicit in the arguments about different 'dialects' in e.g. Dougherty 1970, Carden 1970, Postal 1970, and in discussion of issues such as the status of the verb *remind* (Bowers 1970, Kimball 1970, Wolf 1970, Bolinger 1971 etc.) However, the fact that 'dialects disagree' is in no way a barrier to the use of intuitions, as is shown by Elliott, Legum and Thompson 1969; C.-J. Bailey 1970b; Carden 1972; etc. If they are not used here, it is for quite other reasons.

It is a particular characteristic of the creole continuum that, in the initial stages of investigation at least, intuitions are wholly uninterpretable. As shown in Chapter 5, Guyanese speakers in some sense know the whole system, even when they cannot actualise all of it. Thus, if their responses are based on this knowledge, they must be prepared to accept a wide variety of sentences with equivalent meanings; and indeed there is one type of informant common in creole societies who will accept virtually any sentence he is given, to the inevitable bewilderment of the inquirer. However, the type of informant who bases his judgements on that section of the continuum with which he has most familiarity can be equally misleading, since his judgements will conflict sharply and at first sight irreconcilably both with those of the first type and with those of other informants similar to himself whose responses are based on a different section of the continuum.

The investigator who relies solely on intuitional evidence is thus placed in an impossible position. If he knew the overall system he would be able to sort and arrange his informants' responses, but if he cannot first sort and arrange those responses, how is he ever to arrive at a knowledge of the overall system?

The only way out of this impasse is to obtain data from the actual outputs of the speech community. In the present study, efforts were made to obtain as catholic a sample of such outputs as possible, so that no significant speech variety should escape unrecorded. To this end, a large number of recordings were made under both interview and less formal circumstances; samples were taken of the speech of all Guyana's inhabited areas, of all its social classes and ethnic varieties, and of as wide a variety of speech styles as possible – formal oratory, narrative, process description, conversation (between intimates as well as between acquaintances and strangers), folk-tales, songs and 'jokes' (a joke in Guyana is a story, usually but not necessarily humorous, rather than a wisecrack). The materials thus assembled amounted to approximately a quarter of a million words, and were supplemented by the writer's personal observations over a four-year period and his many discussions with students and others interested in creole speech.

Once the overall system has been roughly laid out in this way, it becomes possible to interpret and utilise the responses of informants. One no longer asks, 'Can one say such-and-such?' but rather, 'If someone said such-and-such, what kind of person would he be? What would he mean by it? Is there anything else slightly different he might say?' In this way, speaker intuitions can be used to confirm, supplement and on occasion modify the description derived from analysis of actual outputs. But that analysis must play a primary role in any investigation of a creole continuum.

In the analysis, implicational scaling played a role which perhaps requires some explanation. This technique, first developed by Guttmann (1944) and introduced into linguistics by Elliott, Legum and Thompson (1969) and DeCamp (1971a), has recently been the subject of some controversy among both linguists and statisticians. It is still far from clear what are the thresholds of significance for any particular type of scale; it has even been claimed that, given full freedom to manipulate rows and columns, any material whatsoever is scalable to a 90% level, though this assertion is decisively refuted by Table 4.10 above.

Some writers (e.g. Fasold 1970) seem to have assumed (a) that implicational scales are simply the arrayed data and (b) that they are somehow a substitute for the writing of grammatical rules. In fact, as claimed in Bickerton 1973c, they constitute an abstract measuring device, essential in the initial data-sorting phase, by which data can be checked against the predictions of a Baileyan wave model (see C.-J. Bailey 1974 for the fullest exposition of this model). For if data scales, it can do so only by virtue of the fact that a succession of rule-changes has spread fairly evenly and consistently through the community as a whole.

An implicational scale consists essentially of a series of ranked isolects. Each isolect is the output of a hypothetical grammar which is assumed to be invariant; each differs from its immediate neighbour in only a single respect, e.g. it lacks or possesses a rule its neighbours possess or lack, or it has a particular feature in two environments while its neighbours have that feature in either one or three. Once such a scale has been set up, outputs of particular speakers can be located on the scale. Let us assume as background a scale such as that in Table A.1, in which the vertical columns represent differing environments for a given pair of variable features, the horizontal rows represent contiguous isolects, and the figures 1 and 2 the expected incidence of the two variables involved. Against this scale we can lay the outputs of three hypothetical speakers, A (1 1 2 2 2), B (1 × 2 2 2), and C (1 1 2 × 2). A (at

TABLE A.1   Model implicational scale

1	1	1	1	1
1	1	1	1	2
1	1	1	2	2
1	1	2	2	2
1	2	2	2	2
2	2	2	2	2

least for the duration of the speech event that we are analysing) has his output identical with that of the fourth isolect in Table A.1, and is therefore no problem. B, since he varies only in the second environment, can be regarded as having an output intermediate between those of the fourth and fifth isolects in the table and therefore as currently undergoing the change necessary to transform the output of the fourth isolect into that of the fifth. The only difficulty is presented by C, whose output is non-identical with those of any isolect, yet who cannot be regarded as unambiguously being located between any two isolects. C's position could be equivalent to that of the fourth isolect, minus a deviation in the fourth environment, or intermediate between the second and third isolects, with a deviation in the third environment. (In practice, there are usually other factors present which enable one to determine where to assign a given speaker or speech event). C must therefore be listed as a potentially deviant speaker.

However, it must be emphasied that an implicational scale compares outputs and not sets of rules; it follows that it cannot itself determine the form of the rules. It is true that, where an implicational scale is deviance-free, the rules may be assumed to be such as would sequentially generate the output of each isolect. However, where the data, placed against the scale, show deviances too numerous to be written off as performance error, these can only be accounted for by the actual rules. It follows that the rules required to produce simply the outputs of the isolects cannot be adequate, and other forms of analysis must therefore be invoked in order to account for the observed discrepancies and to determine the form that the rules must take. One example of such further analysis is found in Bickerton 1973c; a similar case can be found in Table 3.11 above, where the fact that four out of the six observed deviances are found in the V − syll column can be accounted for in part by the differing analyses of *start* described in the text.

Thus implicational scaling constitutes an invaluable discovery procedure – invaluable, not merely as a data-sorting device, but also for determining where a Baileyan model will apply unchecked and where its operation is impeded by other factors. It enables us, too, to rank speech varieties on a scale between remotest-from-English and nearest-to-English, thus providing a rapid and convenient overview of the processes which go to make up the continuum. However, behind the results of any implicational scaling there must lie a set of rules, and it is these rules which any study of grammar is aimed at discovering. Scaling may assist that discovery; it can never substitute for it.

A word should perhaps be said about the relationship between such scales and actual flesh-and-blood speakers. DeCamp 1971a has been sometimes taken to imply that speakers can actually be located on an implicational scale. In fact, only the output of a given speaker on a given occasion can be thus located. At different times and in different circumstances, given the switching capacities described in Chapter 5, the same individual may be located at widely differing points on a scale, and his range must therefore be regarded as potentially spanning all the isolects between its extremes.

Appendix II   Speakers cited in the text

For all speakers whose outputs are either cited directly in the text or analysed in statistical tables, details (in so far as these are known) are given below in the following order: ethnicity; sex; age; education; occupation; place of residence; nationality of interviewer/recorder (G = Guyanese, E = English); speaker's awareness that he/she was being recorded (2 = complete, 1 = doubtful, 0 = presumed zero).

2: Indian; female; 73; primary (3 years); retired labourer; Bushlot, West Berbice; G/2. (See 186.)

5: Indian; male; 20; secondary; schoolteacher; Bushlot, West Berbice; G/2.

6: Indian; male; 23; secondary; rice farmer; Bushlot, West Berbice; G/2.

8: Indian; female; 74; primary (4 years); retired rice farmer; Bushlot, West Berbice; G/2.

9: Indian; female; 59; none; labourer; Bushlot, West Berbice; G/2. (See 188.)

10: Indian; male; 22; primary; mechanic; Bushlot, West Berbice; G/2.

11: Indian; male; 48; primary; carpenter; Bushlot, West Berbice; G/2.

12: Indian; male; 31; primary; shopkeeper; Bushlot, West Berbice; G/2.

15: Indian; male; 34; primary; rice farmer; Bushlot, West Berbice; G/2.

16: Indian; male; 20; secondary; unemployed; Bushlot, West Berbice; G/2.

22: Indian; male; 53; primary; rice farmer; Bushlot, West Berbice; G/2.

24: Indian; female; 40; primary (4 years); housewife; Bushlot, West Berbice; G/2.

25: Indian; female; 40; none; housewife; Bushlot, West Berbice; G/2.

26: Indian; female; 55; primary; housewife; Bushlot, West Berbice; G/2.

27: Indian; male; 42; secondary; taxi owner and mechanic; Bushlot, West Berbice; G/2. (See 168.)

28: Indian; female; 42; none; housewife; Bushlot, West Berbice; G/2.

30: African; female; 43; primary; workshop supervisor; Buxton, East Demerara; G/0.

32: African; female; 55; primary; housewife; Buxton, East Demerara; G/0.

41: African; female; 40; postgraduate; university lecturer; Georgetown; G/0.

43: African; female; 50 +; primary (?); housewife; Wismar, Demerara River; G/0.

44: African; female; 60 +; secondary; housewife; Georgetown; G/0.

67: Indian; male; 60 +; primary; retired labourer; Black Bush Polder, East Berbice; E/2.

87: Indian; male; 70 +; primary; retired labourer; West Demerara; E/2.

92: African; male; 50 + ; college; education officer; Georgetown; G/2.

93: Mixed; male; 40 + ; college; education officer; Georgetown; G/2.

94: African; male; 40 + ; college; university lecturer; Georgetown; G/2.

98: Indian; male; 66; primary; peasant farmer; West Demerara; E/0.

99: African; male; 39; primary; canecutter; West Demerara; E/0. (See 125.)

100: African; male; 52; primary; labourer; South Georgetown; G/2.

101: Indian; female; 60 + ; primary; market stallholder; Essequibo Coast; G/2.

103: African; male; 40 + ; secondary; forestry worker; Bartica, Essequibo; E/2.

105: African; female; 50 + ; primary; housewife; Bartica, Essequibo; E/2.

107: African; male; 60; primary; minibus operator; Batrica, Essequibo; E/2.

108: African; female; 65; primary; housewife; Bartica, Essequibo; E/2.

111: Mixed; male; 30 + ; secondary; timber merchant; Bartica, Essequibo; E/2.

114: African; male; 40 +; primary; nightwatchman; Bartica, Essequibo; E/2.

117: African; male; 65; primary; retired boathand; Bartica, Essequibo; E/2.

118: Indian; female; 50 + ; not known; housewife; West Demerara; G/2.

119: Indian; female; 60 + ; none; retired labourer; West Demerara; G/2.

121: Indian; male; 20 + ; secondary; unemployed; West Demerara; G/2.

122: Indian; male; 71; primary; storekeeper; West Demerara; E/0.

123: African; male; 20 + ; college; student; Georgetown; E/1.

124: African; male; 50 + ; primary; painting contractor; West Demerara; E/0.

125: Same as 99; E/1.

126: Indian; female; 12; primary; schoolchild; Black Bush Polder, East Berbice; G/2.

127: Indian; male; 20 + ; college; student; West Demerara; G/1.

129: Indian; female; 30 + ; not known; peasant farmer; Black Bush Polder, East Berbice; G/2.

131: Indian; male; 11; primary; schoolchild; Black Bush Polder, East Berbice; G/2.

133: Indian; male; 10; primary; schoolchild; Black Bush Polder, East Berbice; G/2.

134: Indian; female; 11; primary; schoolchild; Black Bush Polder, East Berbice; G/2.

135: Indian; female; 20 + ; primary; peasant farmer; Black Bush Polder, East Berbice; G/2.

137: Indian; female; 40 + ; primary; peasant farmer (former nursing assistant); Black Bush Polder, East Berbice; G/2.

146: Indian; female; 40 + ; not known; housewife; Black Bush Polder, East Berbice; G/2.

148: Indian; female; 42; not known; peasant farmer; Black Bush Polder, East Berbice; G/2.

149: Indian; female; 12; primary; schoolchild; Black Bush Polder, East Berbice; G/2.

157: African; male; 40 + ; not known; policeman; Kamerang, Essequibo; E/2.

160: Amerindian; female; 40 + ; not known; peasant farmer; Essequibo Coast; E/0.

162: African; male; 64; not known; comedian; Georgetown; tape of radio interview.

164: African; male; 40 + ; not known; comedian; Georgetown; tape of radio interview.

165: Group (African and Indian); male; 20–50; not known; working class; Essequibo Coast; E/0.

166: Indian; male; 36; college; schoolteacher; Bushlot, West Berbice; E/1.

168: Same as 27; E/2.

169: Indian; male; 40; secondary; storekeeper; Bushlot, West Berbice; E/2.

170–6: Group of Indians; male and female; 20–60; primary; rice farmers; Corentyne, East Berbice; G/2.

177: Same as 12; E/2.

178: Same as 28; E/1–2.

179: Indian; female; 62; primary; housewife; Bushlot, West Berbice; E/0.

180: Indian; female; 50 +; not known; not known; Bushlot; West Berbice; E/0.

183: Indian; male; 66; primary; rice farmer; Bushlot, West Berbice; E/2.

185: Indian; female; middle-aged; not known; not known; Bushlot, West Berbice; E/0.

186: Same as 2; E/2.

188: Same as 9; E/2.

192: African; female; 70 +; primary; retired midwife; Essequibo Coast; E/0.

196: African; male; 54; primary; diamond prospector; Essequibo Coast; E/0.

197: Indian; male; 40 +; not known; not known; Essequibo Coast; E/1.

198: Indian; female; 70 +; none; retired labourer; Port Mourant, East Berbice; G/2.

199: Indian; male; 20 +; college; student; Port Mourant, East Berbice; G/1.

209: African; male; 67; primary; carpenter; Anna Regina, Essequibo Coast; E/0.

210: Indian; female; 16; primary; unemployed; Port Mourant, East Berbice; G/2.

214: Indian; female; 30 +; primary; housewife; Port Mourant, East Berbice; G/2.

216: Indian; female; 40 +; not known; not known; Port Mourant, East Berbice; G/2.

219: Indian; female; 48; none; sugar estate labourer; Port Mourant, East Berbice; G/2.

220–5: Group of Indians; male; elderly; primary; retired sugar estate workers (labouring and clerical); Albion, East Berbice; G/2.

226: African; male; 50 +; secondary; office supervisor; Mackenzie, Demerara River; E/2.

227: Portuguese; male; 30 +; not known; railway foreman; Wismar, Demerara River; E/2.

228: African; male; 40 +; not known; chief mechanic; Wismar, Demerara River; E/2.

229: African; male; 50 +; primary; maintenance worker; Wismar, Demerara River; E/2.

236: African; female; 70 +; primary; retired housemaid; Wismar, Demerara River; E/2.

238: African; male; 40 +; not known; bar owner; Wismar, Demerara River; E/1.

240: African; male; 75; primary; nightwatchman; Wismar, Demerara River; E/2.

241: African; male; 30 +; secondary; electrical engineer; Wismar, Demerara River; E/1.

242: African; male; 50 +; primary; bauxite miner; Wismar, Demerara River; E/1.

248: Indian; male; 20 +; primary; canecutter; Albion, East Berbice; G/2.

252–3: Indians; male; one elderly, one younger; not known; not known; Albion, East Berbice; G/2.

Notes on speakers

The curious reader will naturally wish to know what happened to 'blank' numbers, i.e. those not represented by speakers in the above list (and hence not included in the foregoing analysis) such as 1, 3, 4 etc. There are several contributory factors to this, *viz.*:

(a) Owing to revisions in the system of numbering speakers, as well as (in some cases) accidents of transcription, some numbers (e.g. 29, 33–40) are genuinely null and have no speaker attached to them.

(b) The acoustic quality of a number of tapes of bar conversation proved difficult to transcribe with a sufficiently high degree of accuracy to determine, in a number of cases, whether tense-aspect markers were present or not; therefore, despite the (linguistically and otherwise) interesting nature of this material, it was ignored for purposes of analysis, though it was retained in the corpus for comparative purposes.

(c) Numbers were given to every speaker recorded irrespective of quantity of speech. It therefore happens that in recordings graded 0 or 1, minor participants in, or even interruptors of, ongoing conversations have numbers, even though their intervention may consist of only a single remark. Such speakers have been excluded from all tables (since their presence would obviously not add to the validity of the results, and might very well distort them) and sentences uttered by them are cited in the text only when they appear to be particularly unambiguous illustrations of a grammatical point for which there is substantial evidence from other speakers. The bulk of the citations in the text are from speakers from whom a minimum of 1,000 words was recorded – and often a much higher figure.

(d) In the case of the Bushlot sub-sample, a few speakers were excluded even though they fell under none of the conditions mentioned above. This was done because it seemed advisable (even though there is a very limited amount of purely geographic variation in Guyana) to avoid overbalancing the sample with too many speakers from a single area. In every case, speakers omitted had outputs similar to those of speakers included. Of the whole of the data it can be said that no variant lects or even individual variants have been excluded for any reason whatsoever, and that while inclusion of more (or all) speakers recorded might have affected statistics in some cases, they would in no way have altered the analysis of the verbal system as here represented.

Appendix III
A brief note on the Guyanese community

Guyana, formerly British Guiana, is a former European colony which became an independant republic in 1970. In that year, during which many of the data for the present study were collected, the estimated population was 740,196 (this and other contemporary statistics are taken from Yates 1972). Of this population 51% was of East Indian descent, 31% of African, 11% mixed, and 4% Amerindian, and the remaining 3% consisted of Chinese, Portuguese (regarded as a distinct ethnic category here as in other Nordic colonies) and other Europeans. This somewhat unusual ethnic mixture owes itself to the peculiar history of the country, which will be briefly outlined later in this appendix.

The population as a whole is very unevenly distributed over the country's land area of approximately 83,000 square miles. Of this, some 87% is forested, while much of the remainder consists of low-grade savannah which will support only limited herds of cattle. Probably over 95% of the population lives on less than 2% of the land area – that region which is constituted by a narrow coastal strip about 150 miles long and five to ten miles wide, plus similar strips which border the rivers for varying distances. This coastal and riverine area consists mainly of rich (or once-rich) alluvial land, and is mainly devoted to rice and sugar. The only other major industry is bauxite mining. The proportionate importance of these three industries to the country's economy may be gauged by the export figures for 1970, in U.S. dollars: bauxite and alumina $70 million, sugar $36 million, rice $18 million. Allowance should, however, be made for the fact that, alone of the three, rice is sold mainly on the home market; also, the numbers employed in all three industries are in inverse proportion to export figures.

Over a quarter of the total population is located in the city and suburbs of the capital, Georgetown; however, there are few other towns (the three townships grouped recently into the bauxite-mining complex of Linden – Mackenzie, Wismar and Christianburg – with 29,000, and New Amsterdam with 17,000, were officially the largest in 1970) so that the bulk of the population is rural. However, 'rural' may conjure up a misleading picture to the uninitiated. The rural areas are absolutely flat, criss-crossed by rectangular patterns of drainage and irrigation canals and artificially raised tracks ('dams'); every inch is cultivated up to the courida scrub on the salt-laden land by the 'sea-dam' on one side, and up to the lakes, swamps and jungle ('bush') beyond the 'backdam' on the other. Residential areas, consisting mainly of small one-storey wooden houses raised on stilts because of frequent flooding, are strung out in narrow ribbons along the sides of the 'public road' that crosses the greater part of the country a mile or two inland from the sea; although these areas are described as 'villages', some have only numbers instead of names, and the stranger is often quite unable to tell where one ends and another begins. However, despite this superficial sameness, each one has a vivid sense of its own identity, its own heroes and legends, its eccentrics and its tales of violent or supernatural experiences. Each one has its school, its church (or temple, if it is mainly Indian), its general store, as often as not owned by a 'Potogee man', its 'cake-shop' where the women and children gossip and its 'rum-shop' (often disguised as a 'recreation club' to escape taxes) where the men do the same. It was in villages of this kind that the bulk of the data for this study were obtained.

Paradoxically, these areas are less known to the outside world than is the under-populated interior. The latter has been described in numberless travellers' tales of varying veracity since it was first visited by Raleigh nearly four centuries ago. While it is of some general linguistic interest (at least nine indigenous languages are spoken there), it is of little interest to the creolist, since, apart from Amerindians (who mainly speak either their own languages or a little 'foreigner's English' learnt at European missions), the bulk of the interior population consists of transients – government officials, trade-store owners, gold and diamond prospectors or loggers – who came from the coast and will return there, and who merely carry the speech of the coast with them. Its main relevance to the present study is the inexhaustible fund of stories of the uncanny, of disasters and hairbreadth escapes, of courage, endurance and treachery, which sojourners in the bush bring back with them, and which add instruction as well as entertainment to the study of their speech.

However, no merely synchronic account of the Guyanese community can explain the peculiarities of its sociolinguistic structure. To understand this, it is necessary to know a little of the history of the region, both remote and recent.

Prior to 1640, there was no permanent European settlement anywhere in the Guianas. Although the whole South American continent was officially partitioned between Spain and Portugal along the thirtieth parallel of longitude, the whole area of the Amazon basin, of which the Guianas form a kind of northerly appendage, was unamenable to Iberian methods of colonisation. From the beginning of the seventeenth century, Dutch and English traders had set up temporary posts in the area or had tried, and failed, to establish permanent ones, but it was not until the middle of the century that a substantial force of English planters from Barbados, with their slaves, set up the first durable colony in what is now Surinam. England was forced to cede this colony to the Dutch in 1667, but few English planters left before 1674, and by this time 'Negro English', 'taki-taki', or Sranan, as it is now known, had already become the lingua franca of the colony.

At this period, and for some time afterwards, what is now Guyana did not constitute a political unit, although the Dutch established three distinct colonies in it; Essequibo, the westernmost; Demerara, in the centre; and Berbice in the east. Berbice was the first to be founded, and had always the highest percentage of Dutch population, but at the time the Dutch gained the already flourishing sugar colony of Surinam, the plantations of Berbice were little more than provision-grounds for the Dutch traders (Rodway 1912:62), with few if any African slaves. It seems probable that when sugar was established there, seasoned Sranan-speaking slaves would have formed the nucleus of the work force, and would have taught their language to the larger numbers of *sowatra nengre* imported direct from Africa.

However, from the early part of the eighteenth century, the Dutch welcomed foreign planters, especially Englishmen, who were prepared to invest capital in the region. According to van's Gravesande (1911:292), by 1753 'by far the greater number' of the population of Demerara was 'English or English-speaking'. It is not clear from the context whether he is speaking of the free or the total population; since, after several more years of continued English immigration only a quarter (56 out of 206) of the Demerara plantations were English-owned (ibid.:400), it seems likely that he included slaves and interpreted 'English-speaking' as including 'speakers of English creoles', whether Sranan or some Caribbean variety.

For at this stage, one cannot imagine that there was a great deal of difference between the creole varieties of Barbados, Antigua, Jamaica and Surinam. The original Sranan speakers were slaves brought to Surinam from Barbados in 1650, the majority of emigrants from Surinam (and their slaves) went to Jamaica in 1674, and the slaves of English planters brought into Demerara and Essequibo in the mid-eighteenth century came mostly from Barbados and Antigua, with some from Jamaica. It is quite possible that the actual children or grandchildren of slaves who left Surinam in 1674 may have returned to the Guianas. However, the proportion of whites to blacks in Barbados is and has always been higher than elsewhere in the Caribbean, so it may be that some measure of decreolisation had already set in there by 1750. It would be tempting to suppose, for example, that these slaves had introduced *doz* in competition with Sranan *a*. But one would then only have to wonder how they had not, at the same time, introduced Barbadian *unu* 'you (pl.)'; there are few easy historical answers in the diachronic study of Caribbean creoles.

Whatever the precise relationship between creole varieties, all must have been in contact in Demerara from at least 1750 on, and it seems likely that by the time all three Dutch settlements became officially British in 1803, some degree of levelling must have taken place both there and in Essequibo, where there was less, but noticeable, English influence. However, Berbice, with its almost exclusively Dutch planters, would have retained something closer to Sranan, and laid the basis of a linguistic conservatism, traces of which are still visible.

Except for a relatively small number of house-slaves and freedmen, it is unlikely that anything substantial in the way of decreolisation took place before Emancipation in 1833. From this period on, however, careers were progressively opened to people of African descent, and the sharply segregated castes of slavery days began gradually to give place to the more fluid class system of a modern capitalist society. In order to improve one's social position, one had to approximate ever closer to English norms in language as well as behaviour. Before Emancipation, attempts by missionaries to educate the slaves had been blocked by both official and unofficial means, but now that the ex-slaves enjoyed, at least nominally, the status of British subjects, government regarded it as essential that they should acquire the appropriate loyalties and codes of behaviour. Creole culture was correspondingly deprecated, and its vehicle condemned as 'broken language'; instead of 'Nansi 'tory', children were brought up with the gallery of European heroes whose exploits were recounted in the aptly named *Royal Reader*. This led to the 'dual standard' which Reisman (1965) and many subsequent writers on the Caribbean have observed, by which creole values are overtly despised and secretly respected, and European values overtly respected and secretly despised – a situation which helps to account for the very wide ranges we have observed in the speech of many Afro-Guyanese.

Social factors reinforced this tendency. After Emancipation, most ex-slaves refused to work on the hated sugar plantations; many planters went bankrupt, and the ex-slaves, by clubbing together in dozens or sometimes hundreds, were able to buy their estates and set up communal villages based on subsistence farming. The planters, backed by government, did all they could to ensure the economic failure of these villages, in the hope that the men would then return to the plantations. But their strategies, though largely successful, did not have the desired effect. Instead, a typical pattern of family life developed in which the menfolk went away to work in the interior or the city, while the women cultivated the family holding (for a full account of African family life in Guyana, see R. T. Smith 1956.) Despite the 'dual standard', this trend helped decreolisation by exposing even the less educated to urban lects.

However, the consequent labour shortage on the plantations led to the recruitment of large numbers of indentured labourers. These came from many areas – Madeira and the Azores, South China, West Africa, the Caribbean and even parts of Europe – but the bulk (almost a quarter million over the eighty-year period of indenture) were from India. The first Indians were instructed in their new duties by the few Africans who had remained on the sugar plantations, and thus acquired as a second language the most conservative variety of Guyanese Creole. Skinner (1956), citing contemporary documents, has shown that Afro-Indian relations were good in the early years, but quickly deteriorated when Indians were used to break African strikes. There is some evidence that interracial conflicts were deliberately encouraged by the colonial power in accordance with the *divide et impera* principle.

The Indians, relatively isolated on the plantations from the mainstream of creole society, became still more so when, towards the close of the nineteenth century, workers whose indenture had expired began to set up rice villages on the coast. This filled an ecological niche, since land too liable to flooding to do well under sugar was often ideal for rice-growing, but it brought about growing competition for limited land between Indians anxious to expand their holdings and Africans trying to retain their provision farms. Since African patterns of inheritance tended to fragment holdings, while Indian patterns tended to hold them together, Africans were at a disadvantage and many more moved to the urban areas, thus tilting the country towards a rural-Indian/urban-African polarisation. This process, in turn, speeded decreolisation in the African community while slowing it in the Indian one.

Competition, however, could not become really acute under colonial rule, since the commanding heights of the society were closed to both groups, and both felt equally blocked and disadvantaged by the White and light-skinned ruling class. Indeed, this fellowship of the oppressed was responsible for an unfortunately brief rapprochement between the two which took place with the founding of the People's Progressive Party in 1951 and its victory in the 1953 elections. Fearful of an alleged 'communist conspiracy', the British government sent in troops and resumed direct rule, thus setting in motion a chain of events which is not yet over.

It is no business of this study to embroil the reader in the ongoing political controversy over these events. The interested may consult the following works: for an orthodox radical view of them, Reno 1964; for an orthodox conservative view, Swan 1957; for an orthodox liberal view (and the most sensible of the three), R. T. Smith 1962; and for an extremely unorthodox, independent and often insightful (if not, according to some, always accurate) view, Despres 1968; while for background on the customs, habits and attitudes of the ordinary people involved, Skinner 1956 and Jayawardena 1963 are still unsurpassed. Some of the consequences of the events, however, need to be taken into account. Chief among them was the escalation of racial conflict through a series of strikes, riots and political murders to the so-called 'disturbances' of 1964, which led to some two hundred deaths and the forced homogenisation (by burning, shooting and physical expulsion) of many formerly ethnically mixed villages; some echoes from this period will have been noted by the reader in cited texts. This process has greatly slowed up the linguistic levelling which one would otherwise have expected in a small and developing nation, although it has not yet led to the actual splitting which might have occurred if (as at least one politician urged) actual partition on ethnic lines had taken place. The conflict for political power has, however, also produced an Indian elite, some of whom have broken their links with the rural majority, but many of whom are genuine bi-dialectals, capable of switching between basilect and acrolect (or at least between something approaching these extremes) without touching the mid-mesolectal level, which is perhaps consciously avoided by them as constituting the vernacular of the African proletariat. Yet in a society as small and intimate as that of Guyana, socioethnic polarisation, however vicious, can never tell the whole story; there are still many lines open, at work and at play, between both the two main embattled groups and the other minorities who stand on the sidelines and nervously await the outcome.

What that outcome will be, no-one can say. At the moment, the Africans' control of the towns, administration and the armed forces outweighs the Indians' numerical advantage. Those who know the country well and have friends in both camps can only remain neutral and hope that some fair solution can be found.

Bibliography

Abrahams, R. D. and R. Bauman. 1971. 'Sense and nonsense in St. Vincent; speech behaviour and decorum in a Caribbean community'. *American Anthropologist* 73, 762–72.

Abrams, O. S. 1970. *Guyana Metegee*. Georgetown: Labour Advocate.

Achemann, R. 1965. *Theories of Knowledge: A Critical Introduction*. New York: McGraw-Hill.

Agheyisi, R. N. 1971. 'West African Pidgin English: Simplification and Simplicity'. Ph.D. thesis, Stanford (Cal.) University.

Alleyne, M. C. 1963. 'Communication and politics in Jamaica'. *Caribbean Studies* 3, 22–61.

1971. 'Acculturation and the cultural matrix of creolization'. In Hymes (ed.), 169–86.

Allsopp, R. 1958a. 'The English language in British Guiana'. *English Language Teaching* 12(2), 59–66.

1958b. 'Pronominal forms in the dialect of English used in Georgetown (British Guiana) and its environs by persons engaged in nonclerical occupations'. M.A. thesis, London University.

1962. 'Expressions of state and action in the dialect of English used in the Georgetown area of British Guiana'. Ph.D. thesis, London University.

Arnott, D. W. 1970. *The Nominal and Verbal System of Fula*. Oxford: Clarendon Press.

Austin, J. L. 1946. 'Other minds'. *Supplement to the Proceedings of the Aristotelian Society* **xx**, 148–87.

Ayer, A. J. 1965. *The Problem of Knowledge*. London: Macmillan.

Bailey, B. L. 1966. *Jamaican Creole Syntax*. Cambridge: C.U.P.

1971. 'Jamaican Creole: Can dialect boundaries be defined?' In Hymes (ed.), 341–8.

Bailey, C.-J. N. 1970a. 'Lectal groupings in matrices generated with waves along the temporal parameter'. *Working Papers in Linguistics* (University of Hawaii) 2(4), 109–24.

1970b. 'Using data variation to confirm, rather than undermine, the validity of abstract syntactic structures'. *Working Papers in Linguistics* (University of Hawaii) 2(8), 77–86.

1971. 'Trying to talk in the new paradigm'. *Working Papers in Linguistics* (University of Hawaii) 4(2), 312–39.

1974. *Variation and Linguistic Theory*. Washington, D.C.: Georgetown University Press.

Bamgbose, A. 1966. *A Grammar of Yoruba*. Cambridge: C.U.P.

Berry, J. 1961. 'English loanwords and adaptations in Sierra Leone Krio'. In Le Page (ed.), 1–16.
Bickerton, D. 1971a. 'Inherent variability and variable rules'. *Foundations of Language* 7, 457–92.
    1971b. 'Creole evidence for a causal operator'. *Working Papers in Linguistics* (University of Hawaii) 3(2), 31–4.
    1971c. 'Cross-level interference'. In G. E. Perren and J. M. L. Trim (eds.), *Applications of Linguistics*, pp. 133–40. Cambridge: C.U.P.
    1973a. 'The structure of polylectal grammars'. In R. Shuy (ed.), *Proceedings of the 23rd Annual Round Table*, pp. 17–42. Washington, D.C.: Georgetown University Press. Monograph Series No. 25.
    1973b. 'On the nature of a creole continuum'. *Language* 49, 640–69.
    1973c. 'Quantitative v. dynamic paradigms: the case of Montreal *que*'. In C.-J. Bailey and R. Shuy (eds.), *New Ways of Analyzing Variation in English*, pp. 23–43. Washington, D.C.: Georgetown University Press.
    1974. 'System into system'. In D. Craig (ed.), *Proceedings of 1972 Conference on Creole Languages and Education*. In press.
    MS. 'Towards a unified description of Pan-English'. Mimeographed.
Bickerton, D. and A. Escalante. 1970. 'Palenquero: A Spanish-based creole of Northern Colombia'. *Lingua* 24(3), 254–67.
Bloch, B. 1948. 'A set of postulates for phonemic analysis'. *Language* 24, 3–46.
Bloom, L. 1970. *Language Development*. Cambridge, Mass.: M.I.T. Press.
Bloomfield, L. 1927. 'Literate and illiterate speech'. *American Speech* 2, 432–9.
    1933. *Language*. New York: Henry Holt.
Bolinger, D. L. 1971. 'Semantic overloading: A restudy of the verb *remind*'. *Language* 47, 522–47.
Bowers, J. 1970. 'A note on *remind*'. *Linguistic Inquiry* 1, 559–60.
Carden, G. 1970. 'A note on conflicting idiolects'. *Linguistic Inquiry* 1, 281–90.
    1972. 'Dialect variation and abstract syntax'. In R. Shuy (ed.), *The Georgetown Linguistics Forum*. Washington, D.C.: Georgetown University Press.
Carrell, P. L. 1970. *A Transformational Grammar of Igbo*. Cambridge: C.U.P.
Cassidy, F. 1960. *Jamaica Talk*. London: Macmillan.
    1966. 'Multiple etymologies in Jamaican Creole'. *American Speech* 41, 211–15.
Cassidy, F. and R. B. Le Page. 1967. *Dictionary of Jamaican English*. Cambridge: C.U.P.
Cave, G. 1970. 'Some sociological factors in the production of standard language in Guyana'. *Language Learning* 20(2), 249–63.
Cedergren, H. J. 1973. 'On the nature of variable constraints'. In C.-J. N. Bailey and R. Shuy (eds.), *New Ways of Analyzing Variation in English*, pp. 13–22. Washington, D.C.: Georgetown University Press.
Cedergren, H. J. and D. Sankoff. MS. 'Variable rules: performance as a statistical reflection of competence'. Mimeographed.
Chomsky, N. 1964. Formal discussion of W. Miller and S. Erwin, 'The development of grammar in child language'. In V. Bellugi and R. Brown (eds.), *The Acquisition of Language*, pp. 35–40. Monograph of the Society for Research in Child Development, vol. 29, no. 1.

1965. *Aspects of the Theory of Syntax.* Cambridge, Mass.: M.I.T. Press.

1968. *Language and Mind.* New York: Harcourt, Brace & World.

Chomsky, N. and M. Halle. 1968. *The Sound Pattern of English.* New York: Harper & Row.

Christaller, J. G. 1875. *A Grammar of the Ashanti and Fante Language.* Basel: Evangelical & Missionary Society.

Closs, E. 1965. 'Diachronic syntax and generative grammar'. *Language* **41**, 402–15.

Collymore, F. 1965. *Notes for a Glossary of Words and Phrases of Barbadian Dialect.* Bridgetown, Barbados: Barbados Advocate Co.

Comhaire-Sylvain, S. 1936. *Le Créole haitian: morphologie et syntaxe.* Port-au-Prince: Puillet.

Corder, S. P. 1967. 'The significance of learners' "errors" '. *International Review of Applied Linguistics* **5**, 161–70.

Craig, D. 1966. 'Teaching English to Jamaican Creole speakers'. *Language Learning* **16**, 49–61.

Cruikshank, J. G. 1916. *Black Talk.* Demerara: Argosy Press.

Cunningham, I. A. E. 1970. 'A Syntactic Analysis of Sea Island Creole (Gullah)'. Ph.D. thesis, University of Michigan.

Dance, C. D. D. 1881. *Chapters from a Guianese Logbook.* Georgetown.

Dato, D. P. 1971. 'The development of the Spanish verb-phrase in children's second language learning'. In Pimsleur and Quinn (eds.), 19–33.

DeCamp, D. 1961. 'Social and geographic factors in Jamaican dialects'. In Le Page (ed.), pp. 61–84.

1964. 'Creole language areas considered as multilingual communities'. *In Symposium on Multilingualism (Brazzaville 1962)*, pp. 227–31. London: Commission for Technical Co-operation in Africa.

1971a. 'Toward a generative analysis of a post-creole speech community'. In Hymes (ed.), 349–70.

1971b. 'The study of pidgin and creole languages'. In Hymes (ed.), pp. 13–39.

de Granda, G. 1968. 'Materiales para el estudio sociohistorico de los elementos linguisticos Afro-Americanos en el area hispanica'. *Thesaurus* **23**, 547–73.

1969. 'Posibles vias directas de introduccion de Africanismos en el "habla de negro" literaria castellana'. *Thesaurus* **24**, 459–69.

Despres, L. 1968. *Cultural Pluralism and Nationalist Politics in British Guiana.* Chicago: Rand McNally.

Dillard, J. L. 1970. 'Principles in the history of American English – Paradox, Virginity, and Cafeteria'. *Florida F. L. Reporter* **8**(1–2), 32–3.

Dougherty, R. C. 1970. 'Recent studies in language universals'. *Foundations of Language* **6**, 505–61.

Edwards, J. D. 1968. 'Social linguistics on San Andres and Providencia Islands'. Louisiana State University. Mimeographed.

1970. 'Aspects of bilingual behaviour on San Andres Island, Colombia'. Louisiana State University. Mimeographed.

1972. 'Social and historical aspects of the folklore of San Andres Island'. Louisiana State University. Mimeographed.

Elliott, D., S. Legum and S. A. Thompson. 1969. 'Syntactic variation as linguistic data'. In R. Binnick et al. (eds.), *Papers from the 5th Regional Meeting of the Chicago Linguistic Society*, pp. 52–9. Chicago: University of Chicago Press.

Fasold, R. W. 1970. 'Two models of socially significant variation'. *Language* **25**, 29–50.

1972. *Tense Marking in Black English*. Washington, D.C.: Center for Applied Linguistics.

Ferguson, C. A. 1971. 'Absence of copula and the notion of simplicity: a study of normal speech, baby talk, foreigner talk and pidgins'. In Hymes (ed.), pp. 141–50.

Fillmore, C. 1972. 'A grammarian looks to sociolinguistics'. In R. W. Shuy (ed.), *Sociolinguistics: Current Trends and Prospects* (Report of the 23rd Annual Round Table Meeting). Washington, D.C.: Georgetown University Press, 273–88.

Grimes, J. E. and N. Glock. 1970. 'A Saramaccan narrative pattern'. *Language* **46**, 408–25.

Gudschinsky, S. C. 1967. *How to Learn an Unwritten Language*. New York: Holt, Rinehart & Winston.

Guttman, L. 1944. 'A basis for scaling qualitative data'. *American Sociological Review* **9**, 139–50.

Hall, R. 1958. 'Creolized languages and genetic relationship'. *Word* **14**, 367–73.

1966. *Pidgin and Creole Languages*. Ithaca, N.Y.: Cornell University Press.

Halle, M. 1964. 'Phonology in generative grammar'. In J. A. Fodor and J. J. Katz (eds.), *The Structure of Language*, pp. 334–52. Englewood Cliffs, N.J.: Prentice-Hall.

Hancock, I. A. 1969. 'A provisional comparison of the English-derived Atlantic Creoles'. *African Language Review* **8**, 7–72.

Herskovits, M. J. and F. S. Herskovits. 1934. *Rebel Destiny: Among the Bush Negroes of Dutch Guiana*. New York: McGraw-Hill.

Hockett, C. F. 1958. *A Course in Modern Linguistics*. New York: Macmillan.

Hodge, C. T. 1958. 'Non-native Hausa'. In W. Austin (ed.), *Proceedings of the 9th Annual Round Table*, pp. 57–64. Washington, D.C.: Georgetown University Press. Monograph Series no. 11.

Hsieh, H.-I. MS. 'On listing phonological surface items in the lexicon'. Mimeographed.

Hymes, D. 1971. 'Sociolinguistics and the ethnology of speaking'. In E. Ardener (ed.), *Social Anthropology and Linguistics*, pp. 47–94. London: Tavistock.

Hymes, D. (ed.). 1971. *Pidginization and Creolization of Languages*. Cambridge: C.U.P.

Jayawardena, C. 1963. *Conflict and Solidarity on a Guianese Plantation*. London: Athlone Press.

Jones, E. 1968. 'Some tense, mode and aspect markers in Krio'. *African Language Review* **7**, 86–9.

Kay, P. and G. Sankoff. MS. 'A language-universals approach to pidgins and creoles'. Mimeographed.

Kimball, J. 1970. 'Remind remains'. *Linguistic Inquiry* **1**, 511–23.

Kiparsky, P. 1968. 'Tense and mood in Indo-European syntax'. *Foundations of Language* **4**, 4–29.

    1971. 'Historical linguistics'. In W. O. Dingwall (ed.), A *Survey of Linguistic Science*, pp. 577–640. College Park, Md.: University of Maryland Press.

Klima, E. 1964. 'Relatedness between grammatical systems'. *Language* **40**, 1–20.

Labov, W. 1963. 'The social motivation of a sound change'. *Word* **19**, 273–309.

    1964. 'Phonological correlates of social stratification'. *American Anthropologist* **66**(6) part 2, 164–76.

    1966. *The Social Stratification of English in New York City*. Washington, D.C.: Center for Applied Linguistics.

    1969. 'Contraction, deletion and inherent variability of the English copula'. *Language* **45**, 715–62.

    1970. 'The study of language in its social context'. *Studium Generale* **23**, 30–87.

    1971a. 'The notion of "system" in creole languages'. In Hymes (ed.), 447–72.

    1971b. 'The place of linguistic research in American society'. In *Linguistics in the '70s*. Washington, D.C.: Center for Applied Linguistics.

    1972. 'Negative attraction and negative concord in English grammar'. *Language* **48**, 773–818.

    MS. 'On the adequacy of natural languages'. Mimeographed.

Labov, W., P. Cohen, C. Robins and J. Lewis. 1968. A *Study of the Non-Standard English of Negro and Puerto Rican Speakers in New York City*, vol. I, II. New York: Columbia University Press.

Lakoff, G. 1968. 'Instrumental adverbs and the concept of deep structure'. *Foundations of Language* **4**, 4–29.

Lakoff, R. 1968. *Abstract Syntax and Latin Complementation*. Cambridge, Mass.: M.I.T. Press.

    1972. 'Language in context'. *Language* **48**, 907–27.

Lawton, D. 1963. 'Suprasegmental phenomena in Jamaican Creole'. Ph.D. thesis, University of Michigan.

Lenneberg, E. H. 1967. *Biological Foundations of Language*. New York: Wiley.

Le Page, R. B. 1957–8. 'General outlines of English creole dialects'. *Orbis* **6**, 373–91; **7**, 54–64.

Le Page, R. B. (ed.). 1961. *Creole Language Studies*. London: Macmillan.

Le Page, R. B. and D. DeCamp. 1960. *Jamaican Creole – An Historical Introduction*. London: Macmillan.

Loflin, M. D. 1967. 'A note on the deep structure of nonstandard English in Washington, D.C.'. *Glossa* **1**, 26–32.

    1970. 'On the structure of the verb in a dialect of American Negro English'. *Linguistics* **59**, 14–28.

Loman, B. 1967. *Conversations in a Negro American Dialect*. Washington, D.C.: Center for Applied Linguistics.

Mafeni, B. 1970. 'Nigerian Pidgin'. In J. Spencer (ed.), *The English Language in Africa*, pp. 95–112. London: Longman.

Magens, J. M. 1770. *Grammatica over det Creolske sprog*. Copenhagen: Gerhard Giese Salikath.

McIntosh, A. 1966. 'Predictive statements'. In C. E. Bazell et al. (eds.), *In Memory of J. R. Firth*, pp. 303–20. London: Longman.

Mitrovic, P. 1972. 'Deux sabirs balkaniques'. *La Linguistique* 8(1), 137–40.

Naro, A. J. 1970. Review of Carvalho, *Estudios Linguisticos*. *Foundations of Language* 7, 148–55.

Ogunbowale, P. O. 1970. *The Essentials of the Yoruba Language*. London: London University Press.

Peet, W. 1972. 'Omission of subject relative pronouns in Hawaiian English restrictive relative clauses'. Paper presented at 8th SECOL meeting.

Pimsleur, P. and T. Quinn (eds.). 1971. *The Psychology of Second Language Learning*. Cambridge: C.U.P.

Politzer, R. L. 1949. 'On the emergence of Romance from Latin'. *Word* 5, 126–30.

Postal, P. 1970. 'On the surface verb *remind*'. *Linguistic Inquiry* 1, 37–120.

Pulgram, E. 1961. 'French /a/; statics and dynamics of linguistic subcodes'. *Lingua* 10, 305–25.

Quow (M. McTurk, pseud.). 1877. *Essays and Fables*. Georgetown: Argosy.

Reibel, D. 1969. 'Language learning analysis'. *International Review of Applied Linguistics* VII(4), 283–94.

1971. 'Language learning strategies for the adult'. In Pimsleur and Quinn (eds.), pp. 87–96.

Reinecke, J., D. DeCamp, I. A. Hancock, S. Tsuzaki and R. Wood. 1974. A *bibliography of pidgins and creoles*. Honolulu: University of Hawaii Press.

Reisman, K. M. L. 1965. 'The isle is full of noises; A study of Creole in the speech patterns of Antigua, West Indies'. Ph.D. thesis, Harvard University.

Reno, P. 1964. *The Ordeal of British Guiana*. New York: Monthly Review Press.

Rens, L. L. E. 1953. *The Historical and Social Background of Surinam's Negro English*. Amsterdam: North Holland Publishing Co.

Richards, J. C. MS. 'Social factors, interlanguage and language learning'.

Richardson, I. 1963. 'Evolutionary factors in Mauritian creole'. *Journal of African Languages* 2, 2–14.

Rickford, J. MS. 'Insights of the mesolect'.

Robson, B. 1972. 'Individual vs. community grammars: English /h/ in Jamaican Creole'. In D. G. Hays and D. M. Lance (eds.), *From Soundstream to Discourse*. Columbia: University of Missouri Press.

1973. 'On the stability of underlying forms across individuals'. In C.-J. Bailey and R. Shuy (eds.), *New Ways of Analyzing Variation in English*, pp. 164–70. Washington, D.C.: Georgetown University Press.

Rodway, J. 1912. *Guiana – British, French and Dutch*. London: T. Fisher Unwin.

Ross, J. R. 1967. 'Constraints on variables in syntax'. Ph.D. thesis, Massachusetts Institute of Technology.

1969. 'Auxiliaries as main verbs'. In W. Todd (ed.), *Studies in Philosophic Linguistics, Series 1*, pp. 77–102. Evanston, Ill.: Great Expectations.

Samarin, W. J. 1967a. A *Grammar of Sango*. The Hague: Mouton.

1967b. *Field Linguistics*. New York: Holt, Rinehart & Winston.

Sankoff, G. MS. 'A quantitative paradigm for the study of communicative competence'. Mimeographed.

Sankoff, G. and S. Laberge. 1973. 'On the acquisition of native speakers by a language'. *Kivung* 6(1), 32–47.

Schneider, G. D. 1966. *West African Pidgin English*. Athens, Ohio: G. D. Schneider.

Schuchardt, H. E. M. 1914. *Der Sprache der Saramakka-Neger in Suriname*. Amsterdam: Muller.

Schütz, A. 1972. *The Languages of Fiji*. London: O.U.P.

Silverstein, M. 1972. 'Chinook jargon; Language contact and the problem of multilevel generative systems'. *Language* 48, 378–406, 596–625.

Sivertsen, E. 1960. *Cockney Phonology*. Oslo: University Press.

Skinner, E. P. 1956. 'Ethnic interaction in a British Guiana rural community'. Ph.D. thesis, Columbia University.

Smith, F. and G. A. Miller. 1966. *The Genesis of Language: A Psycholinguistic Approach*. Cambridge, Mass.: M.I.T. Press.

Smith, N. V. 1969. 'The Nupe verb'. *African Language Studies*, x, 90–160.

Smith, R. T. 1956. *The Negro Family in British Guiana*. London: Routledge & Kegan Paul.

1962. *British Guiana*, London: O.U.P.

Solomon, D. 1966. 'The system of predication in the speech of Trinidad: A quantitative study of decreolization'. M.A. thesis, Columbia University.

Speirs, J. 1902. *The Proverbs of British Guiana*. Demerara: Argosy.

Stampe, D. 1969. 'The acquisition of phonetic representation'. In *Papers from the 5th Regional Meeting, Chicago Linguistic Society*, pp. 443–54. Chicago: University of Chicago Press.

1972. 'A dissertation on natural phonology'. Ph.D. thesis, University of Chicago.

Stewart, W. A. 1965. 'Urban negro speech; Sociolinguistic factors affecting English teaching'. In R. Shuy (ed.), *Social Dialects and Language Learning*, pp. 10–18. Champaign, Ill.: National Council of Teachers of English.

Swan, M. 1957. *British Guiana, the Land of Six Peoples*. London: H.M.S.O.

Taylor, D. 1956. 'Language contacts in the West Indies'. *Word* 12, 399–414.

1959. 'On function versus form in "non-traditional" languages'. *Word* 15, 485–9.

1960. 'Language shift or changing relationship?' *International Journal of American Linguistics* 26, 144–61.

1963. 'The origin of West Indian creole languages: evidence from grammatical categories'. *American Anthropologist* 65, 800–14.

Thompson, W. A. 1961. 'A note on some possible affinities between the creole dialects of the Old World and those of the New'. In R. B. Le Page (ed.), 107–13.

Todd, L. 1971. Review of Schneider 1966. *Lingua* 28, 185–97.

1973. ' "To be or not to be" – What would Hamlet have said in Cameroon Pidgin? An analysis of Cameroon Pidgin's "Be"-verb'. *Archivum Linguisticum* iv (N.S.), 1–15.

Traugott, E. 1973. 'Some thoughts on natural syntactic processes'. In C.-J. Bailey and R. Shuy (eds.), *New Ways of Analyzing Variation in English*, pp. 313–22. Washington, D.C.: Georgetown University Press.

Tsuzaki, S. 1971. 'Co-existent systems in language variation'. In D. Hymes (ed.), pp. 327–40.

Turner, L. D. 1949. *Africanisms in the Gullah Dialect.* Chicago: University of Chicago Press.

van Sertima, I. 1905. *The Creole Tongue of British Guiana.* Berbice: New Amsterdam.

van's Gravesande, S. 1911. *Despatches,* ed. C. A. Harris and J. A. J. de Villiers. London: Hakluyt Society.

Visser, F. T. 1969. *An Historical Syntax of the English Language,* Part III. Leiden: E. J. Brill.

Voorhoeve, J. 1957. 'The verbal system of Sranan'. *Lingua* 6, 374–96.
    1961. 'A project for the study of creole language history in Surinam'. In Le Page (ed.), 99–106.
    1962. *Sranan Syntax.* Amsterdam: North Holland Publishing Co.

Weinreich, U. 1958. 'On the compatibility of genetic relationship and convergent development'. *Word* 14, 374–9.

Weinreich, U., W. Lablov and M. I. Herzog. 1968. 'Empirical foundations for a theory of language change'. In W. P. Lehmann (ed.), *Directions for Historical Linguistics,* pp. 95–195. Austin: University of Texas Press.

Westermann, D. 1930. *A Study of the Ewe Language.* London: O.U.P.

Whinnom, K. 1965. 'The origin of the European-based creoles and pidgins'. *Orbis* 14, 509–27.
    1971. 'Linguistic hybridization and the "special case" of pidgins and creoles'. In Hymes (ed.), 91–116.

Williamson, K. 1965. *A Grammar of the Kolokuma Dialect of Ijo.* Cambridge: C.U.P.

Wilson, W.A.A. 1962. *The Crioulo of Guinea.* Johannesburg: Witwatersrand University Press.

Wolf, M. 1970. 'A note on the surface verb *remind*'. *Linguistic Inquiry* 1, 561.

Wolfram, W. A. 1969. *A Sociolinguistic Description of Detroit Negro Speech.* Washington, D.C.: Center for Applied Linguistics.

Yates, J. (ed.). 1972. *International Year Book and Statesman's Who's Who,* 20th ed. London: Burke's Peerage.

Index